D1131821

TRANSPORT POLICY

TRANSPORT POLICY:
Geographic, Economic and Planning Aspects

PATRICK O'SULLIVAN

Bowling Green Univ. Library

BARNES & NOBLE BOOKS
TOTOWA, NEW JERSEY

First published in the USA 1980 by
Barnes & Noble Books
81 Adams Drive
Totowa, New Jersey, 07512
ISBN: 0–389–20143–X

First published 1980
© Patrick O'Sullivan 1980

Printed in Great Britain

Contents

CHAPTER·1

Transport Issues

━━

Transport routes and vehicles are our means of gaining access to other people, for company and to make a living. To fulfil this task the transport system is geographically pervasive and persistently impinges on all our lives. Even on the mountain tops we cannot escape the presence of aircraft. The means of transport cause irritation to their users in the shape of the need to pay for them, to share them with others, the need to wait for them and spend time on them and bear the burden of wear and tear on the body and the senses involved. Both users and non-users are assailed by the noise, smell, danger and ugliness which transport generates. These irritations form the seedbed for entre-preneurial, political or administrative actions to improve the per-formance of our means of mobility. Whether for the carriage of goods or persons, the artefacts and effluvia of transport are seldom out of sight or sound. In addition to these negative aspects of our relation to the means of mobility, we have a more than intermittent positive involvement. Some of our more deliberate habitual actions involve using transport to get to work, school, shops, to buy and sell goods and to disport ourselves. The operations of the transport system affect our actions by intrusions on our privacy, in terms of danger to life and limb and in terms of the cost of movement. The structures of the system affect us in terms of the accessibility to other people and activities and thus the geographical frame they provide for our lives, as well as in terms of aesthetics. We identify the places we use with reference to transport structures and we mark our passage from place to place by such landmarks.

In a piece of simplistic physiological materialism, MacKinnon (1978) has made a case that man's big brain developed to solve logistic problems in gathering sustenance over a wide territory. Human walking is suited to carrying things over long distance but is essentially slow. It puts a premium on taking the shortest route and knowing that the journey will be fruitful when you arrive. On this argument, our nature is determined by our need for efficient access to the means of life. Certainly from the dawn of man's tectonic activities, since he began to consciously fashion the landscape, the friction of distance has governed his cultural arrangements. The pattern of man's occupancy of the land, where he places shelters and grows crops, reflects the balancing of the need to employ land and scattered resources against the pain and energy expenditure involved in covering distance. The geography of rural and urban settlement mirrors this balance, and changes in the ability to overcome distance are to be seen in the shifting geographical arrangements of society. The impetus behind the economic and political actions which bring about these changes is discontent with the shortcomings of the present structures and operations. Discontent over potholes, congestion, availability of service, pollution, noise, danger, fares, bridges and routes, encourages competition or political commitment, often translated into ideological terms. Whatever the grand scheme within which this discontent is mustered, its genesis is displeasure at the friction occasioned by our habitation of a world with the dimensions of distance and direction.

In poorer countries the chief issue is usually a lack of facilities and services. High transport costs prohibit the extension of commercial agriculture and increases in well-being by eroding market prices too steeply with distance into the hinterlands of urban markets or exporting ports. The crucial problem is how to make the most of limited means in extending lines of communication and commerce and how to pay for this.

In the regions of modern, commercial economies, including the cities and developed areas of the third world, the problem is one of finding a balance between the fabric of our cultural landscape and our mobility needs. At the local, personal level this involves the deleterious and costly effects of travel, the alleviation of congestion, noise, smell and visual intrusion set against desired objectives in terms of the geographical arrangement of employment, services and habitation. At a broader geographical scale, similar considerations arise where the nuisance of air travel, trucks and trains impinge on the integrity of private and public space. The carriage of goods in developed economies does involve issues of the provision of sheer capacity to some geographical locations. At other points, however, problems of excess capacity and obsolescence arise. New means of transport cause a problem of managing the decline or demise of their predecessors. With competition among different means of transport for the same traffic, the stability of prices and services availability become matters of grave concern.

Many transport policy issues enter the political arena first in terms of particular roads, bridges, rail services, airports or particular nuisances. The process of politics weights and summarizes these, translating them into general preferences and social values which promote constitutional, regulatory or administrative acts or programmes of public works. The political expression of these issues is often clothed in economic ideology, formed and manipulated by the interests which coalesce in partisan positions. Transport policy, however, presents some significant departures from simple correspondence with the usual alignment of interests to the left and right of centre. Economic ideology has traditionally opposed leftist central control to rightist market solutions to allocation problems. Nevertheless, right-leaning governments have in the past been encouraged to increase collective control of transport services by regulation to buy stability with 'fair' shares of monopoly profits. Both unions and big operators, in radical opposition on other matters, would like to flourish under a government-arranged cartel. Users and small owner-operators would prefer a greater degree of competition.

Structure of the book

Faced with dissatisfaction over transport in one aspect or another, the commonsense procedure is firstly to take stock of the existing situation and secondly to project the future so as to identify present and future problems more precisely. Having specified the problem in its present and future shape, then a whole range of feasible solutions to it ought to be devised, tested and evaluated against some established criteria of desirability. Having done that, the task of making choices and implementing them as actions remains.

To take stock one needs analytic insight, capable of deducing the crucial relationships governing the workings of the phenomena in question. Some body of theory, extracting generality from unique circumstances, is of value. In chapter 2 we present some of the components of such a theoretical framework. To choose and act wholly on the basis of the heroically simplified and conjectural abstractions of theory is clearly foolish. Generality must be embellished with sufficient unique detail to provide historical perspective. An historical appreciation reveals the extent of the simplification involved in theory and the true complexity of life. Wise judgement and decisions emerge from achieving a level of resolution in understanding which focuses attention on the problem so as to retain relevant detail balanced against what we might regard as underlying causes. There are those, particularly historians, who seriously doubt that we will ever be able to generalize our behaviour and thus predict our future with any accuracy. Certainly to stand a chance at it, theories must be tempered by historical understanding. To this end, in chapter 3 some historical sketches of the evolution of man's employment of the face of the earth and his conquest of distance are presented.

From these beginnings in theory and history we may be able to translate what are general feelings of dissatisfaction into specific issues and thus derive clearer statements of the problems involved. Greater clarity should reveal if the issue is amenable to the resolution of policy, involving government action for its remedy. In chapter 4 transport issues are reviewed, chiefly drawing upon the recent experience of the two nations with which the author is familiar, the UK and USA.

Having come to some understanding of a problem, the prospects for its solution are clarified. Chapter 5 discusses a frame-work for problem-solving after typifying the kinds of solution which can be applied to improving the performance of transport. To decide between solutions it is necessary to weigh their outcomes, and this implies measurement. The positive and negative impacts, the benefits and costs, of any course of action must be gauged, and chapter 6 addresses this question of measurement.

The process of making a decision or choice, if it has some consistent rationale, can be represented formally. Once we have determined what we want to achieve in general, specific choices involving some complexity of relationships may be determined as the solution to an analogous mathematical problem, if it is tractable. In other words, the logic and circumstances of a decision, the objective and the constraining limitations on freedom of choice and the criteria of selection may be translated into their mathematical equivalents and the readier solution of the mathematical problem will yield the appropriate concrete choice. This, of course, providing that the mathematical problem has a unique and determinable solution. Chapter 7 presents some calculi of decision which can, in theory, be applied to making decisions on transport policy and investments.

Whether we employ a structured rubric for making decisions or not, choice is for the future and implies trying to foresee the state of things to come. For transport planning we have to try to predict future demands and performance. The methods of forecasting which are used are considered in chapter 8.

The process relating the parts of the transport system and describing its impacts on users and non-users operates through space as well as time. The geographer, therefore, has a special contribution to make in tackling transport problems since they manifest themselves in his domain of interest. One traditional *modus operandi* of geographers is the establishment of discrete units of the earth's surface as regions. This can be put to good use in the delimitation of transport problems, the forecasting of impacts of change in the system and the solution of problems, limiting the allowance which must be made in calculations for the interrelatedness of the parts of the system to as circumscribed a scope as possible. The application of regionalization to transport networks in a practical context may be applied at a variety of scales, from the global to the urban. Chapter 9 presents some thoughts and evidence on the importance and applicability of regionalizing transport systems in the setting of urban planning.

The variety of geographic scales at which transport systems operate and problems exist provides the organizing principle for a review of the range of current problems and solutions in chapters 10, 11 and 12. The theme of geographical scale of the problem's incidence is employed to order a large array of particulars. The realities of politics and happenstance intervene to disrupt the naïve postures which the theoretical formulations in chapter 7 might encourage. Distinguished according to whether they operate at the international, interregional or local level, the variety of solutions applied to resolving the shortcomings of the means of movement and exchange are displayed in these three chapters. These then provide for a conclusion with some sense of the texture of society and its relationship with the means of mobility and how these are changing in the last quarter of the twentieth century.

CHAPTER·2

Transport and Geographical Economics

━━━━━━━━━━━━━━━━━━━━━━━━━━━━━━━━━━

In analyzing the operation of the transport sector as a preparation for prescribing methods of intervention and decision-making, we must keep in mind the intimate association of choices of place and movement. Where we locate activities is strongly conditioned by those activities' transport requirements, while transport decisions are constrained by where activities are located. We can better inform ourselves about the nature of this interrelation by considering a series of partial formulations of the interactions involved. The three phenomena of investigation are networks, flows and locations. The complex interplays of this triad may be simplified by holding one or the other of them to be determined and studying the relations of the other two. In this way we produce a tripartite theoretical structure of network theory, flow theory and location theory. Having analyzed the circumstances of our livelihood by these three parts we should be in a better position to appreciate the nature of the whole. Since the subject of concern in this volume is the provision of facilities for transporting people and goods it is appropriate to commence with a consideration of the best set of transport facilities to meet some given needs. From this we move naturally on to questions of the demand for movement and flows of goods and people over these transport networks. The flows are generated by the geographical distribution of production and consumption, which is the subject matter of location theory. The three sets of constructs do intertwine to provide a partly articulated body of theory with which to address questions of the public weal in transport matters.

Facility networks

The primary man-made contribution to a transport system is the set of ways joining points on the surface of the earth so as to better facilitate movement between them. These may consist of road, rail or waterways or even airways and seaways. In some fashion or another man has invested resources in lowering the cost of traversing these channels. In some cases, as with roads, it is a matter of using material, labour, capital and energy to lay out a travelling surface physically. In the airway, seaway and riverine cases the investment is largely in the means of charting, monitoring and controlling the routes and terminals of the network. This activity has mostly been a very conscious matter of design. Because of their political significance and the externalities associated with them transport networks have often been provided on a collective basis and the deliberation was a public matter. It is not appropriate, therefore, to treat the cause of a network's configuration as arising from the individually motivated actions of many buyers and sellers in the usual fashion of economic theory. To deal with collective decisions it may be postulated that the agency of government charged with building transport facilities seeks the best arrangement in terms of some measure of general well-being.

Suppose there are some locationally fixed points, say two existing towns, where a case may be made for building a road between them. The first question to ask is whether it is worthwhile building the link at all. Is the reduction in transport cost brought about by building the road sufficiently greater than the cost of constructing and maintaining the route to outweigh alternative uses of the resources involved? To answer this question we need to measure the additional benefit generated by the investment, the cost of providing the facility and the yields of alternative uses.

Benefit measurement

A measure of benison long advocated and frequently employed for measuring discrete changes in economic circumstances confined to narrow locality is the change in consumer surplus arising. Consumer surplus is the difference between what each individual involved is willing to pay for a product in the last resort and what they have to pay, summed over all the relevant individuals. This can be measured by integrating the area under the demand curve for the product in question (figure 1). For a road the price axis would be given in terms of the cost of passage in time and money which we can call generalized cost. The quantity axis we shall deem to be in terms of the number of vehicle trips between the two towns on the presumption that these are homogeneous units. The consumer surplus accruing from travelling before the road was built would be given by the area A in figure 1, the area under the demand curve above the supply line. Building the road will reduce the cost of travel to say C^2 from C^1 and induce more people to travel, increasing demand for T^1 to T^2. The consumer surplus associated with this arrangement would be given by $A + B + C$. The change in consumer surplus resulting from building the road would then be the sum of $B + C$. This is the quantity to judge against the cost of providing the road.

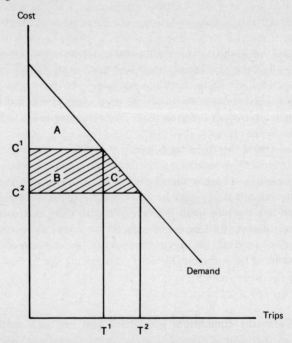

Figure 1

In preparation for dealing with more complex circumstances later on, it is instructive to elaborate on the nature of this quantity at this juncture. Suppose that travelling the original track between the two

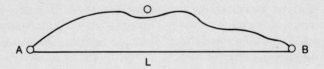

Figure 2

towns had cost C_O. The new road with better alignment and geometry is laid down beside it with a lower generalized cost C_N (figure 2). If the demand for travel does not change in response to the new lower cost and if all travellers merely switch to the new lower-cost road, which operates without congestion, then the benefit of the new road is the savings in generalized cost $T^1 (C_O - C_N)$. If demand is elastic to a reduction in travel cost so that a greater demand T^2 ensues then for a linear demand curve the consumer surplus will be given by:

$$\tfrac{1}{2} (T^1 + T^2) (C_O - C_N).$$

The assumption implicit in all of this, that transport route cost does not change with different levels of use, is contrary to experience. Transport systems are subject to relationships between speed and flow and the congestion phenomenon. As the number of users of a road increases, so the safe headways of operation decrease and speeds are reduced to avoid the danger. If we allow for velocity to decrease beyond a certain volume of traffic then the time component will push up the generalized cost of travel. If we suppose that travellers are indifferent between routes on which the generalized cost of travel is the same, then the possibility exists that as people leave the original route, increasing speed on it, and join the new link, decreasing velocity there, a situation may arise where the cost on both routes is the same and travellers will be found on both routes. In this case the consumer surplus would have to be measured on both routes, as:

$$\tfrac{1}{2} (T^1 + (T_O^2 + T_L^2)) (C_O - C_*)$$

where C_* is the equilibrium generalized cost on both routes after changes in total volume of travel and the choice between the two routes has settled down.

It is more usual that the links between A and B are part of a network of routes with which they have relations of complementarity as well as competition. The links between A and B are parts of paths connecting a great many other origins and destinations. Reducing the generalized cost of travel between these two places is likely to increase demand from much further afield, thereby changing costs on other links of the network. To pick up these effects of building link L, consumer surplus must be measured over all parts of the network affected. If there are n affected origins or destinations labelled i and j then the appropriate expression is:

$$\frac{1}{2}\sum_{i=1}^{n} \sum_{j=1}^{n} (T_{ij}^1 + T_{ij}^2) \ (C_{ij}^1 - C_{ij}^2).$$

Cost characteristics

The cost characteristics of the new route are a matter of engineering the solution to an economic problem. For some expected volume of traffic the obvious design objective for road-building is to minimize the joint cost of the movement of traffic and of building and maintaining the facility. There is a problem in dealing with these two sets of costs since construction costs occur as a one-off expenditure before the road is used, while maintenance and movement costs are incurred continuously over the life of the road. This can be resolved by amortizing the construction costs. We can express construction costs in annual terms as a constant payment over the lifetime of the facility, covering the principal and interest on the debt incurred for its construction. For simplicity we can assume that traffic is constant over the life of the road and that maintenance costs do not vary from year to year. The design problem can thus be solved in terms of a year's costs. On a flat plain with no rivers or bad drainage the obvious alignment would be a straight line between the two towns, which minimizes both cost elements. If, however, the terrain is differentiated so that construction costs vary geographically, the trade-off between building costs and movement costs may result in a diversion of the best route from the straight. The reduction of the cost of providing the facility brought about by taking a detour around more costly terrain is bought with an increase in the length of the journey and thus of movement costs. In the case of a river intervening between the two towns as in figure 3, since bridge-building costs can be considered overwhelmingly greater than any movement cost increase caused by a slight diversion, the route may be refracted so as to minimize the bridge span by crossing the river at right angles to its direction of flow.

Since drainage and foundations are more costly in swamp and the cost of culverting, earthworks and the mileage necessary to provide a negotiable gradient are greater in hilly terrain, then diversions increasing movement costs to avoid additional construction costs may be in order. The nature of such solutions is indicated notionally in figure 4.

Road network decisions are seldom made with respect to only two places to be served. To elaborate on the design problem arising from trying to join more than one place we can reintroduce the simplification of a flat plain on which construction costs are uniform and least-cost

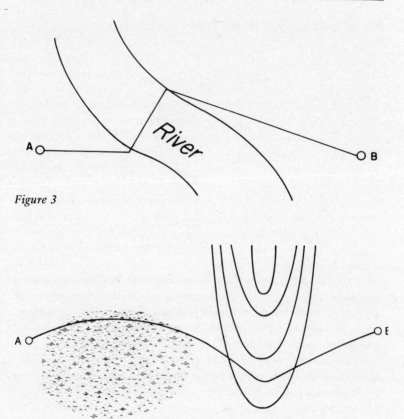

Figure 3

Figure 4

alignments are straight lines. As a step towards generality let us first consider the case of joining three points like A, B and C in figure 5. For a start let us deal with the case where the demand for travel between the three places is equal and symmetric:

$$T_{AB} = T_{BA} = T_{BC} = T_{CB} = T_{AC} = T_{CA}.$$

If the cost of building and maintaining the roadway is not very large compared with the potential for saving travel costs by providing routes as direct as possible between the places involved, the solution would be a triangular network joining A, B and C directly as in figure 5a. At the other extreme, if construction is so costly as to overwhelm movement-cost considerations the minimum span between the three places would

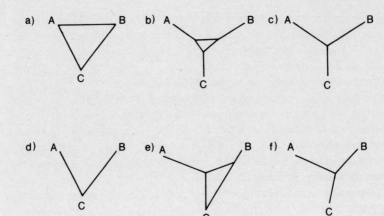

Figure 5

form a Y-shaped network as in figure 5c. If the relationship between the two sets of costs is not dominated by one or the other but there is some active trade-off the outcome will have the general form shown in figure 5b, with an interior delta and three intermediate junctions. As movement-cost considerations become more important the delta increases in size, tending towards the triangular extreme. As construction costs weigh more heavily, so the delta reduces, approaching the limiting case of the Y junction.

To approach real circumstances more closely the prospect of an imbalance of traffic between the end points must be allowed. If the traffic between A and B is negligible and that between C and A and C and B equal, then the configuration in figure 5d would be appropriate if construction costs are not too onerous. If some demand exists between A and B but is less than that between A and C which is less than that between B and C ($T_{AB} < T_{AC} < T_{BC}$), and construction costs are somewhat weightier, then the solution would look like figure 5e. For the same general demand configuration and with movement costs dominated by construction cost, the shape in figure 5f would result. Figure 5 illustrates the considerations which have to be taken into account in solving this type of problem. The precise method of calculation is given in Beckmann (1967). Beckmann also points out that what is a tractable problem in joining three places becomes unmanageable for four or more, requiring the proximate calculus of engineering or geographical intuition to produce an answer.

If we are willing to sacrifice a degree of geographical resolution and specify the location of routes and junctions at the outset of the analysis, numerical methods can be employed to determine which of a set of possible routes of a network connecting several places ought to be built with a fixed construction budget so as to minimize the cost of movement throughout the system. The solution to such a problem indicates which pre-specified links ought to be built and what capacity existing links ought to be expanded to. Route alignment and the location of junctions must be determined *a priori*. We shall return to this kind of specification of the problem and method of solution in chapter 8 when we consider what methods can be applied to transport network planning in theory at least.

Returning to the solution of the geometrical as well as the capacity problem, when we reach the extreme case of a continuum of points to be served, with demand being construed as a continuous surface, the prospect of finding a best arrangement for the uniform density case does exist in terms of finding that regular lattice of roads which serves the plain at a minimum joint cost of construction and movement. The only polygons which pack into a regular lattice are the square, the hexagon and the triangle. Thus, we need merely evaluate the relative merits of the three configurations. With a continuous representation of demand it is necessary to standardize the level of local access which the three networks provide as a basis for comparison. They are not joining a set of points, but providing access to areas. If we require that the average distance from the area delimited by the lattice elements to the roads, which are the lattice edges, be the same in all cases, then we will be comparing like with like. For this average distance to a road to be the same in all three cases, the networks must be constructed so that the perpendicular distance from the road to the centre of the elementary square, hexagon and triangle is the same (Melut and O'Sullivan 1974). When this is the case the density of the three networks turns out to be the same, for each length of road will serve the same sized area. On the assumption that construction and maintenace costs are proportional to density, this implies that the comparison rests solely on the relative merits of the three networks in terms of movement costs. These latter can be gauged in terms of 'route factors'. The route factor for a network is the average divergence between straight-line and over-the-road distances. For an isotropic plain the divergence between Euclidean and route distance is, obviously, zero. For the square lattice network the relationship between Euclidean distance (s) and network distance (d) between any two points with an angular deviation between the grid and the azimuth θ is:

$d = s (\sin \theta + \cos \theta)$

Since the square grid is symmetric in eight $45°$ arcs, we need only average this relationship over $45°$ to produce a route factor of $4/\pi$. Similar calculation over the relevant $30°$ arcs of the hexagonal and triangular lattices produces the same value of $4/\pi$ in the hexagonal case and a superior value of $(2\sqrt{3})/\pi$ for the trianglar network. The triangular network is thus the best, excelling in terms of movement costs. The hexagonal and square grids are inferior equals. Even if square grids are laid down for ease of surveying and because farming and building technology dictate square fields and lots, it is not surprising that the logic of transport cost encourages their bisection by radial routes connecting foci of activity directly, imparting a triangular component to road geometry.

In discussing the composition of benefits arising from transport investment, allusion was made to another cost to be taken into account. The design problem, and thus the appropriate construction cost, is not merely a matter of which places to join by a length of road, but also of what capacity to build the road to. Transport networks characteristically display a variation of cost of use with the amount of traffic flowing over their links. They are subject to capacity relationship between flow and speed. As volume increases the phenomenon of congestion reduces the velocity with which a given piece of road can be traversed, thereby reducing capacity measured over a given time interval. The form of this relationship is such that speeds are only slightly decreased as traffic builds up until a critical level is reached where the headways between vehicles are dangerously small, so as to inhibit free flow and bring about a reduction in safe speed. The general form is as in figure 6. The design problem is to decide on the standard of network link appropriate to the expected volume of traffic. What complicates the issue in most transport systems is the temporal fluctuation of demand, giving rise to a peaking of volume at certain times. Urban systems suffer the twin peaks of the commuter tide. Freight traffic tends to peak at the end of the day's production. Airline traffic peaks at holidays. Agricultural commodity carriers face an enormous peaking at harvest time. The engineering solution to the problem is to design for the peak load and carry the cost as excess off-peak capacity rather than as a peak time queue. When viewed from an economist's perspective the problem often appears to have arisen from a failure to price for the use of the facility appropriately. Obviously road space is more valuable in the peak as is an airline seat. Presenting the appropriate signal of the opportunity cost

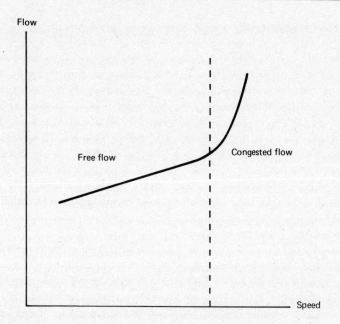

Figure 6

involved to a potential user may alleviate the problem by inducing an adjustment of his time of use, reducing the need for excess capacity by trimming the peaks and filling the troughs, as in figure 7.

Congestion represents a deadweight loss to society. This arises from the disparity between private perception of the cost of using the transport system and the social cost. The most serious problem is that

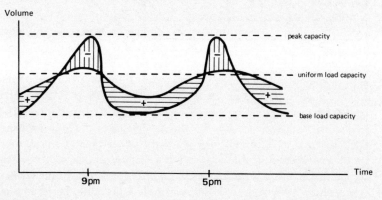

Figure 7

in urban road systems, where the price paid is in terms of generalized cost of travel which incorporates the private evaluation of the time taken for a journey. The individuals deciding to join a stream of traffic may be aware that their entry will reduce the speed of the stream by one second. They take this average increment to journey time and match it against the extra value they get out of making the trip. If the utility of the trip exceeds the cost of the effort involved at the existing speed, plus the extra second their joining the traffic will incur, they will undertake the journey. People will continue in this until the average journey cost just equals the utility of making the trip. What these people have not taken into account in their decisions is the increment to travel time they imposed on all of the existing travellers. From a social point of view the appropriate measure of cost is the increment to total travel time over all travellers, i.e. the marginal travel time. Individual decisions are made in terms of average journey time. In a system such as we have described where cost increases with volume, marginal cost will exceed average cost as in figure 8. The level of use of the system will be in excess of the socially desireable level, and a deadweight loss equal to the shaded area in figure 8 will be imposed on

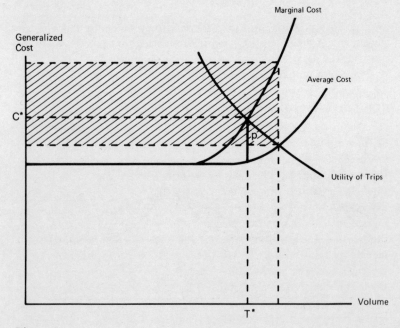

Figure 8

society. The social optimium is found where marginal cost equals utility at C^*, T^*. This can be brought about by imposing a cash charge on users equal to p in figure 8, which raises the perceived value of average cost in travel time terms to the level of marginal costs. This is the basis for proposals to impose road pricing on urban road users.

The implication for investment appraisal is that if we use current levels of use in a congested system as a basis for extrapolating the benefits of expanding capacity, we are in grave danger of overestimating these benefits. Current levels of use are excessive in terms of collective well-being. The proper level of use to determine future capacity is that at which marginal cost and demand are equated.

The opportunity cost of capital

Having discussed the measurement of benefit from transport investment and the design of least-cost solutions to an investment problem, we are left with the question of the opportunity cost of the resources involved. To decide if a scheme is worthwhile we have to gauge what else might have been achieved by the resources involved in alternative uses. When we spoke of amortizing construction costs, the means of incorporating this consideration was introduced as the relevant interest rate. The ultimate reason for investing, or foregoing present consumption, is to achieve increased consumption in the future. Consuming less now in order to build roads will, we hope, reduce the cost of transport, increase the productivity of the economy and the amount available for consumption in the future. The productivity of investment has, however, to be set off against the fact that consumption now is more valuable to us than consumption at some future date. The reconciliation of the excess of future over present consumption generated by investment with the preference for consuming now rather than later, is brought about by the price of funds for investment — the interest rate. In a perfect market for capital funds, the interest rate is determined by the set of asset prices which equates the net worth of all investments no matter when their stream of earnings arises. We compare the worth of investments with different time profiles of outlays and income by transforming the yield of income over outlay back to some present value. The excess of benefit over cost arising at any time over the lifetime of the asset is translated to its present value by discounting by the interest rate, and these net present values are summed over the relevant lifetime of the investment. Disregarding inflation, a pound's worth of income in ten years is not the same as a pound's worth now.

Discounting represents this reality. Money invested at interest rate i grows at a rate of $(1 + i)^t$, where t is the number of years involved. To get the present discounted value of the outlays and income generated by an investment t years hence, we invert this expression as $1/(1+i)^t$. Faced with many potential uses of limited resources, the decision rule for selecting investments must be to pick those which give rise to largest net present values.

In dealing with this matter we have relaxed the need for the earlier simplifying assumption that the stream of use and, thus, benefits and operating costs of road or track was constant. We can now treat a time profile of costs and benefits. Much of the cost of a project occurs as a knot of construction cost at the start of its life, but some costs, such as those of operating and maintenance, are spread unevenly over its life. Maintenance costs in particular increase with age. Benefits of an investment build up with use, often in a regular fashion through time. There is, however, the prospect of a sudden attenuation or surge of demand, as a result of competition or demographics. If we estimate a series of prospective costs k_t and benefits b_t of each investment over its lifetime of n years, the decision rule is to select projects where the net present value of benefits exceeds the net present value of cost, i.e.:

$$\sum_{t=1}^{n} \frac{b_t}{(1+i)^t} > \sum_{t=1}^{n} \frac{k_t}{(1+i)^t}.$$

Flow theory

What was presumed in our discussion of networks was that the demand for their use was known, although we did allow for its variation in response to the the cost of movement when we treated congestion. An allusion was made to the utility which derived from making a trip over a piece of road. Apart from the strange joys of taking a spin or cruising, we mostly travel or ship goods because of the place utility which this movement imparts, getting us or our products to places where our pleasure or our market value is greater. Transport, for the most part, is not consumed for its own sake. The demand for transport is derived from the access it provides to other places, goods and people. In general transport has negative utility, the less of it one has to consume the better off one is. It is a costly concomitant of the world of space and time we live in. The flows of goods and people we see represent an expenditure of effort to overcome the friction of distance.

The clearest demonstration of how the demand for transport derives from that for other goods and varies with their supply and demand conditions is provided in the time-honoured Cournot solution to finding the equilibrium trade in a commodity between two regions. This has been presented by Scott (1971) complete with back-to-back demand diagrams. O'Sullivan *et al.* (1979) display the extension of the equilibrium to take in the supply and demand for transport services, so that a three-way competitive equilibrium between the two commodity markets and the market for transport services can be established. Transport prices need not be taken as given. The deeper theoretical significance of Cournot's analysis was drawn out by Samuelson (1952). Starting with the classical back-to-back diagram, it is possible to construct excess supply functions for the two markets (S_1, S_2) by subtracting demand laterally from supply at every price as in figure 9.

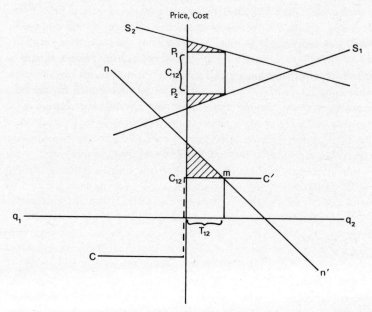

Figure 9

Rather than as a shift in the price axis, transport costs are represented by the discontinuous function CC'. The competitive equilibrium is found where the gap between the excess supply functions is just equal to the cost of transport C_{12}. This same level of exports from region 1 and imports to region 2 is determined by the intersection of a net excess supply curve nn' constructed by plotting the vertical difference between S_1 and S_2, and the transport cost function at m. This formulation of the problem leads us back to the consumer surplus measure of utility. The area under the net excess supply curve is equal to the consumer surplus accruing in both regions, since the area under S_2 is consumer surplus in region 2, the area under S_1 is equal in magnitude and opposite in sign to consumer surplus in region 1, and *nn'* was constructed by subtracting the value of S_1 from that for S_2. The socially optimal level of trade and the set of prices and demand for transport can now be determined by finding the level at which consumer surplus less transport cost is maximized. This maximum is found where the net consumer surplus curve *nn'* and the transport cost function *CC'* intersect at *m*. The consumer surplus in both markets net of transport costs is given by the shaded triangle, which summarizes the two surplus triangles shown in the upper portion of the diagram.

Samuelson next extended this extremum form of the problem to the many-regions, one-commodity case by reference to the Koopmans-Hitchcock linear programming transportation problem. If we simplify the problem by assuming a set of fixed supplies and demands in various regions separated by known and constant transport costs, the optimum trade configuration and set of prices can be determined by solving a linear programme. Suppose *m* exporting regions have quantities O_i available and *n* importing regions require quantities D_j and that the unit cost of transport between each pair of regions C_{ij} is a known constant with volume, i.e., transport enjoys constant costs. In this case the net consumer surplus problem is reduced to the simpler problem of minimizing transport costs. The objective of the exercise then is to minimize:

$$\sum_{i=1}^{m} \sum_{j=1}^{n} T_{ij} C_{ij} .$$

The set of flows T_{ij} which achieve this must lie within the domain of feasibility in terms of requirements and availability and being non-negative, i.e., the minimand is subject to:

$$\sum_{i=1}^{m} T_{ij} = D_j , \quad \sum_{j=1}^{n} T_{ij} = O_i , \quad T_{ij} \geq 0.$$

There are well-tried and proven ways of finding a unique solution to this problem (Scott 1971). The theoretical interest in this construction lies in the optimal prices arising from the simultaneous maximization of its dual, the two meeting at a minimax saddlepoint. The maximand is:

$$\sum_{j=1}^{n} p_j D_j - \sum_{i=1}^{m} p_i O_i$$

and this is subject to the limiting conditions:

$$p_j - p_i = C_{ij} \; ; \quad p_j, p_i \geq 0 \, ,$$

where the ps are regional prices and C_{ij} is the unit transport cost for the commodity in question.

Takayama and Judge (1964) relaxed the fixity of supply and demand quantities required for a linear programme by formulating the maximization of net social surplus for linear representations of supply and demand as a quadratic programme. For one commodity the maximand is:

$$\sum_i \int_o^{\sum_j T_{ij}} p_i \, dT_{ij} - \sum_j \int_o^{\sum_i T_{ij}} p_j \, dT_{ij} - \sum_i a_i - \sum_{ij} T_{ij} C_{ij}$$

subject to

$$p_i - p_j \leq 0; C_{ij}, p_i, p_j \geq 0$$

where a_i is the sum of producers' and consumers' surplus in region i at pre-trade equilibrium prices. This conversion of a market equilibrating problem to a collective optimizing one has been extended to many commodities and transformed into an operational model with efficient algorithms for its solution. Most recently Meister, Chen and Heady (1978) have applied it to the evaluation of the geographical implications of proposed policies for US agriculture.

Models of movement such as these arise from assumptions of perfect markets and discrete, omniscient rationality on the part of buyers and sellers and shippers. The commodities involved are homogeneous and infinitely divisible, and their utility is made explicit by the equality of supply and demand in terms of money prices. Although one can conceive of such a world, it is hard to discern its shadow in reality. This is especially so when we consider the motives for personal travel — and this is the largest component which must be grappled with in addressing the crucial questions of urban transport policy. The bewildering array of preferences and potential substitutions lying behind even the daily journey to work has led to the adoption of a probabilistic approach in theorizing and modelling some elements of the demand for transport. Much theorizing about the demand for personal travel has grown up around efforts at forecasting for the planning of networks for towns. The models of behaviour employed were designed to provide quantitative estimates of demand in terms of the operation of the whole transport system. To do this it is necessary to know how many people will be travelling between various points in a given time interval, by what means and what routes. The decision to travel is conditioned by where the actor is, where he wants to get to, for what reason, what means are available and what alternative routes present themselves. The choice between means of transport clearly depends on their performance in terms of the generalized cost measure introduced earlier, the most important element of which, along with money, is time. The selection of a means of travel depends on a comparison of performance, and this in its turn depends upon the selection of an appropriate route for the journey. In selecting which route to take, the actor must consider the numbers of others using the route — since performance is a function of volume travelling. Obviously the array of means and routes available and their relative merits may influence people's choice of destinations, if not whether to travel at all and, in the long run, where to locate their home, workplace and patronage of services. To break into this tangled complexity the travel decision has been broken out into a sequence for operational purposes. If we keep in mind that the reality is a skein of connections rather than single knots along a string of time, this simplification may provide some clearer vision of what is involved. The decision process is spun into a thread with decision knots made representing the choice of whether to travel, where to travel, how to travel and by what route to travel.

For practical purposes the decision to travel or not has to be translated into an aggregate of people who wish to load on to the transport system in particular times at particular places. Dividing the town into zones appropriate to the operational character of the transport system, the objective of modelling is to predict the numbers of trips generated by a zone. This obviously depends on the numbers of people doing various things in the zone and the generality of their travel behaviour. Since the critical time for design purposes is the peak and workers' daily travel is mostly from one home site to one work site, the theorizing involved in predicting traffic generation concerns the selection of residential locations and production locations. We will turn to these matters in the final section of this chapter. In forecasting operations the modelling involves establishing statistical regularities regarding the numbers of trips of various kinds as a function of the people resident or employed in zones and their wealth, potential for mobility and occupations.

Having established where people wish to start and finish their travels in aggregate terms the next step is to determine which origins and which destinations are connected by a flow of what magnitude. If the trips were for the same purpose by the same type of transport and the satisfaction available at destinations did not vary in quality, the programming solution of the last section would represent a competitive equilibrium and a social optimum. The real heterogeneity of any sizeable town is too great to handle even if different occupations and activities were treated as many different commodities.

Faced with this heterogeneity the chief response has been to abandon an aggregate of precise decision-makers in favour of a statistical model of the behaviour of a large number of randomly motivated individuals. Wilson (1967) postulated a system of zones from and to which there were given numbers of trips emanating O_i and terminating D_j. The feasible states of the system in terms of flows between origins and destinations (T_{ij}), were limited by constraints requiring the satisfaction of these availabilities and requirements and a constraint on the total energy available, that it be the same for any state. Thus, we have a structure where the minimand of the transportation problem discussed earlier constitutes one of the constraints of the system. along with limits on flow matrix row and column sums. What drives the system is not the minimizing of energy expenditure but a tendency towards sameness among system states. The probability of any particular configuration of flows existing is given by the total number of individual arrangements of origin/destination choices which conform with it. This is calculated as the product of the number of ways each element of the flow matrix could be selected from the total of trips, given the magnitude of the other flows. The probability of a particular matrix of flows is given by the binomial product

$$\frac{T!}{\prod_{ij} T_{ij}!}$$

where T is the total number of trips in the matrix. Wilson asserted that over all possible arrangements the distribution of this quantity was so peaked at its maximum that this was overwhelmingly the most likely set of flows. To get the general expression for this most probable array, the logarithm of the binomial product is maximized subject to the availabilities, requirements and energy constraints defining the feasible domain. Any monotonic function of the probability will produce the same expression and the logarithmic transformation enables the ready approximation of the factorial terms involved. The outcome of this algebra is an equation:

$$T_{ij} = A_i \, B_j \, O_i \, D_j \, \exp\left(-\beta C_{ij}\right)$$

where

$$A_i = \left(\sum_j B_j \, D_j \, \exp\left(-\beta C_{ij}\right)\right)^{-1}$$

and

$$B_j = \left(\sum_i A_i \, O_i \, \exp\left(-\beta C_{ij}\right)\right)^{-1}$$

where A_i and B_j are the solutions to the Lagrange multipliers associated with the row and column sum constraints. Since the value of the energy constant is unknown, the Lagrangian involved with this constraint cannot be solved for. That multiplier remains as an unknown B, which is then estimated from current behaviour.

This is the familiar gravity model, derived as the most probable state of movements in a system of randomly activated individuals upon whose behaviour we can only impose limits in terms of endpoint capacities and a total transport expenditure budget.

The resemblance between this model and the linear programming formulation is striking. Following Wilson's intuition, Evans (1973) has shown formally that the transportation problem solution is a limiting case of the most probable gravity model, where the value of the exponent of the cost of travel has been pushed to infinity and the budgetary constant effectively becomes a minimand. Wilson and Senior (1974) suggest that the probabilistic relaxation of deterministic programming models of behaviour using Wilson's 'entropy maximizing' structure may be an appropriate way of allowing for the imperfections of real markets and knowledge in trying to forecast the state of the world. Williams (1976) has shown that the entropy measure employed as a maximand by Wilson can be interpreted as a measure of consumer surplus and used in the evaluation of projects where demand is forecast with the appropriate model.

Some have seen programming and entropy maximizing formulations as an abdication of actual or potential knowledge of behaviour in theorizing about all aspects of the demand for travel. Rather than assume simple uniform motivation, it is deemed more valid to seek to measure components of individual choice functions and then aggregate these behavioural tendencies to forecast demand. As far as the choice of destinations is concerned, this approach is a response to observations that all persons do not inevitably choose the closest destination to satisfy a need which can, on the face of it, be gratified equally at a closer or a further place. Choices between close alternatives characteristically display an S-shaped relationship when accumulated over many

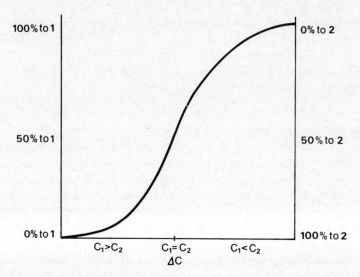

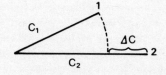

Figure 10

people. The proportion of people going to a closer rather than a further destination for the same purpose increases as the difference in cost of travel between pairs of places increases in the fashion shown in figure 10. Faced with this it is still necessary to make some assumption about the nature of motive and choice to articulate a model of rational behaviour. This usually takes the form of assumptions about the distribution of utility values between people or from time to time in the same person (McFadden 1973). One approach is to postulate that the values attributed to the utility of a good are stochastic but that choice is deterministic, selecting the highest utility value down to an infinitely small difference. An alternative is to assume that utilities are measured with deterministic precision but that choices are subject to random error. O'Sullivan and Ralston (1978) have suggested how a similar model form can be derived without recourse to the unobservable abstraction of utility. Even if we assume that people are identical in tastes, income and mobility and obey the *lex parsimoniae*, their choice between destinations differing only in terms of the distance involved in getting to them will display a degree of ambiguity arising from the limit to perception of differences in distance. The introduction of a tolerance level below which differences are imperceptible, with a distribution in the magnitude of this among a population, will yield a sigmoidal regularity such as that shown in figure 10.

Modal choice

These probabilistic models of choice have their original transport planning application in the forecasting of choice of means rather than destinations. This conception and representation of behaviour arose from trying to generalize the basis for selecting car or public transport for travel. The difference in stimulus was that of the generalized cost of making the same journey and the choice was between modes. In essence the traveller was faced with making a choice between two goods in terms of two currencies, time and money. The car is obviously less time-consuming and more money-consuming. The bus is slower but cheaper in cash terms. Given differences in the evaluation of time and money among the population of trip makers one would expect aggregate behaviour to exhibit some ambiguity of choice. The earliest overtly behavioural analysis was Warner's (1962) use of regression and discriminant analysis to estimate the probability of choosing one form of transport over another as a function of travel time, cost and the characteristics of the journey and person. Quarmby (1967) postulated a disutility-minimizing traveller. The disutility of one mode of transport compared with another he wrote as a linear function of the relative performance of that mode compared with other media, relative time, relative cost, relative convenience, etc. If we assume that the threshold at which differences in performance translate into the critical level of disutility is normally distributed among the population, then the probability of choosing one mode over the other will be a logistic function similar to that in figure 10. The empirical problem is to find the weights of the components of the disutility function so that they generate a sigmoid function which describes real choices best. Statistical procedures such as regression, discriminant, probit and logit analysis have been applied to this task, extending the disutility function to reflect the appropriate characteristics of the travellers, such as their mobility, income and purpose in travelling. Hensher and Stopher (1979) have assembled a compendium of the state of the art in this field.

One sought-after by-product of this kind of analysis of travel demand is an average value for time spent in travel of the population in question. The statistical procedures establish the set of coefficients *a* on the relative measures of modal performance which best fit a set of observed choices. For a linear disutility function where a_i is the coefficient for the time difference and a_j is the coefficient for the cash outlay difference in a choice between car and bus say, a_i/a_j reveals the sample's value of travel time. If the time differences have been dis-aggregated according to the walking, waiting and in-vehicle times involved in trips, it is also possible to induce the relative value of these components of generalized cost of travel. Bruzelius (1979) summarizes the theoretical and estimation problems involved in this.

Rather than deal with the specifics of transport, Quandt and Baumol (1966) proposed to follow Lancaster (1966) in theorizing in terms of the attributes of a good rather than the good itself. What is chosen, they proposed, is not a bus trip but some combination of speed, frequency and comfort at the appropriate cash outlay. Both destination and modal choice are modelled at the same time in terms of abstract modes. Modes are characterized in terms of speed, frequency, comfort and cost. A traveller's decision to travel and choice of mode is considered to depend on the absolute performance level of the 'best' mode on each criterion and the performance level of each mode on each criterion relative to the best mode. Since the model is couched in terms of abstract criteria, to forecast the use of new or proposed modes, their performance characteristics are merely inserted into the estimating formula. The demand for travel between two places by a particular mode is estimated as a function of the generative and attractive forces of these places, the number of modes serving them, the best performance in terms of time, cost, frequency over all modes and the relative time, cost and frequency for each mode. This function is taken to be linear in the logarithms so that it can be estimated using least squares. Some restrictions have to be placed upon the form of such models to ensure that irrelevant alternatives are excluded from influencing choices. Carelessly specified models of modal choice are prone to what in transport modelling parlance is called the 'red bus–blue bus' problem. Suppose there is a rail service and bus service of similar disutility joining two places so that the initial state is an even split of traffic. If it is now proposed to introduce another bus service differing only in the colour of buses, under assumptions of fixed total demand and no congestion effects, an abstract mode model will split the traffic in three equal parts, giving a bus : train split of 2 : 1 and an effective shift to the bus mode which denies the choice theory axiom that requires that irrelevant alternatives be independent.

Route choice and assignment

One way to avoid the irrelevant alternative problem is to assume that the choice of means of transport is made prior to the choice of route. This is a strong assumption about the way people view the travel process, but consideration must give it a good degree of credibility. It seems plausible that a decision is made on the mode to use on the basis of an approximation of disutility of alternatives and that the precise selection of a route on that mode's network is a matter for more precise calculation. To discuss the selection of a route and the aggregation of route choices into flows on network links, which are the crucial quantities for planning purposes, we will proceed on the basis of this assumption.

For public transport some notion of the schedule of services on alternative routes and their reliability should be sufficient to determine the way between a given origin and destination which minimizes disutility on what are usually sparse systems. For the case of car drivers, matters are complicated by the relationship between speed and flow. The cost of using a particular link varies as a function of the number of drivers who select it. Speed and flow are related as in figure 6. We can in effect treat this as an optimization problem in the market for road space. It is reasonable to assume that drivers will try to minimize absolute travel time, presuming that all other generalized cost components are a function of time taken within any single mode — or that we can transform any tolls to time penalties by the application of a suitable value of time. In selecting a path of travel between a given origin and destination the drivers are motivated to minimize their perceived private cost of travel. In selecting a particular link as part of this path, a driver influences the travel speeds of others using the link. This can be described by the general supply relationship between increasing vehicle numbers and decreasing travel speeds as in figure 6. Such a change causes all other users to reappraise their choice of routes, thus possibly changing route volumes and speeds, and so on. By a series of convergent iterations such a market arrangement can be brought to a balance between the sum of individual desires to minimize travel time and the capacity of the road system. The results of improving the capacity of the system can then be measured as the difference in traffic equilibrium volumes and speeds on roads after the proposed investment.

To express this in formal terms we designate the nodes of the network in general by i, k and j, there being a total of n of these. Trips start or finish in a subset m of these, labelled r as origins and s as destinations. The set of links ij in the network is signified by N. The flows along these links are given by T_{ij} with T_{ijrs} denoting the trips between origin r and destination s which use link ij. The total number of trips incident on any node is D for destinations and $-D$ for nodes generating trips. The time taken by a vehicle to traverse a link is taken to be a differentiable, monotone increasing function of volume. The travel-time relationship governing the performance of link ij is designated $X_{ij}(t)$. We can define the total travel time incurred on link ij as

$$f_{ij}(T_{ij}) = \int_{o}^{T_{ij}} X_{ij}(t)\, dt \,.$$

The stable set of flows on the network T_{ij} will be those which minimize the total travel expended over the entire network, i.e.

$$\text{minimize} \quad f(T) = \sum_{ij\,\epsilon\,N} f_{ij}\left(\sum_{r,s=1}^{m} T_{ijrs}\right).$$

The solution values to this problem must not be negative and must be such as to draw no more trips from an origin than it generates, send no

more to any destination than it requires, and clear all the traffic from
non-terminal junctions of the network. These requirements can be met
by placing the following constraints on the minimand:

$$\sum_i T_{ijrs} - \sum_k T_{jkrs} =$$

$$\begin{cases} -D\,(r,s)\,j = r & j = 1, \ldots, n \\[1.2em] O & j \neq r, s \quad r, s, = 1, \ldots, m \\[1.2em] D\,(r,s)\,j = s & r \neq s \end{cases}$$

and

$$T_{ijrs} \geq o \quad ij \; \epsilon \; N, \quad r, s, = 1, \ldots, m, \quad r \neq s.$$

It has been shown that a unique solution exists to this nonlinear
programme (LeBlanc, Morlok and Pierskalla 1975).

Location theory

To this point we have taken the location of production and
consumption activities as given, examining the movements between
them and the provision of channels for these movements. It is now
time to consider the motives of location selections and their aggregation
into patterns of land use.

The simplest specification of the location problem is in terms of a
constant cost producer who draws materials from several sources and
processes them at costs which do not vary geographically for
distribution to punctiform markets demanding fixed amounts at given
prices. The entrepreneurial decision then reduces to finding the location
for a factory for which the total transport bill is a minimum, for this
will maximize profits if they are to be had at all. The optimal location
will be the point of minimum aggregate travel in terms of both
assembly and distribution costs. It is easiest to formalize this on the
Euclidean plane surface where shortest paths are straight lines and
movement is equally costly in all directions. Solutions come more

readily on a graph-like representation of transport networks space, since the median point must be one of the vertices of the graph. However, we usually theorize on an isotropic surface and project the results into the relevant transport space as a map of isotims. These are lines of equal transport cost from some fixed point. In the Euclidean space they will be circular. In geographical space they will reflect topography and the structure of transport networks. Determination of the mapping function which transforms circles into the geographical loci will enable the transfer of solutions from Euclidean space into terrestrial space. For regular lattice networks we have already established these mapping functions in our discussion of route factors.

On the isotropic plain the total transport cost K at coordinates x_o, y_o is:

$$K(x_o, y_o) = \sum_i w_i c_i d_{io}$$

where w_i is the weight of input i per unit of product and is unity in the case of the product itself, or a proper fraction representing the market share in each of several markets, c_i is the transport rate applicable to good i and d_{io} is the distance from the source or market at x_i, y_i to x_o, y_o. There is no analytic method of finding a minimum value of K because of the fundamental interdependence of the x and y variables with respect to which the transport cost function is differentiated. In this case we are forced to seek numerical solutions for particular versions of the problem, using an interative process to make a series of approximations that approach an exact solution. In this case a method devised by Newton can be used to trace a path towards the bottom of the basin of cost lying within the polygon joining the material sources and markets. A modern version of this is given by Kuhn and Kuenne (1962). Another means of solution is exhaustive enumeration, a complete mapping of the transport cost surface within the polygon, summing the isotims of individual materials and markets to form an isodapane, total transport cost, surface, which can be inspected to find its minimum point. It is frequently the case that one material or market overwhelms other considerations and leads to a corner point solution at one of the vertices of the polygon. Whether this is the case can be ascertained before undertaking any extensive computations by finding if for any source or market j:

$$w_j \, c_j \geq \sum_i w_i \, c_i, \quad \text{for} \quad i \neq j.$$

If such a dominant weight exists, transport costs will be minimized by locating at its source. Even if such a dominant weight does not emerge, the best location may still be at a terminal, for at that juncture one set of terminal transport costs can be avoided. The methods involved do not take account of this, and any intermediate location selected by them must be set against the endpoint locations where these costs are not incurred. What further enhances terminal location is the tapering of rates characteristic of freight costs. This taper would translate into a wider spacing of more distant isotims on the transport cost map. To enjoy this advantage of longer hauls, it is tempting to ship one product as far as possible and thus locate any processing plant at the extremity of the maximum journey, rather than shipping the materials and product over two short hauls.

The above analysis holds for fixed quantities, prices and production costs, reducing profit maximization to transport cost minimization. If these restrictions are relaxed, then the transport cost minimizing location will not necessarily coincide with the profit maximizing one. Implicit in the formulation above is the assumption that the quantity of a factor of production used per unit of product is constant. This assumption is employed in input-output and other linear representations of economic relations. We do, however, in general recognize the potential for adjusting the mix of factors and reducing costs with increasing output. Moses (1958) showed that if factor substitution is allowed, since the delivered price of inputs will vary from place to place, the best factor mix will vary in such a fashion that the ratio of the marginal productivity of the factors will equal the ratio of their prices. It will only be a matter of chance that the profit maximizing location coincides with the transport cost minimizing one.

Central places

If we are concerned with the manufacture and distribution of consumer goods and services it is necessary to extend the representation of demand geography from a point to an areal extent. For many products the minimum size of market necessary to sustain the activity and the maximum distance from which customers will purchase the good are far less than the breadth of the regional and national market contemplated. The location problem becomes one of delimiting market areas for the functions of towns as central places providing goods and services to their hinterlands. Under the assumptions of a boundless plain with an evenly distributed population for the case of a single good where customers bear delivery costs, both Christaller (1966) and Lösch (1954) generated hexagonal lattices of equilibrium market areas. Most recently Eaton and Lipsey (1975) have conjectured that no such equilibrium can exist for three or more firms competing in the plain and Shaked (1975) has proved this to be so for three firms.

To deal with the gathering of several functions into towns and the nesting of market areas of functions with different ranges, Lösch built up an hierarchically ordered landscape starting with the function with the most 'local' market. Having constructed lattices for all possible functions he anchored them on the largest city, which served all functions and rotated lattices until the agglomeration of functions in towns was maximized. Christaller started with the most 'national' good's market area and the premier city providing all goods and divided its market area up by the location of towns with fewer and fewer functions and smaller and smaller hinterlands. Depending whether the driving force of the process was commercial competition, the minimization of transport investment or administrative convenience, different symmetrical landscapes based on stacks of different-sized hexagonal lattices emerged. Obviously the symmetrical economic landscapes of both theorists arise from the service of widely spread customers and their symmetric patterns of movement and transport demand. Although they provide a neat explanation of city size and spacing relations and have been applied to the historical analysis of development processes (Johnson 1970), their degree of abstraction makes them of little value for policy application.

Land use and value

From a strategic, macrogeographic viewpoint, it may be reasonable to consider production and service activities as having no areal extent, as points to be located. This will obviously not do for agricultural production nor to address policy issues where competition for land is concerned. In dealing with the effect of building roads in towns, for example, the main concern is with the extent and value of residential land and its encroachment on farm land. In such circumstances it is more realistic to consider the market to be a central fixed point, the place of work or market for agricultural produce, and to determine the type and intensity of land use in relation to this central focus.

Whether the product of the land is workers destined for a centre of employment or agricultural produce which must be sold at a market, the surplus accruing from its use is the difference between the market price of its product and production and transport costs. We can write this in terms of a unit of land as:

$$R = q(p\text{-}k) - qcd$$

where q is the amount of product per unit of land, for example, workers or bushels per acre, p is the market price at the central point, k is production cost per unit produce, c is the transport rate for the product per unit distance and d is distance to the centre. If we assume production costs and productivity per acre are everywhere the same, then the surplus is a simple function of distance as in figure 11. This is at a maximum at the market where distance is zero and declines with increasing distance until at the margin of settlement or cultivation the surplus becomes zero at a distance $p\text{-}k/c$. Beyond that point production and transport costs exceed the wage or price available at the centre. In the case of labour we might think of production cost as a reserve price determined by unemployment payments. This difference in the surplus achievable at various locations will incite competition for land. People will be willing to pay either higher rents or purchase prices for land nearer the place of work or the market. Supposing that the land is rented, competitive bids will continue to the point where the surplus is consumed by rent, for only at that juncture will users be indifferent between locations. Rents will be at a maximum at the centre and decline to zero at the margin of active land use. Thus, the return which equilibrates the competition to use land is rent and in this instance is equivalent to consumer surplus in the market for transport services. The reserve price for transport, which all producers would pay in the last resort, is that paid by the marginal producer. If we sum the difference between this value and what is actually paid we get as a measure of consumer surplus the same quantity we have just called rent. If all other considerations than pure position are set aside, the geographical margin of participating producers with respect to a fixed central market is the locus which maximizes their surpluses, i.e. the radius at which willingness to sell just equals the central market price minus unit transport cost. The peculiarity of land — that it has unique position as well as homogeneous extent as its primitive attributes — means that this surplus, enjoyed by purchasing transport to ship a good or travel to work at a central point, can be arrogated by the owners of land. The owner of land is the ultimate in discriminating monopolists for he owns, in effect, one or many unique goods and can charge what the traffic will bear. Competition cannot force a single market clearing price. Rather there is a pattern of rents which absorb the surpluses arising from geographically variable transport costs. The surplus is at a maximum where transport cost is zero at the centre and decreases to zero at the margin where transport cost is maximal. Geographical equilibrium is achieved where rent absorbs the surplus and rent and transport cost sum to a constant amount, which makes farmers or residents indifferent between locations. From this it follows that changes in circumstances, for example, changes in transport costs due to investment, can be evaluated in terms of their contribution to rent or its equivalent, consumer surplus in the transport market. Much of location theory is an elaboration on this simple theme, with the surplus which becomes rent remaining the driving force.

One obvious elaboration is to allow for more than one type of occupancy competing to use land. This would be different crops with different prices, costs, yields and transport costs in the case of farming. In the urban case it might be different classes of workers with different wages, tastes in dwelling space and mobility in terms of car ownership. In general each activity will have a potential surface of prices for land diminishing from the market centre outwards as in figure 11a in accordance with price yield, costs and transport costs. The activity with the highest such 'bid price' surface will drive all other

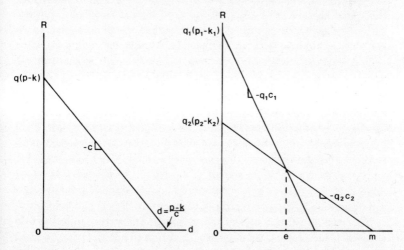

Figure 11

uses out over the range of its superiority. In a simple two-use case as in figure 11b, activity 1 has the superior rent function over the range *oe*, whence 2 becomes dominant with its occupation of land extending out from *e* to the margin at *m*. Rotating this through 360° produces a land-use map consisting of concentric circular boundaries between 1 and 2 and 'no use'. The conditions necessary for competition to yield annuli in this fashion with rent bid surfaces crossing are that the rent surface of one use must have a steeper slope ($-q_1 c_1 < -q_2 c_2$) at the same time that its intercept value is greater ($q_1 (p_1 - k_1) > q_2 (q_2 - k_2)$). Obviously a use with a smaller slope and higher intercept will exclude any inferior competitor, while a larger slope with a lower intercept value will render an activity non-competitive. This analysis can obviously be extended to many activities producing a 'tree trunk section' pattern of land uses. The construction can be employed to examine the comparative static effects of changes in prices, yields and transport costs on the margins between uses. General reductions in transport costs can be evaluated in terms of the increase in total rent and the extension of the outer margin of use.

In the case of residential use, the assumption of a constant yield or different yields for different classes may be an inadequate description of the real thing. Even among groups of people similar in occupation, income and mobility, there are differences in the amount of space they consume. If the demand curve for space is in general elastic, sloping down to the right so that at a higher cost per acre people consume less land, then there is going to be a reduction in the density of residential land use with distance from the centre of town as in figure 12. At the higher rents near the centre, people will consume less space and density will be greater, diminishing as rent per acre diminishes until it becomes zero where the rent bid surface for agricultural use becomes superior. To determine where this margin lies it is necessary to consider the market for labour in this economy which will give the total number of persons to be accommodated. The limit to which the density function must spread in order to encompass this total population will locate the outermost commuters. The wage to be paid to all workers must be sufficient to overcome the travel costs of these most distant participants. The surplus over actual travel costs for those located at less than this generates equilibrium values of per-unit rent, and multiplied by density these give rents per dwelling.

The duality of rent maximization and transport cost minimization we have just explored in location theory was displayed by Stevens (1961) exploiting the same linear programming framework which

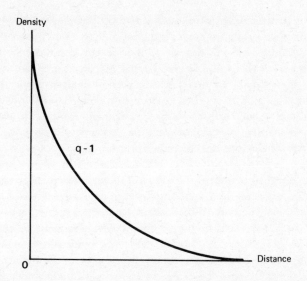

Density

q - 1

Distance

Figure 12 0

Samuelson employed when treating interregional trade equilibrium. The prices generated by the dual of the transportation problem which we examined in our treatment of flow theory, can be interpreted as location rents if we introduce an element expressing production costs including normal profits which we will assume to be a constant k among all locations. The constraint on the dual then becomes

$$(p_j + k) \leq (p_i + k) - C_{ij}.$$

This will not alter the incidence of these limits and, since k now appears as both a positive and a negative in the dual maximand,

$$\sum_j (p_j + k) \, D_j - \sum_i (p_i + k) \, O_i,$$

the value of this will be unaffected. With this adjustment $(p_i + k)$ becomes the ex-works or factory gate price at i and $(p_j + k)$ is the delivered price at j, and the constraint expresses the usual condition for geographical price equilibrium, that there is no excess profits. For any one destination the equilibrium delivered price is established by the delivered price from the source actually supplying the good which is most distant in transport cost terms, the marginal supplier. This furthest supplier earns zero rent. Closer locations receive differential location rents equal exactly to the amounts saved on transport on units supplied by them rather than by the marginal supplier. Under assumptions of a common responsiveness to variations in transport costs and prices, this quantity can be seen as consumer surplus in the transport market. This is zero for the marginal purchaser of transport and maximal for the most locationally advantaged participant in the market. The perfect discrimination of the land market results in an equilibrium identical to that of perfect competition. Under perfect discrimination, marginal revenue is identical to demand, and profit maximizing results in efficient marginal cost prices. The maximized surplus is merely transferred to the owners of land.

With this treatment of location theory we have completed the circuit of interwoven relations between land uses, flows of goods and people and the channels carrying these between places. As yet no one has provided successfully for the general treatment of these phenomena simultaneously, but the components of such a creation have been articulated as displayed here. It could be said, of course, that the network construction element of the whole should not be treated as arising from a market process. The public sector is inevitably involved in these decisions and the government ought to insist on the planning of transport network developments as a conscious optimization problem with collective welfare as its optimand.

CHAPTER·3

Social and Economic Evolution and Transport Technology

Many of the significant political, social and economic changes man has experienced were associated with new, more efficient means of locomotion, both in terms of ways and vehicles. Certainly his ability to occupy and exploit the face of the earth was related to the ease with which he could overcome the friction of distance. To flesh out this proposition we will consider some particular historical examples. To explore politics and economy in a pre-industrial society as a response to transport technology, the evolution of man's occupancy of Ireland from the Boreal to the twentieth century will be traced. This is followed by an investigation of the process of colonization. The relations between transport, settlement and territorial hegemony are exemplified by the expansion of the frontier in what is now the USA. This has obvious parallels with the Russian experience of Muscovy and then Tsardom expanding control and the Slavic presence into the southern river basins and beyond the Urals. A related and contemporary phenomenon was the explosion of industrial activities with its epicentre in Great Britain. The connections between canals, railways and industrial growth will be viewed in the setting of the British Industrial Revolution in the first place. Discussion of the role of railways in the industrial take-off process naturally extends to the national railway network experience of Italy and France and then to the continental American and Russian cases, where there was a great deal more geographical enterprise involved. Since it was Fogel (1964) who stirred the controversy in economic history with the US case, it is this we will concentrate attention on. At a more local scale industrialization and improved means of personal transport spawned the vast urban growth of the last 150 years. The most recent focus of concern over man's cultural evolution in transport terms has arisen as the <u>internal combustion</u> engine and reinforced concrete provided the prospect of a universal means of individual travel. Provisioning this new-found freedom of movement generated a major expansion of the industrial complement of developed economies in the car industry and its auxiliaries and generated political pressure to expand the public facility for using the product. After the improvements and additions to existing roads designed for horse carriages and carts in the 1920s and 1930s, roads specifically designed for motor vehicles were built in Italy and Germany and then, after World War II, in the US and UK. The relative, and in some cases absolute, decline of rail's fortunes as a result of improved roads, pipelines and air passenger services, has presented political problems of some consequence. As inter-city routes probed the edges of sprawling suburbia, the demand for comparable facilities for intra-urban movement gave rise to the most significant planning problems of our urban fabric faces. The service of mobility needs within the city by different means of transport and its effects in terms of the evolution of urban shape and size will be illustrated by reference to Chicago, which grew most rapidly in the era of mass transit, and Los Angeles, a city of the middle twentieth century.

Transport and the human geography of Ireland

Let us trace the changes in man's occupation of Ireland as his mastery of distance developed. We can start with a clean slate in the Boreal, when the ice sheet last retreated from this part of the world. The people who reached the place by a land bridge across the North Channel, or by craft across a shallow sea, formed the basis for the future population. After the separation of the island with rising sea level, there is no skeletal or archaeological evidence to indicate further mass immigration. The degree of archaeological continuity found suggests that Ireland's population followed the common line of European development, but by absorbing in indigenous forms cultural and economic changes introduced by small groups of seaborne traders and warriors.

An extreme 'diffusionist' view of the process sees all advance impinging from outside. Sir Cyril Fox (1959) labelled Ireland part of the European 'zone of fusion of cultures'. The Atlantic fringe of the offshore islands, because of their remoteness and physiognomy, with a lower density of population scattered over a thinner resource base than the central area, was seen as absorbing ideas and changes at a slower rate. Innovation waves were seen as sweeping from hearths in the Middle East and Mediterranean Basin, picking up speed across lowlands amenable to movement and breaking against the intractable bogs and blocks of the western periphery. The validity of this simple picture is called into question by the discovery that the carbon-14 clock used to collaborate this view of prehistory was miscalibrated. It appears now that many northwest European artefacts were contemporary or prior, not just pale reflections of Mediterranean and Levantine originals. Nevertheless, innovations did come from the east and were slowed in their spread by forest, bog and upland. Bog, and land over 1000 feet, still take up one-third of the island. Stone or bronze tools could not effectively hack the temperate forests of Ireland — only cheap iron tools and a climatic change from the moist Atlantic period to the drier sub-Boreal gave man a start in mastering this aspect of the environment.

Early settlement was coastal and riverine. The coast afforded the first way for travel and trade. 'Until men became tillers of the soil and road makers, the edge of the sea was their highway'. Through the Stone Age and early Bronze Age people could only gain access to limited inland areas which were not heavily wooded nor subject to bog formation. Spreading out from early north-eastern coastal and riverine sites people penetrated along lines of least resistance into the open grasslands of the north central drift plain, the limestone tracts of the northwest coast and the unforested plateau of the north. Apart from these open areas the only possible sites for human habitation were the tops of drumlins and eiscirs, on sandhills by the sea, in river valleys or on hillslopes between 600 and 1000 feet.

The drowning of the north-eastern land bridge in the Atlantic period led to a period of isolation, reflected in Irish flora and fauna. In the early Bronze Age a seaborne trade in copper led to ties with Iberia via the Atlantic trade route, which extended north to Scotland and Scandinavia. Prehistoric scholarship conventionally divides the Bronze Age into early and late phases at about 1000 B C. This marks a reordering of linkages and interactions in Ireland away from Iberia and towards central Europe. The occupants of the Alpine foreland, athwart transalpine and Danubian trade routes between the Mediterranean and the north, became the dominant influence in Western Europe. As the Celtic hegemony emerged, Iberia lost its monopoly of trade and the southern half of the Atlantic trade route fell into disuse. It was replaced by an overland route through north Wales and by ridgeway to the English Channel. This east-west connection predominated through the late Bronze Age and early Iron Age. For Ireland, this shorter link with southern England was to prevail over the more tenuous Iberian link through the centuries. There is no evidence of wholesale Celtic invasion and replacement of population. There were incursions of warrior bands of iron users forming two epicentres for the diffusion of iron use, one in the north-east with Scottish ties and the other in the Central Plain, with southern British connections. Late Bronze Age and early Iron Age settlement expanded into formerly unoccupied areas by clearing forest, commencing in the Plain of Meath opposite the gateway to Britain.

Parallel with the growth and spread of population ran an enlargement in size of the territorial arrangements of society. From the family unit of mesolithic hunters, there arose clan and tribal units among neolithic pastoralists and tillers. In the Bronze Age a very stable basic unit of political economy emerged. The island was divided into about 100 regions of about 10 miles in radius. These varied in size according to variations in the physical base, being larger in upland areas. They were political entities based on a rural economy, each having its own dynastic family and court of law and state. These units were variously combined into regional groupings under the leadership of the family of one of their members. At the start of the Christian era Ireland was divided into five such divisions. These fifths had central places where periodic gatherings (hostings) for fairs, legal and political assembly took place. By the fifth century the political pattern had resolved itself into a somewhat insecure high kingship over a seven-fold division of the island. This approached the stature of a unified state briefly about A D 1000, under Brian Boru.

The clearest evidence of the widespread centralization of military and political power is to be seen in the archaeological remnants of a network of roads radiating from the Plain of Meath and extending to the periphery of the country, which is conjectured to have reached its fullest extent by the second century A D (Figure 13). This structure is redolent of political centralization. It connects the centres of the seven provincial kingdoms to the seat of the high king on the Plain of Meath. This is the area nearest the centre of gravity of the island capable of supporting a large military establishment. That Tara, the focus, is inland indicates that it sprang from local enterprise. No doubt this network facilitated some trade, but probably the chief movement of wealth was of tribute and the chief use of the roads was military (i.e. for cattle thieving). The continual battle for control of the whole island was essentially a fight for control of the Meath hub.

The emergent Roman Empire played an indirect role in all of this. Irish warrior bands made a living from raiding Roman provinces and picked up ideas along with plunder. Epic tales suggest a change from Homeric individual fights and the use of chariots to the use of organized

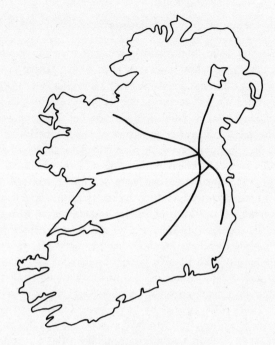

2ND CENTURY ROAD NETWORK

Figure 13

mercenary foot soldiers based on the Roman model. Christianity returned with raiders in the shape of a slave in about A D 430. The institutional influence of Christianity, which had inherited and spread Roman centralism in the form of hierarchy elsewhere, was infused with the native political order here, producing a decentralized tribal, monastic structure.

From A D 800, Scandinavians in clinker-built boats presented a new external influence on the course of Irish history. The Vikings, first as raiders then as traders, gained permanent footholds on the seaboard, even though their attempts at conquering the interior were rebuffed in 1014. The major towns of Ireland have their origins in Viking forts which grew into trading towns. These were the places with the readiest access to the interior. The effect of this intrusion was to expand the horizons of the Irish economy and introduce it to overseas markets and supplies. Although the land of saints and scholars had exported learning, Christianity and artworks from the sixth century, the Viking ports enabled trade to extend to imports of wine, salt, metals and luxuries for hides, wool and provisions.

Conquests

The process by which the island was engulfed in the economy with
its centre on the English plain began in 1169. Henry II arrived in
1171 to ensure that the acquisitions of his wilder bucks became part
of the realm. Dublin was chosen as the capital from which to administer
these gains and in 1200 Dublin Castle was built, standing where one
of the roads from Tara crosses a navigable inlet — the Liffey. Thus the
centre of the transport network was pulled to the coast, indicating
the exterior focus of the new order. The method of conquest was en-
castellation. Permanent garrisons were set up at strategic points on
the lines of communication. Fifty years after the first landing, conquest extended to two-thirds of the island. The native aristos retreated
with their fighting men into the remote and rugged reaches of the land.
For most people there was just a change of rulers. The native kingdom
became the barony with a feudal rather than a tribal lord.

The English kings, contesting for power with the English barons,
were unable to keep control of Ireland. After 1315 there was a re-
surgence of the Gaelic aristocracy who regained much territory. By the
early fifteenth century, the Pale had shrunk to a radius of 25 miles
from Dublin. Of the 90 baronies outside the Pale, 60 were ruled by
Gaelic chiefs. Most of the Normans beyond the Pale went native, becoming *'ipsis Hibernicis Hiberniores'*. Moats and castles meant to
maintain unitary control became centres of defiance against the central
government. The aristocracy, now a mixture of Fitzgeralds, Butlers,
Burkes, Lynches and deLaceys along with the Macs and O's, continued
to fight to extend their several interests. The traditional structure had
overcome a geographically precocious attempt at unification — distance
friction triumphed.

The economy was still basically a subsistence one, with farmers
paying tribute rents out of any surplus to a warrior elite. Some of this
surplus accrued to the English monarchy, when it could make its power
felt. The major direction of a mounting overseas trade was to the
continent, especially to Spain. Southern and western ports boomed on
the basis of the wine trade. Dublin's importance was due to its position
as political capital, taking little part in continental trade. There was a
fairly even distribution of traffic between the 16 chief ports as a result
of the high cost of overland transport, reflected in the division of the
country into many small political and economic units.

The fifteenth century saw a start of a radical rearrangement of
affairs. The introduction of ordnance, the *ultima ratio regis*, to warfare

assisted in the concentration of power in England. Supported by the existence of a large unitary state under the stable Tudor monarchy, there was an acceleration of English mercantile activity seeking new markets and raw material sources. Ireland presented the first target for this expansion. Henry VII and Henry VIII tried to reconcile the lords of the land to the new order, but it became obvious that to control the island and make it amenable to commercial intercourse with England would require 'extirpation'. Fighting and planting continued throughout the sixteenth and seventeenth centuries and was accompanied by the building of roads, bridges and passes through forests and by drastic deforestation. There is a constant repetition in state papers of the period of orders to the military to impress labour for constructing and maintaining causeways, roads and passes. The Dublin Parliament of 1613-15 established a regular highway system with a view to territorial dominance.

The old order sustained itself longest in the remote corners of the island but, despite reverses, the suppression succeeded and by 1700 control was firmly in the hands of the English central government, with a satellite administration and parliament in Dublin. The confiscation of the lands of the clans was accompanied by the planting of settlers from Great Britain. Lowland and border Scots proved more durable than English farmers. Many who did settle, especially in Ulster, were induced to remove themselves to North America by native competition, by English mercantilist restrictions on their manufacturing enterprises and by rent increases when the initial 99-year leases came up for renewal. The first surge of Scotch-Irish swelled the population of the 13 colonies in the 1720s, their bitterness at England providing a core for revolt. Outside Ulster, plantation meant the substitution of absentee, rack-renting, Anglican gentry for the native warrior elite. Through the eighteenth and for much of the nineteenth century, power lay in the hands of the landlords of the Protestant ascendancy. This group was backed by the power of the English central government *but* it was also inhibited by the mercantile and English landed interests which the London government most keenly responded to. The landlords' main concern was the extraction of rent. Legislation limiting trade discouraged investment in their Irish property. The low level of economic and social life encouraged absenteeism and resulted in most of the rental income being spent or invested in England. These same limits on trade resulted in the rapid decline of the southern and western ports engaged in continental trade and the rise of the eastern ports trading with England through Chester, Liverpool and Bristol. The mercantilist desire to cut the ties of trade with Spain and France was reinforced by military fears for the soft western flank.

Transport investment

The road network in 1700, resulting from three centuries of military actions, showed clearly how the country was being focused on the Dublin satellite (figure 14). It radiated from this nexus with English power, producers and markets. The majority of the population was, as usual, engaged in surviving periods of destruction and famine under a system best described as tribute agriculture. They subsisted, and any surplus was drawn off as tribute rent and taxes by whosoever could command them. By the 1650s the use of the potato was widespread and this, plus comparative peace after 1700, helped to produce a rapid expansion of population from 2,000,000 in 1680 to 8,000,000 in 1840.

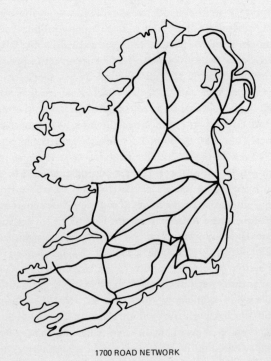

1700 ROAD NETWORK

Figure 14

With the growth of industry and its city population England became a net importer of food after 1750 and, thus, released restrictions on imports from Ireland. In 1759 an embargo on Irish cattle imports was lifted and the Dublin Parliament offered a bounty for the inland transport of wheat to Dublin for export to England. The subsistence of the majority did not depend on trade and good communications, but the payment of rent and taxes did — especially when grain production was encouraged. Thus, it is not surprising that the governmental promotion of agricultural production was accompanied by an increase in public investment in transport to facilitate this intensification. The road network of 1750 was in bad repair. In 1759 statutory labour on roads was abolished and aristocratic county grand juries were authorized to use tenant taxes to repair and build roads. This grand jury presentment system reduced the cost of movement to and from mountainous and formerly remote western areas, extending the margin of commercial agriculture. Improvements in roads enabled the winning of great tracts of land between the 1780s and 1840s. Mountain and bog property increased in value as a source of turf and for growing the subsistence crop of potatoes, thereby releasing better land for cash grain production. Some landlords even used their own capital to build roads. A denser and more extensive road network made policing the population easier, reduced tax evasion, made illicit whiskey making more risky and less necessary and provided famine relief work. In the 1830s 40 per cent of the land tax was directed to roads and bridges. In 1784 a Post Office was established in Ireland with power to widen and strengthen old roads and construct new ones for the benefit of the mails. In 1799 soldiers were employed building military roads in the Wicklow and Waterford mountains after the rising of 1798. Board of Works famine relief work resulted in many improvements. All of these efforts intensified the network in the lowlands near the ports and extended coverage into the Atlantic littoral and mountains (figure 15).

In the late eighteenth and in the nineteenth century there was widespread belief that investment in canals or railways would solve the problems of recurrent famine, rural underemployment and discontent. The government was induced to invest in the Grand Canal (1804) and Royal Canal (1817) connecting Dublin to the Shannon. The outlay never yielded a positive return. There was little freight that could bear the tolls and passenger traffic was soon captured by railways. The main rail trunk lines of Ireland were laid down during the 1840s along three axes radiating from Dublin. By the 1860s many cross links between provincial centres and feeders had been added, especially

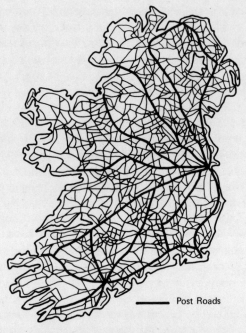

1850 ROAD NETWORK

Figure 15

in the northeast. But, as early as 1860, the railway companies found themselves in dire financial straits. Ireland did not have the perennial freight traffic which sustains railways. Building slowed up except in the north-east and where subsidized light railways were pushed into the western peninsulas and mountains.

The outcome of the transport improvements of the eighteenth and nineteenth centuries was a greater involvement of Ireland in the British economy and thus with rapidly developing world markets. This was accompanied by a catastrophic adjustment of population and production. The increase in grain production of the second half of the eighteenth century met slackening demand in 1815 when the Napoleonic wars were concluded. Cattle offered a better return as meat consumption increased in England and as Baltic, American and Australian grain supplies grew steadily. As the price of grain decreased so the value of labour used to produce it declined. Thus, landlords desired to reverse the trend of subdivision of land which they had encouraged when grain prices were high and get rid of surplus labour. Leinster, in closest proximity to England, exhibited the most rapid response to changed conditions. Subdivision was halted and farms consolidated into grazing ranches. Labourers and farmers ejected in this change either moved to Dublin or crossed to the industrial centres or to the canal- and railway-building navvy gangs of Great Britain. Thus in the 1830s and 1840s Leinster had the slowest rate of population growth and the lowest density of population on arable land. The change from tribute to commerical agriculture commenced in the most accessible part of the country. To some degree this change was a redirection of the provisions trade, drawing on livestock from the pastures of the south-west and midlands, which had formerly served the American seaboard. Increased competition from the Ohio Valley combined with rising English demand to swing its course.

The wool and silk industries of Ireland, started in the late eighteenth century, withered rapidly when subjected to the full blast of English competition. Only the linen industry survived by concentrating in the north-east. In Down and Antrim, free from competition for labour and capital, it was able to expand when the linen industry of England and Scotland gave way to cotton. The concentration of the industry led to emigration from those areas where the domestic linen industry had flourished — the rest of Ulster and adjacent parts of Connacht and Leinster. This was the second surge of Scotch-Irish to North America in 1771-3. Outside the north-east the only manufacturing to concentrate and grow was brewing — which localized in Cork and Dublin.

The death of a million people in the famine of 1845-8 awakened the survivors, especially in the west, to the risks of subsistence on the potato. Improvements in communications and travel drew the alternatives to their attention and eased the path to the burgeoning industrial economies of Great Britain and North America. Cheap trans-Atlantic travel enabled one million to leave for the shores of America in the 1840s, while a quarter of a million provided the expanding British economy with cheap, unskilled labour. Only the north-east increased in population, with Harland and Wolff siting their shipyard in Belfast Lough. These population changes were part and parcel of the centripetal flow from peripheral and rural areas to the growing cities of Europe and North America. The population of Ireland declined in this fashion from 6.5 million in 1851 to 4 million in 1931, at which level it has remained since.

The emergence of a fully commercial agriculture in Ireland was diverted by the political battle for control of land. There had always been local resistance to landlords but the arrival of cheap newsprint and railways enabled the growth of nationwide parties whose leaders' clout came to outweigh that of the landed class with the British cabinet. The high cost of policing a discontented people was an added incentive to the central government to address their demands. By the 1860s the condition of the tenantry was a matter of great government concern. In an effort to placate their antipathy, the Ashbourne Act of 1885 finally made tenant ownership possible. The holdings which resulted were in many cases too small to be commercially viable and to attract capital. Despite the rapid reduction in population, the problem of small fragmented holdings barely sufficient for subsistence persists in the far-flung Atlantic fringe, subsidized by emigrants' remittances or itinerant labour in England, and now grants to sustain a Gaelic-speaking and small farming stock. In the last century efforts such as the building of light railways were made to generate commerce where people spoke no English and had little experience of a market economy. One persistent source of income from outside which those railways first introduced was the tourist trade, which was drawn to the rugged drama of the west's landscape which appealed to romantic and pre-Raphaelite tastes.

The emergence of government responsiveness to popular interests in the last century is complicated in Ireland by the issue of nationality. The separatism of those representing Catholic tenant interests in the nineteenth century was a demand for Home Rule — a parliament in Dublin closer to social and economic problems. Republicanism had its origins among the Protestant middle classes. It picked up romantic notions of the preservation of folk identity and formed a focus for popular sympathy in times of crisis when sides were chosen. The countervailing sentiment of loyalty to the British Crown was not strong among people for whom the Crown and landlordism were synonymous. The exception to this was among the nonconformist Protestants of the north-east. They chose to forget past woes and close ranks with their Anglican landlords and governors against the threat of papist domination. More importantly, the welfare of industry in the north-east was obviously tied to the fortunes of the British economy, and the bitterness between landlord and tenant had been ameliorated by a more favourable rental custom than the tenancy at will which prevailed outside Ulster. Aside from immediate causes and events the separation of 26 counties of the island from the US in 1922 represented resistance to cultural and economic assimilation into a 'British' entity, while the perceived interests and sympathies of many people in the north-east with the British connection, combined with the power of the UK, resulted in six counties remaining outside the new state.

Political separation of the Republic has not resulted in any lasting change in direction for trade and the economy. If anything there has been a more intense focusing on Dublin, which remains the nexus with the English economy. The patterns of economic and social inter-action with the bigger island, which have been in the weaving at least since 1700, cannot readily be unravelled. The inertia of trade relations and comparative advantages is massively stable, not easily disrupted by politics. The process of transformation from Arensberg and Kimbal's 'Irish peasants' (1968) into agricultural entrepreneurs continues slowly. A trickle of people leave the countryside, especially from the west, to emigrate or increase the small growth of urban population. Migration and the realities of the market place are aided and abetted by govern-ment schemes for improvement and resettlement.

At a cost in tax concessions and subsidies, the government has attracted a number of manufacturers to locate in Ireland, expanding the limited employment in this sector. It has even persuaded some to locate beyond the Shannon. The problem is that an operation which will readily go to Ireland for a temporary advantage can as readily go elsewhere should the occasion arise. Now with both the Republic and the UK in the EEC, political separation looks, from a historic perspec-tive, like a brief experiment which brought about no fundamental change in Ireland's economic landscape.

The US frontier and transport

Drawing on the authority of Brown (1948), it is evident that the political and economic evolution of the USA is written in routes, roads, rails and trails as much as it is in a constitution, amendments, claims, purchases and cessions. Those beyond the political boundary or settlement frontier were crushed or integrated as a web of routes increased access to markets. These encouraged commerical settlement, stripping lighter forms of exploitation of their resource base, and drew together a coherent, unified economy and polity. To explore the relations between transport, settlement, production and com-merce we have merely to follow the expansion of the frontier of European settlement from the coastal colonies and missions of the early seventeenth century to the Census Bureau's official announce-ment of the closure of the frontier in 1890.

By 1700 there was a tidewater tracery of rural settlement along the

Atlantic coast, petering out in the Dismal Swamp of southern Virginia. The original coastal sites, often in clearings made for Indian shifting cultivation, shot off planned extensions into the interior along lines of weakness to penetration. Lobes of settlement spread up the Connecticut, Hudson, Potomac, James and Susquehanna. Starting in the 1630s the French had parcelled out and occupied the banks of the St Lawrence as far as Rapides de la Chine, with strip farms, one-tenth of a mile long, running back from the channel of intercourse provided by the river. This pattern was repeated in the Illinois settlements of the Mississippi bottom lands at Kashaskia, founded in 1682 and later along the channels and bayous of Louisiana. The Spanish had tried to make something of Florida on and off from the 1560s, selecting San Augustin as its nucleus in 1562. By 1700 there was a track, grandly entitled El Camino Real, from San Augustin to San Marcos on the Gulf. More lasting marks were left by expeditions up the Rio Grande and Gila in the 1630s. From El Paso the Spanish reoccupied Santa Fe in 1690, having been repulsed by the Pueblos in the 1680s. Alburquerque was settled in 1706. Missions and military stations were spun off from El Paso along the Gulf coast with San Antonio as the regional headquarters.

Apart from the Spanish missionary incursions into California in the 1770s and 1780s, the main flood of expansion after 1700 stemmed from the British settlement of the Atlantic shore, so it is on these that we concentrate. By 1720, New England's largely planned extension of settlements, with pre-arranged towns, roads and platting, included eastern New Hampshire, much of Massachusetts, Rhode Island, and Connecticut with a finger probing up the Connecticut valley. In New York and Pennsylvania the spread was a more spasmodic leap-frogging of single farmsteads, especially after the arrival of the first wave of Scotch-Irish in the 1720s. These colonial shock-troops, having learned to survive in the face of native hostility in Ulster, now turned their expertise on America's indigenes. They provided the typical frontiersman, often out making a living well in advance of the unbroken line of settlement. The line of the frontier did remain stationary at Fort Stanwix at the head of the Mohawk Valley from 1740 to 1790. The Iroquois, with the aid of the imperial government in London, held the line in defence of their territory. They bled the pressure for settlement up the Mohawk by not discouraging expansion into the Ohio Valley, from which they had previously expelled a rival tribe. Avoiding the bleaker Appalachians of Pennsylvania, people trickled into the more southerly ridge and valley country along animal trails connecting the salt licks of the interior. By 1780 there were outliers of the frontier in the Kentucky Bluegrass at Boonesborough and Harrodsburg.

The economy of the South was also on the move. The plantation complex inundated vast tracts of the Piedmont from the Potomac south to Georgia, where settlement dates from 1732. Tobacco plantations were being established on the Virginia Piedmont while cotton was beginning to emerge as the plantation product in South Carolina. Along with the younger sons and surplus slaves of the English squire-archical system, this westward push was powered by Pennsylvanians, Germans and Scotch-Irish who occupied the interstices of the plantation mosaic as yeoman farmers. A distant satellite of this southern drive westward was founded at Natchez on the bluffs overlooking the Mississippi around 1775. In 1763 the Acadians, thrown out of what the British then called Nova Scotia, added to the French presence at the mouth of the Mississippi. These gave the western surge some fixed points of reference.

The victory of the USA and the Treaty of Paris in 1783 signalled an abrogation of the British Crown's alliance with the Six Nations and its defence of the interior. The nations were then at the mercy of colonial land hunger. Sullivan and Clinton's campaign in the Mohawk Valley in 1779 and Clark's capture of Kaskaskia, Cahokia and Vincennes in 1778 and 1779 broke the English and Iroquois hold on the lake trough and the Ohio Valley. As a result, in the two decades after 1790 60,000 people entered the New Military Tract, Genesee Country and West Geneseo through the Mohawk gap. The Military Tract was surveyed and plotted in square sections and made available for patenting by veterans of the War of Independence, who mostly sold it to real-estate speculators. Genesee Country was developed by a Scots entrepreneur, Sir William Pulteney. The settlers, whose places were named in the classical revival fashion of the time, for example, Rome, Syracuse, Ithaca, were mostly Pennsylvanians and New Englanders. Above and beyond the need of subsistence they were soon producing a surplus of wheat and beef on the hoof to the seaboard cities.

The settlement of the valleys of Appalachia was more atomistic, with bold spirits following the winding trails through the mountains. There were three principal tracks westwards. Firstly, the Forbes Road, Juniata Road and National (or Cumberland) Road met the headwaters of the Ohio river system at Pittsburgh — the Forks of the Ohio. Settlement in this vicinity produced provisions, whiskey and ironwork to send down river to Kentucky and the towns of Spanish Louisiana, including New Orleans. Secondly, the way along the Shenandoah Valley struck through the Cumberland Gap to reach the headwaters of the

Kentucky River, Bluegrass country and the Nashville Basin via the Wilderness Road blazed by Daniel Boone in the 1770s. Finally, the track which, following along the Valley of Virginia (Shenandoah), leads into the valley of East Tennessee. Settlements sprang up at Watauga, French Broad and Halston, spilling into the Cumberland Valley and the basin around French Lick (later Nashborough and, after 1812 when the English manner became unpopular, Nashville in the French fashion). The valleys which these routes traversed attracted many to stay in the hills, frequently to subsist as isolated pockets of eighteenth-century rural life and language. Further south, Georgia Western Territories (later to be Alabama and Mississippi) remained in the hands of the Cherokees, Chickasaws, Choctaws and Creeks. Their suppression and removal commenced in 1814, accelerating under Jackson's frontier democracy in the 1830s.

Transport policy

In 1807 the Congress ordered that a survey be made of transport problems of the republic. This was done by Secretary of the Treasury Albert Gallatin. His report and recommendations at that juncture provided the basis for both national policy and private investment for a good while. State and local governments had made some efforts to build roads, often financing them from tolls. Hard-surfaced, macadamized roads made heavier loads and greater speed possible. This was a clear demonstration to private investors that there was money in road building. An upsurge of turnpike investment in the 1790s connected up much of the eastern seaboard by 1800. Gallatin suggested that a National Road be made to link the growing interior cities of Detroit, Cincinnati, Nashville, Vincennes and St Louis to the Atlantic network. His advice was taken, and the National Road was built beside the Potomac, across a narrow watershed to the Youghiogheny Valley and thence westwards, reaching its terminus at Vandalia, Illinois in 1820. Gallatin also recommended that a canal be cut to join the Lake system to the Hudson-Mohawk route.

The river

Meanwhile the flood of settlers poured down the Ohio and along the Connecticut Western Reserve of Lake Erie's shore after the Treaty of Greenville of 1795, when the Delaware, Shawnee, Wyandotte and Miami let themselves be pushed further west. Cleveland and Cincinnati emerged as the urban foci of these two lines of advance, springing up from fort locations. Below Cincinnati settlement stuck more closely to the river as the Indians held out longest, in the less accessible sections of central and northern Indiana and Illinois. The frontier pushed apace along the Ohio then up the Wabash to Vincennes, which had stood waiting for 75 years. By 1815 the frontier had engulfed southern Illinois and joined up with St Louis. Along the river the frontier advanced to ten times the pace to the north of the river overland.

Though for the most part their origins were on the Atlantic coast, the commercial connections of these settlers were downriver with the South. The Ordinance of 1787 prescribed a chain of forts along the Ohio and its tributaries. Riverbound they guarded the downstream flatboat and keelboat traffic of emigrants seeking land and provisions seeking markets. Louisville sprang to prominence as the place where you recovered from or bypassed the Falls of the Ohio. Although a steamboat was built at Pittsburgh in 1810, it was not till 1820 that powered vessels dominated the traffic. Tobacco, bacon, corn, pork, beef, whiskey, flour, beans, cider, apples, lard, butter and hay were floated downstream while a counter flow of sugar, and cotton from the South and cod and mackerel from the east along with European imports were hauled upstream. Further west, the lead deposits of Missouri attracted riverine exploitation and by 1820 steamboats had penetrated to the Galena-Dubuque area and what had been a native gathering industry became a European mining one. The same channels provided for the export flow of those pelts of the fur trade which did not follow the Lakes basin through the Astors' Mackinac headquarters.

The Erie Canal

In 1825 deWitt Clinton's 'ditch', the Erie Canal from Albany to Buffalo, was completed, and the stage was set for a polarization of the American economy and polity. This canal gouged the grain of the land sufficiently to drain the Northwest Territory trade to the east more than the south. The spectacular reduction in east-west transport costs which it wrought, reoriented the economy of the Upper Mississippi, Ohio and Great Lakes Basin, in the original sense of that term. When the canal was opened freight rates from New York City to the Lakes fell from $100 to $15 a ton. The combination of metalled roads and canals reduced transport costs and increased the range and carrying capacity of wagons and barges. This in its turn extended the potential market for producers geographically. The interior could now supply food to the cities of the seaboard, which in some cases had been buying provisions from across the Atlantic. Seaboard manufacturers could reciprocate with cloth, shoes, ploughs, nails, stoves and hollow-ware. Geographical specialization of production according to comparative cost advantages, with manufacturing concentrated in New England and wheat and provisions production in the Northwest Territories, resulted in greater overall productivity. The specializations reflected soil and climatic conditions and the distribution of population and skills, but the catalyst which brought these components of thriving regional economic integration into ferment was the improvement of transport. The participants in this boom recognized that the cost of the necessary transport facilities was compensated for by the increasing farm incomes and land values generated by easier access to markets. There was a surge of enthusiasm for financing canals and turnpikes, and the clear understanding of the relationship between low transport cost and agricultural prosperity was written in the preambles of many local laws appropriating money for such projects. Abraham Lincoln's rise to prominence as an Illinois politician was based largely on promoting this enthusiasm.

The pressure for more land met with a hindrance as the Indians stemmed the tide of invasion into northeastern Illinois and southeastern Wisconsin until they were crushed in the Black Hawk War of 1832. Until that date they were merely hemmed in by forts at Howard, Winnebago and Dearborn. American encroachment was channelled up the Mississippi seeking minerals and furs. Galena on a navigable branch of the river was the focus of lead mining, connected to St Louis by steamer service from 1822 on. Welsh and Irish immigrants arrived in the diggings in the 1820s, followed by Cornish men fleeing the depression in English tin mines in the 1830s. Mining activity peaked in 1845 and petered out in 1849 as the miners headed for the banks of the Sacramento. However, a penumbra of agricultural settlement surrounded the diggings at Mineral Point, Platteville, Belmont and Galena, spreading along the edge of the Driftless Area in southwest Wisconsin and northwest Illinois. With the defeat of Black Hawk, the eastern parts of the states rapidly filled up. This was largely a matter of individual enterprise, but collective investments such as road building followed close on the heels of settlement. By 1860 only the north woods of Wisconsin remained unsettled.

Cotton

The other element polarizing the USA had its genesis in Eli Whitney's

invention of the cotton gin (1793). The other products of the plantation South were neglected in favour of serving the growing appetite
of the mills of New England and Lancashire with cotton. The institutions of the plantation and slavery, and the technology of cotton
growing developed in Maryland, Virginia, the Carolinas and Georgia
were carried along with the surplus population, white and black, into
the broad fertile plains of north Florida, Alabama, Mississippi and west
Tennessee. The gentry and managers of the Old South were joined by
adventurous hill farmers coming down the Natchez Trace to try their
hand along with hard-eyed immigrant entrepreneurs. Jackson's administration cleared the way by pushing the Nations into Oklahoma. The
Cotton Belt spread across the Mississippi in 1821 and into east Texas
soon thereafter, carrying slavery into Mexican territory in defiance of
the Mexican constitution. This occupation spread rapidly through the
Republic of Texas from 1836. By the time Texas joined the Union in
1845, population, black and white, was approaching the 100th
meridian, which coincided with the 20″ isohyet and the limit for
unirrigated cultivation.

The West

In both North and South then, around 1840 the frontier washed to
the edge of the Great Plains and faltered in its advance. What the
Plains were and could be remained unclear. For a while they were
employed as a land of passage to more attractive prospects in the
western cordillera. Trade connections with the upper Rio Grande
valley were established along the Sante Fe Trail from Independence,
Missouri in 1822. Settlers from the USA had made it to the Willa-
mette Valley, still in dispute between the Hudson's Bay Company
and the Astors, in the 1840s. In 1847, following the Fremont expe-
dition, the Mormons headed for the Great Basin. Then in 1849 gold
was found in the race of Jacob Sutter's sawmill on the Sacramento.

The way west for the more northerly movements was along the
banks of the unnavigable Platte, watched over by Fort Kearney and
Fort Laramie. Following this way traffic crossed the continental
divide as a gentle swell at South Pass, Wyoming, rather than taking on
the Rockies. There were routes on both banks of the river. On the
north side, the Mormon Trail started from Nauvoo, Illinois, springing
off across the Plains from Council Bluffs on the Missouri. The southern
route drew threads from Independence, Westport, Kansas City and
Atchison together at Fort Kearney. Beyond South Pass at Fort Bridger

the trails diverged. The Mormon Trail cut through the Uintas at Salt
Lake. The California and Oregon Trails continued on to the Snake
River. From here the Oregon Trail followed the river via Walla Walla
to Fort Vancouver. The California Trail took the valley of the Humboldt
and surmounted the Sierra Nevada via the Donner Pass. The Overland
Mail Company took a more southerly route from Fort Smith, Arkansas
via El Paso and Yuma to Los Angeles. The route which Lewis and
Clark blazed in the north along the Missouri attracted few. The Missouri
Basin remained the preserve of trappers and miners and soldiers in
uneasy coexistence with the natives. Their needs were served by the
turbulent but navigable river, at a high risk.

These trails and the auxiliary services for travellers were the fore-
runners of Plains settlement. In 1865, just prior to the advent of the
railroad, the Platte route was described as:

'lined with telegraph poles, having every 10-15 miles a stable of stage
proprietors and every other 10 or 15 miles an eating house. Perhaps
as often a petty ranch or farm house, whose owner lives by selling
hay to the trains of emigrants or freighters. Every 50 to 100 miles
was a small grocery and blacksmith shop and about as frequently
is a military station with a company or two of US troops for protection against Indians. This makes up the civilization of the Plains.'
(Quoted in Brown 1948, pp. 397-8.)

Railways

The construction of railways is credited with welding a continental,
industrial nation in the USA, instead of the maritime, colonial one it
had been. Not only did they lower the cost of land transport and bring
new areas and products into the commercial sphere, increasing the
volume of US exports, but they also drew European capital to finance
the development of the internal workings of the US economy.

From the first 15 miles of the Baltimore and Ohio laid in 1830, the
mileage extended to 9000 by 1850. This consisted of many short,
independent lines with large transshipment costs. The trip to the
west coast still had to be by conestoga or over the Panama isthmus.
The reason for spanning the continent with rails and the alignments
chosen must be seen in power political terms. The setting is the urge
to create a continental state and the competition for hegemony over
its westward extension between the northern and southern systems.
This battle had commenced in the 1850s over the settlement of Kansas,

as Missourians and abolitionist New Englanders vied with each other and shot each other for control.

The War Department did the surveying for four proposed routes from the Mississippi to the Pacific, and it is not coincidental that Lincoln signed the bill authorizing construction of the Union Pacific from Omaha and the Central Pacific from Sacramento in 1863. Grants of public land were provided for a right of way, and to sell off to settlers as a means of financing the railway and to encourage the competition in building between the Union Pacific and Central Pacific. State and local governments eager to improve their competitive position also offered the companies inducements of land and money so that they could get on the map of rails. By 1860 40% of railway investment in the North was from the public fisc while in the South the proportion was 60%. The private component came chiefly from England. In the 1890s 65% of Illinois Central stock was foreign owned, 73% of Louisville and Nashville stock and 52% of that of the Pennsylvania Railroad.

In addition to decreasing the cost of freight and travel, the boom of railway building directly increased demand for rails, ties, locomotives, rolling stock, buildings and bridges and thus indirectly for iron and steel, timber, iron ore, coal and so on. We shall return to the role of railway building in the process of industrialization and the debate over its significance later in this chapter. What is clear is that an excess of capacity was provided in some instances, never making a return to the resources invested. Many western lines especially only signified in the landscape as 'twin streaks of rust across the prairie'. It has been argued that the progress of the USA would have been less wasteful if some of the funds poured into rails had been diverted to lower-order transport facilities, especially the roads which fed the rail system with traffic. Nevertheless, the political imperative, urging the creation of an extensive and all-embracing rail system as a necessary condition for the moulding of a coherent nation state, seems more powerful than the logic of cost accounting.

One thing that the rails laid down between 1860 and 1893 did, in conjunction with the Homestead Act of 1862 and the rising demand for bread and meat in the industrial belt of the USA and Europe, was to populate the High Plains. Agricultural occupancy here was commercial from the outset, rather than arising from subsistence producers finding an outlet for a surplus. The intensity of exploitation of the Plains varied in rough consonance with prices of agricultural produce as well as with the unstable climate of the region. Up to the edge of the

Plains subsistence settlement had forged ahead of commerce, preceding much in the way of transport improvements and trade.

The first commercial use of the Plains was the fleeting passage of the open-range cattle industry which followed the eradication of buffalo herds and Indians in the 1860s and 1870s. The mainstay of this industry were the longhorn descendants of Andalusian cattle in the Nueces country of Texas. In the 1840s and 1850s these were spasmodically driven to New Orleans, Ohio, California and Illinois. Cut off from the hunger of the Old South by Union control of the Mississippi, these herds grew apace during the Civil War. From the end of the war, this reservoir of beef was tapped to meet northern urban, military, Indian and stocking needs. The connection was made by droving trails, delivering cattle on the hoof to the railhead for shipment north and east. The point of delivery shifted westward with the advance of settlement and railroad building west of Kansas City. The early destination was Sedelia, Missouri on the Missouri Pacific. Getting there involved crossing settled country, and Texas cattle fever, the herds and herdsmen did not endear themselves to sedentary farmers. The construction of the Union Pacific made it possible to deliver cattle over trails beyond the fringe of settlement during the brief spell before settlement overtook the trails at Abilene and Caldwell in 1867-71, Wichita and Ellsworth in 1872-5, Dodge City and Ellis between 1876 and 1879 and Dodge City and Hunewell in 1880. Other herds moved beyond the railheads destined to stock northern ranges or for butchering at Indian agencies. By 1880 in central Texas, rails had taken over from the trails and the cattle industry had shifted into the dry Great Plains of west Texas and eastern New Mexico. From the great ranches of the Pecos Valley the Goodnight Loving Trail continued to funnel cattle north. The peak of the open range was passed in 1884, as prices collapsed and farmers pressed for more land. Surviving where lack of rain deterred farming the cattle industry changed from ranging to ranching by the 1890s, abetted by barbed wire and various subterfuges with the provisions of the Homestead Act to maintain large, unified holdings.

What followed the rail tracks was settlement. By 1884, along with the Union Pacific, the Northern Pacific, Southern Pacific and Santa Fe railroads straddled the Plains. The promotion of settlement to ensure traffic and revenue which these companies pursued was epitomized by the work of James J. Hill, who created the human geography of Minnesota, North Dakota and Montana with his Northern Pacific. Minnesota Territory had been opened up to settlement in 1849. The

War Department built military roads from St Paul and St Anthony into southeast Minnesota and settlement followed behind. In 1862 the combination of statehood and the Homestead Act prompted the start of railway building. The Sioux and drought held things up for a year or two, but then settlement spread apace. The first railways driving north from Iowa and west from Wisconsin passed through a settled landscape to end at full-blown towns. After this initial phase of building the tracks struck out ahead of the frontier, ending at nowhere but heading for a distant target. The arrangement of places and affairs which followed these pioneering railways was not like the individualistic, spontaneous developments which followed the military roads of the 1850s. The railroad company located towns in terms of its operational needs as stops, division points and freight yards. The company named towns, designed towns and platted them. This relationship finds its clearest expression in the urban landscape in the main street axis of cities such as Cheyenne, Wyoming, linking the state capitol directly with the Union Pacific depot, the ordering of the city being geared to the alignment of the tracks. Settlement of the Dakotas had to wait upon the suppression of the Sioux. The gold rush to the Black Hills of 1878, followed by their defeat, drew cattlemen and farmers to South Dakota. As the plough pushed west so the open range dwindled. A spell of wetter weather between 1875 and 1880 encouraged a westward extension of wheat growing. A drought in 1886 acted as a signal of the riskiness of this area and settlements were abandoned. Since then the margin of cropland ebbs and flows with the price of wheat and with rainfall, with the cattle industry taking up the slack. However, the sod had been turned over a great enough tract, so in 1890 the Bureau of the Census declared the frontier closed.

A similar, longer but as yet unfinished story could be told of the Russian drive east and south from the Muscovite heartland. When Ivan the Terrible had established dominance over the middle Volga, by 1580, a feverish hunt for furs led to the extension of the hegemony of Muscovy to the Pacific shores of Siberia within three generations. To the south Muscovy harnessed the Cossacks to dominate the Ukraine by the middle of the seventeenth century. The empire was extended to the shores of the Black Sea in 1783 and into central Asia a century later. The tsarist beginnings of a transport web stringing this together, epitomized by the Trans-Siberian Railway started in 1891, is still in progress, as the new regime intends to complete the Baikal-Amur Mainline (BAM) to complement the Trans-Siberian nearly a century later.

Transport investment and British industrialization

For this section I have drawn on the works of Dyos and Aldcroft (1969).

At the end of the seventeenth century Britain's essentially rural economy was laced together by a dense network of muddy tracks and a few metalled roads linking penetrating rivers and estuarial ports with their regional markets. Improvements to roads, river navigation and harbours in the sixteenth and seventeenth centuries provided the necessary channels for the beginnings of economic expansion. Till 1740, however, the accumulated surplus of any surge of production was soon consumed. A burst of activity in the 1740s produced a doubling of output which was sustained and increased, outstripping a rapid growth in population to give an increase of output per head of near 1% per annum. This was the first demonstration of the ability of improved methods and productive organization to sustain growth in wealth, and signalled a radical reordering of society. In the landscape this revolution made clear marks. The hedged enclosure of land signified the commercialization of the communal inefficiency of the open fields. The burgeoning industrial population was housed and worked in rapidly growing towns and their food, raw materials and products flowed along the sparse web of roads and waterways. These were the realization of the ability to invest resources in increasing future production, the physical manifestation of putting some 8% of production into new investment. In the prolonged sequence of events which transformed the island from fuedal underdevelopment to a society of ever-rising expectations, the crucial element in the build-up of the structure to support the general economic advance was the improvement of roads and waterways. The important improvements in internal transport were made before the factory came to house most manufacturing activities. The main roads were in place by 1775 and the canal system was put together in the last quarter of the eighteenth century. Although some additions to networks were responses to new demands, for the most part the transport system was laid down as a permissive prerequisite to growth. Parts of the system did not justify the expectations which conceived them, and a major experimental cost of the process of growth was given rise to by the cataclysmic technical obsolescence to which transport facilities are prone, with a slightly inferior form of transport being abandoned wholesale with the introduction of a new means.

Road building

A flurry of export activity in the middle and at the end of the eighteenth century placed a heavy traffic in textiles, metals and their raw materials on the roads leading to Liverpool, Hull, Glasgow and London from their industrial hinterlands. The roads were rutted and holed and there was no unified responsibility for their provisions. The engineering problems of draining road surfaces and improving their load-bearing capacity were tackled by Macadam, Telford and Metcalfe. The obvious value of roads as an investment first drew a private entrepreneurial solution, with 870 turnpike acts passed by Parliament in the 1750s and 1760s setting up road companies. By the 1830s there were 1000 trusts controlling 22,000 miles of road, most of whom were suffering financially. The improvements wrought did give rise to a steady rise in traffic. Although the investment involved was large, the building of the turnpikes did not spin off any new manufacturers nor galvanize the investing activities of the country. It did spark local initiative and meet local needs quite efficiently.

The canals

The chief ways of movement in England during her take-off into industrialization were not roads but waterways. It has been claimed that the chief breakthrough of the industrial revolution was in hydraulics, controlling and channelling rivers and their connections to coastal waters. The second breakthrough was the sequel to this in the cutting of navigable ways to any point on the land that they were needed. This was essential if growth were to continue apace, for by 1720 the potential of natural waterways was fully employed. The way ahead was shown in 1761 when Brindley and Gilbert linked the Duke of Bridgewater's coal mines at Worsley to the growing Manchester market with a canal. The feverish burst of building which followed linked the major river basins of England with a set of trunk routes. Twenty years later a second boom of canal construction began which did not cease till the opening of the Liverpool and Manchester Railway in 1830. During these forty years the intense Midlands network focused on Birmingham was built and connected with London via the Grand Junction Canal.

The significance of the canals lay firstly in the fact that they dramatically increased transport efficiency. The energy efficiency advantage of barges over wheeled traffic is 12 : 1 and over pack horses 16 : 1.

Linking the river navigations into a unified network the canals generated a system's economy, encompassing the natural waterways and coastal trade. For the roads, canals provided a complement, reducing the heavy traffic which was gouging the turnpikes up. In terms of technical innovation the canal companies pioneered the use of horse-drawn railways as their feeders among the collieries or as overland links in their system. Greater efficiency in transport in its turn improved the productivity of other factors by keeping men and machines more regularly and economically employed than previously. Probably the chief contribution of the canals, however, was that they forestalled an impending fuel crisis. The new methods of production required lots of low-cost coal as fuel, power source or raw material. The canals broke the bottleneck and provided sufficient cheap transport capacity to cope with these demands. In their building the canals employed a horde of men and generated an increase in spending power at a time of strategic consequence for the growth of industries looking for mass markets. Their finance made more people familiar with shareholding. Their design enhanced engineering science and the execution of these designs provided a training ground in the managerial talents required to handle the logistics of large-scale contracting.

The railways

By the 1820s, the volume of industrial and commerical activity had surpassed the road and canal capacity which had permitted their expansion in the first place. Congestion and unsatisfied demand was especially marked in Lancashire. Bales of cotton took longer to move from Liverpool's Pierhead to the Manchester Cotton Exchange than it took them to move from Savannah or Mobile to the Mersey. Exasperation at this state of affairs incited local capitalists to risk money in railways. Cheaper, quicker more regular and reliable transport would benefit manufacturers and merchants, consumers would gain from more certain and less expensive food supplies. In particular freezing would not push up the price of food and coal in winter. Given this incipient demand, the success of the railway venture required that certain technical and financial preconditions be satisfied. Building on the experience of colliery tramways, culminating in Trevithick's nine-mile steam locomotive operation between Merthyr Tydfil and Abercynon in 1804, flanged wheeled wagons on iron rails drawn by a coal-fired locomotive achieved technical viability by 1820. In 1821 Parliament sanctioned the Stockton to Darlington Railway. But the railway era really began with the opening of the Liverpool to Manchester in 1830. This was the first line built for the stated purpose of carrying passengers as well as goods, relying only on locomotive traction and monopolized operations. The financial requirement of a large amount of capital for start-up funding was assured by the dramatic growth of wealth from 1740 to 1830. Following the success of the Liverpool and Manchester especially in passenger traffic, lines were built joining the principal foci of the economy so that by 1845 the beginnings of a national network had been built piecemeal. In the following year Hudson began to put the Midlands Railway together by consuming small companies. The mania of building was over by 1870 and only a few gaps needed filling to bring the network to its maximum expanse in 1914.

Railways and Economic Growth

For long the myth reigned supreme in economic history that railways were the very sinews of industrialization and that their development set the tempo and direction of growth. This view is epitomized in Rostow's (1960) identification of railways as the leading sector in the US take-off into sustained growth. Fogel (1964) has countered that the railways' contribution was not the pre-eminent force embedded in mythology, and sought to demonstrate this econometrically. If this is true for the US, it is all the more likely to represent the course of events in Britain. If the period from 1740 to 1830 witnessed the most radical transformation of the economy, then clearly it was previous to the building of the railways. It could be argued that the extensive road and canal networks of 1830 would merely require some augmentation in order to serve the needs of the booming Victorian economy. Before taking up the question in general, extending our geographical coverage to the US, it is worth detailing the results of railway building in the innovative hearth.

In Britain the railway builders were not as venturesome as the canal builders. Routes were selected primarily to capture existing road and canal traffic. Lines were not thrown out to pioneer new settlement and create a value for land beyond the current margin of settlement. The only settlement frontier the railways encouraged was the suburban one, where commuter stations were established as loss leaders in expectation of the more lucrative freight traffic that provisioning the resulting suburbs would generate. The railway company towns of Swindon and Crewe did grow at the centres of the companies' networks, providing for their power units and rolling stock. Some villages became towns because they chanced to be on the chosen alignment of a railway, and in some cases, such as Watford and Slough, because their more exclusive neighbours resisted the intrusion of their peace. In the case of the simultaneous extension of mining on to the western coalfield in Northumberland and into the valleys of South Wales with the building of railways, it is not clear which caused which, and whether these developments would have occurred had the tracks not been laid.

The more direct impact of the railways was in the increased demands for coal, iron and mechanical engineering they involved. Considering both the modest amount needed to raise steam and the greater requirements for the making of rails and equipment, there is no evidence that railway demands overheated the market for coal during the building boom. During the 1840s demand for iron by the railways soaked up most of the increase in pig iron production. The switch to steel rails in the 1860s caused some localized effects within the iron and steel sector, but there was little impact on the total magnitude of production. In the process of starting up the railways did take 20% of the output of the engineering industry in the 1840s and created a new branch in that industry, but thereafter their requirements were quite limited. What railway technology did not do was to spin off a slew of innovations leading indirectly to general increases in efficiency. Railways peaked out technologically very early on, and the performance of trains had nearly reached its limits by the mid 1870s.

The construction of the railways was clearly a major perturbation of the national economy. The wages of the navvy gangs assembled to shift muck and lay track rippled through the economy, creating employment in agriculture and manufacturing. At the height of building activity in 1847 250,000 men were employed on railway contracts and their wages bill accounted for 3% of the national income. This had a pronounced multiplier effect at local and national levels. For a brief period the building of railways absorbed nearly all the free capital available for investment in the country, amounting to 6.7% of national income in 1847.

Railways in the USA

In answer to Rostow's leading-sector thesis, Fogel sought to measure the incremental contribution of railways to US national out-put. He did this with an explicitly geographical estimation of the amount by which the production possibilities of the nation would have been reduced if agricultural commodities could not have been shipped by rail. This involves establishing the margin of commercial agriculture which would have prevailed with alternative forms of transport. The gains or losses associated with railway building can then be assessed. The other component to estimate is the direct calls for output needed to build and maintain railways in the take-off period just prior to the Civil War. From his measurements he concluded that despite the drama of their construction and their hegemony in transport by 1900, the railways did not make an overwhelming contribution to the wealth of the nation. Economic growth was won with a myriad of innovations over the entire spectrum of products. These applications of scientific knowledge of production were facilitated by sweeping political, geographical and social rearrangements, all of which were well under way before the emergence of railways. We have seen that the British Industrial Revolution was virtually complete before the first railways were built. The millions of people who migrated to the interior plains of North America before 1840 did not do so in expectation of windfall gains in land values when the railways arrived to increase the accessibility of the region. They moved west because even without rails the growth of population and wealth in Europe and on the Atlantic seaboard made investment in new lands profitable. In more direct terms it was the demand for nails, stoves and hollow-ware rather than for rails which caused the leap in US pig iron production in the 1840s. The acceleration of city growth that paralleled the growth of manufacturing and commerce also preceded the railways.

Fogel concluded with the indisputable proposal that the overwhelming significance accorded to the railways was fostered by the competitive process that led to slightly less efficient substitutes being discarded, creating an illusion of singularity. The set of institutions, auxiliaries and the geographical configuration of the economy that best accommodate the chosen alternative seem like necessary parts of progress and enhance its appearance of inevitability. These accessories — time tables, fast freight services, types of rail, particular locations chosen for particular activities — impart no independent contribution to the wealth of the nation. They are merely the circumstances under which the primary innovation imparts its contribution to growth.

Although he could not be taken to task for reiterating the economist's basic tenet that the potential for substitution always exists, his treatment of US railways' contribution is subject to dispute. David (1969) points out that the phenomenon of railways was a large enough component of the economic structure to change the constellation of outputs and prices over the entire economy, and thus rightly warrants an attempt at a general equilibrium evaluation. Fogel had reduced the problem to a partial one essentially by assuming constant unit cost for canal and wagon movement and for storage. An increase in volume on existing waterways after 1840 would have spilled excess demand on to more circuitous and costly routes and called for new building in difficult terrain. Fogel also assumed ubiquitous access by road to waterways and no need to focus overland traffic at a port. This strongly underestimates overland wagon costs, which constitute a large part of the cost difference between rail and road and water systems. David's most telling criticism is that Fogel's evaluation dismissed a cost difference amounting to 5% of gross national product as trivial. The more usual measure of value of an investment is its rate of return compared to alternative investments. The existing evidence collated by David suggests that by 1890 railroad capital formation was not yielding much more than could be got in alternative uses. However, prior to this, in its building phase, the returns to railway investment must have been quite spectacular. The inference is that Fogel was mistaken in dismissing the contribution to the general well being that the building of railways in particular provided when compared with an alternative configuration of transport investment.

Providing for cars and trucks

To trace the impact of the internal combustion engine and the response to it in terms of social change and public facilities we will stick with the USA, keeping in mind that developments there had their parallels on the other side of the Atlantic. However, by this time the American economy was beginning to outpace that of Great Britain, and the US entered the motor age well in advance of other nations.

Preoccupation with laying down the rail network from 1850 to 1900 diverted resources and attention from the roads, which deteriorated badly in that time. The turnpikes had fallen into disuse faced with railway competition and public roads were neglected because there were no administrative or financial provisions for their maintenance. In 1893, in response to lobbying for a system of highways, the Congress established an Office of Road Inquiry, providing it with a pittance for research. The absence of highway departments in all but seven states presented a major obstacle to any programme of improvement. But the pressure of demand was building up. In 1900 there were less than 1,000 trucks registered in the USA; by 1920 there were over

1 million. In 1900 there were 4,000 cars sold; by 1920 there were over 2 million on the road. The car makers and the construction industry lobbied strongly for the government to cater to the needs of these vehicle owners. In 1916 the Federal Aid Law started a building programme. This and subsequent legislation contained provision for federal assistance to states in road building. The states were required to match any federal funds, to establish highway departments, to designate a system of routes on which federal funds would be spent and to adhere to federal standards of design and maintenance.

The geographical process which accompanied this growing demand for road space was the explosion in size of major cities drawing in the surplus labour of rapidly mechanizing agriculture. As we have seen, the sweep of the frontier filled in the Dakotas, Nebraska and Kansas between 1870 and 1890. Oklahoma and the Mountain and Pacific states were fully settled by 1910. Since the Civil War blacks had been leaving the cotton fields and heading for the cities of the South, the Atlantic seaboard, the Midwest and the Gulf coast. These were paralleled by a growing trickle of poor whites. All of this was part of a general trend from rural to urban occupations which had been under way since the early eighteenth century. The smaller towns of the country were enhanced by the local rural population. The major metropolitan areas also drew on local sources but to a major degree they were fed by foreign immigration. This flood tapered off during the early twentieth century until it was all but choked by the quota restriction of 1921. In 1920 the nation reached the 50% urban mark and the major urban agglomerations continued to expand apace, spreading suburbs served by rail lines and the Model T. The most phenomenal rise was that of Los Angeles and the other cities of the Pacific and Mountain states. They drew population from the entire country, including the cities of the Midwest, which continued to grow themselves by drawing in blacks and poor whites from the South. In the 1920s the rural migration to the city picked up, fuelled by the failure of many to reach an accommodation with the risks of the Plains. The 'Okies' swelled the movement west, heading for the delights of Bakersfield and its vicinity. This was the era of southern California's oil-, movies- and aircraft-based boom which soared on through the war years and crested in the 1950s when 2 million people arrived to push the population of Los Angeles and Orange counties to 6.5 million. The inward flow tapered off in the late 1960s and now there is a rough balance of inward and outward migration. The cities of the Northeast and Midwest continued to extend their periphery through the century with a spurt of suburbanization in the 1950s and 1960s, slowing as the cities of the Sunbelt now siphon off their surplus growth.

The feeding, clothing, heating and housing of this burgeoning urban population, the exchange of their specialized products and their own travel, generated a massive growth of trade and traffic. To meet these needs there was an enormous building effort in the two decades from 1920 to 1940. One million miles of road were surfaced and 1.5% of gross national product was spent on building and maintenance. This was financed in part by the gradual imposition of user charges. Registration fees from vehicle owners were collected in most states from an early date and fuel tax, first introduced in Oregon in 1919, spread rapidly to other states. In 1921, vehicle owners were only paying 12% of the highway bill. By 1941 taxes incident on road users amounted to half the total road budget. Since 1941 the contribution has been augmented by the collection of federal road taxes that have brought the users' contributions closer to the total amount spent on roads. The expenditure of these revenues was first concentrated on main highways connecting principal cities and centres of local government, comprising up to 10% of total road mileage. The most important 1% of these roads, forming the nationwide Federal Aid Primary System of some 40,000 miles, was 90% paid for through special federal taxes. The next most import 20% of the links were designated Federal Aid Secondary Roads. Farm to market roads shared state-collected user revenues through state aid to local government. Outside these there remained a large mileage of lightly trafficked roads under local jurisdiction. Urban roads were solely the responsibility of the cities.

The road-building programme responded to political pressure and, given the over-representation of rural interests in the US political system, it is not surprising that an economically inefficient allocation of resources resulted. There was a serious imbalance in favour of inter-city and rural roads as opposed to urban transport. The power of the rural interests represented by Florida's Pork Chop Gang, for example, finds concrete expression in the splendid and empty highways cutting through north Florida's pinewoods. Prestige projects, to show that government is doing something, appear more magnificent per dollar in a rural setting where they are easier to design and execute. Many unnecessary roads were built and more were built to excessively high standards for the use which transpired. In 1950, 148,000 miles of roads in the USA were providing no essential traffic function.

There was an unprecedented surge of demand for cars following World War II as ownership diffused through society, approaching saturation level in the late 1950s. The taste for low-density suburbs, encouraged by the income tax structure and Veterans Administration and Federal Housing Administration loans, engendered a tremendous growth of car usage. From 1947 to 1957 motor vehicle registration doubled from 34 million to 68 million. Miles of travel rose by 80% from 340,000 million to 650,000 million vehicle miles. Car production tripled from 2 million to 7 million vehicles. By 1960, 77% of households owned at least one car and spent over 10% of family income on car travel. During this period the mileage of surfaced roads only rose from 1.7 million to 2.3 million and the level of road investment remained virtually constant. By the mid 1950s existing roads were unable to handle the increased numbers of motor vehicles especially in cities and suburbs without stress. Bad surfaces, increasing congestion and climbing accident rates stoked the discontent which the road lobby focused on Congress.

In 1944 the Federal Aid Highway Act had provided the first significant federal aid for urban roads. The Federal Aid Primary System was extended to include the portions of its roads which passed through urban communities. Federal funds were authorized for selected highways in urban areas with more than 5,000 people. The Bureau of Public Roads was directed to cooperate with state highway officials in designating a 40,000-mile national system of Interstate Highways, 'located as to connect by routes, as direct as practicable, the principal metropolitan areas, cities and industrial centers to serve the national defence and to connect at suitable border points with routes of continental importance in the Dominion of Canada and the Republic of Mexico'. With the Federal Highway Act of 1956, the federal government assumed 90% of highway construction costs for any portion of this interstate system. The army and navy were involved in its designation and the 'defence' goal made the enterprise a sacred cow in an era of intense chauvinism. Nevertheless the road lobby claimed that it would achieve more mundane objectives as well. The 35,000 miles of limited access intercity routes would improve speeds and safety. The 6,000 miles of many-laned urban routes would reduce downtown congestion by bypassing through traffic and would permit a reduction of commuter stress and strain. The proponents of the system stressed the user benefits accruing through reduced accidents and lower operating costs. The opportunity cost of the $41,000 million worth of construction was ignored. The estimates of benefits were optimistically extravagant and the value of the system was never subject to close scrutiny. The political price for obtaining some relief of urban congestion was a vast expenditure on excess capacity in the rural setting.

While the main burden of growing activity was borne by roads, the railways shared some part of the expanding commerce of the nation, but with mounting competition from trucks, barges and pipelines. The absolute volume of freight on rail increased slowly but the share decreased radically. Passenger traffic peaked out in 1916 and fell off rapidly with competition from cars, buses and then airlines until in the 1970s it was back to pre-1870 levels. Struggling to shed this loser, the railroad companies managed to get it surreptitiously nationalized and carried by taxpayers as Amtrak. A similar, though supposedly temporary arrangement, was made for the ailing Penn Central giant, which muddled management and circumstances had conspired to reduce to a mess. Rather than allow its rivals to buy up pieces of the northeastern system to put together a coast-to-coast system, Union Pacific persuaded government to nationalize the regional network as Conrail. As part of the same package the over-extended rail networks have finally been given more latitude in adjusting their geographical coverage downward. At the inter-city level the main questions which remain to be settled concern the regulation of prices and entry and the provision of subsidies, intervening in the competition to meet the nation's needs for movements of goods and persons. The answers to these questions may well affect the relative merits of different locations for different activities in a small way, but seem unlikely to bring about dramatic sweeps of people and their products across the land.

Transport in towns

The principal arena requiring the exercise of ingenuity and good judgement in governance of the means of mobility is in the cities. Dissatisfaction with transport facilities provides a focus for many of the real or imagined grievances arising from the stress and strain of an unfamiliar way of life. We have not yet come to terms with the aggregations we have come to live in, nor devised appropriate ways of moving around them. To characterize the growth of these conurbations we shall examine a city which was structured by nineteenth-century growth, Chicago, and one which experienced its most rapid expansion in this century of the car, Los Angeles.

Chicago

Chicago grew at the centre of the vast fertile interior plain, the capital of the most productive agricultural region in the world. It stands at the national crossroads where the deepest southwesterly penetration of Great Lakes provides low-cost connections to the east and overseas; where land traffic between east and northwest refracts around the southern end of the lake and where a few miles of watershed separates the two great national waterways of the continent. It was incorporated in 1833 when its population was 350. By 1848 when the Illinois Central Railroad was under construction and the Illinois and Michigan Canal had cut the portage between the Lakes and the Mississippi, its population was 20,000. Becoming the hub of ten trunk rail routes its population increased tenfold during the Civil War to reach 300,000 by 1870. The layout of the city was determined by the Federal Ordinance of 1785 and its land survey provisions. The major arteries as they developed followed section lines, with shopping centres developing at intersections. The stubborn persistence of sensible Indian trails, for example in Ridge, Greenbay and Archer, gave rise to the few diagonal routes. Destroyed by the fire of 1871, the city was rebuilt by 1875, providing the genesis of the Chicago tradition in architecture and of the combination of outward suburbanization and tall buildings downtown. By 1890 the population reached 1 million and by 1930 3.4 million, with an ever-increasing outwash of suburbs around its fringe.

The commuter stops located every few miles along the railway spokes radiating from the downtown hub generated beads of suburbs. These suburbs were quite small, since the radius of development permitted by foot or horse was limited. The main body of the city was served first by horse car lines in the 1860s, then by cable cars in the 1880s, which were ousted by electric streetcars introduced in 1892 at the same juncture as the L (elevated railroad) was placed on the landscape. The L had the effect of encouraging high density apartment developments for Loop-bound commuters along its routes. After World War I, the motor vehicle began to show its paces and by the end of the 1920s the bus was replacing the streetcar. The private ownership of motor vehicles picked up at the same time, hesitated in the depression of the 1930s and during World War II, to take off rapidly in 1947. The rate of suburban growth was pretty much in consonance with this. The car first enabled rail commuters to live further from their stations, expanding the beads along the trunk routes. As roads were improved, direct commuting independent of rail services became feasible and the interstices between the railroad spokes began to fill in. The prosperity of the 1950s and 1960s saw the most rapid rate of car, road and home building ever. Whatever the motives, this low-density spread now extended forty miles from the Loop, in ribbons along the expressway alignments.

Not having a completely commerical remit, but being hemmed in by regulatory control, the mass transit companies were having a hard time in competition with the car. In 1947 the Chicago Transit Authority was given a monopoly over bus and L services to overcome this financial problem — but has failed to produce enough revenue to cover its costs. It is burdened in doing this by its statutory obligations to provide an extravagant level of service (24-hour operation on the L and a section grid of bus services) and political obligations to the Democratic machine. The heavy load of rail commuters to the dense employment focus of the Loop has sustained the city's commuter railroads in operation at some small financial loss. Since the 1940s, the distribution of manufacturing employment in Chicago has been dispersing and the mass facilities developed to feed a central employment core offer no ready access to these jobs. Chicago was fortunate in putting most of its expressway network together before rising antipathy froze urban road building, so the low-density spread of jobs and houses and car commuting is fairly well catered for. The Crosstown expressway, the last major element of the region's system, after a long contentious battle has been reduced to a much more limited improvement of road capacity. In an effort to overcome the difficulties of subsidizing mass transit facilities in the face of political fragmentation, with the poorer central city providing the tax base for subsidizing suburbanite commuters, a Regional Transportation Authority was set up extending over the six counties of northeastern Illinois. Whether this will provide a solution remains to be seen.

Los Angeles

The migration of people to southern California during and after World War II created a new type of city — whose image we see repeated across the US Sunbelt in Houston, Atlanta and Miami, for example. The flood of 2 million people who arrived in Los Angeles and Orange counties in the 1950s continued through the 1960s, with population reaching nearly 10 million by 1970. Thereafter growth decelerated until it now approaches stability. This inundation filled the southern California coastal plain and its tributary valleys with a low density of residences interspersed with several more intense nuclei of commercial and industrial occupancy, all strung together with a graticule of freeways. The rail and streetcar facilities which gave Chicago its spoked structure did exist in Los Angeles. However, before the arrangement of settlement had crystallized along these lines, the advent of near universal car ownership freed the developer from the need to offer proximity to the rail lines to customers. The services on these lines became unremunerative and were withdrawn, leaving the provision of movement to the car. The overwhelming reliance on the car is a reflection of the time of the agglomeration's greatest growth. Cars were available and the climate was convenient for cars. Many of the migrants in the area were country people used to personal transport and unused to public transport. The preference was not a cost-accounting decision, because its rationale included considerations of individual control and status which went far beyond the value of time. The freedom from reliance on railways to accommodate the diurnal flow to work released the city's form from the monocentric, steeply increasing density gradient shape which Chicago classically exemplifies. Los Angeles is a polynuclear mass with its downtown in half a dozen places. There are some signs of a concentration of activities taking place in the Los Angeles core, especially since they found that tall buildings can be built to withstand earthquake shocks. Thus some centripetal force such as impressed the structure of Chicago exists, though in a muted form.

CHAPTER·4

Transport Problems and Policies

Transport and government

The ideal objective of government in regulating and controlling the provision of transport facilities is to provide for the geographical coherence of the nation in the most efficient manner possible. By 'geographical coherence' I mean to imply the integral operation of its economy and political and social life. Efficiency is a matter of meeting the needs for movement at the least social cost. The social cost of transport is the cost of network capacity, including the cost of building and maintaining the ways and terminals of the various transport systems and any deleterious results which their presence imposes on their surrounds. These capacity costs increase as the stock of roads and tracks and terminals is increased. Beyond some point in their provision diminishing returns to scale set in and the cost of facilities increases at an increasing rate, which can be represented by drawing the capacity cost curve upward-concave as in figure 16.

The second component of social costs is that associated with movement on a particular stock of networks. These decrease as the stock of facilities is expanded. More network capacity diminishes the circuity of routes and levels of congestion. As more and more capacity is provided the incremental saving that can be achieved is likely to dwindle, so that the curve of movement-related costs will also be upward-concave. From this it is evident that the function describing the total social cost of the transport system will be U-shaped, as shown in figure 16. Adding two upward-concave functions, one of which is decreasing while the other is increasing, will in general yield a curve which decreases to a singular minimum and then increases. Thus there will be a minimum-social-cost, i.e. more efficient, stock of transport facilities lying somewhere between zero and infinity. Given the com-

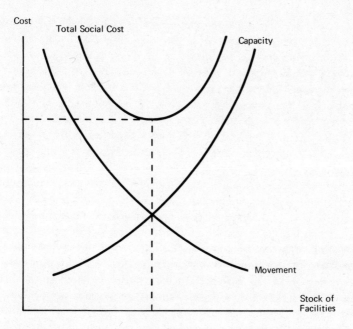

Figure 16

position of the social cost function, this minimum will lie at the juncture where the increment of productivity arising from expanding transport capacity just equals the increment of cost resulting from this expansion. It is worth increasing the capacity of the transport system until the decrease of movement cost just offsets the increase of capital costs, i.e. while benefits measured in operating cost savings exceed incremental capacity costs.

This analysis is based on the presumption of a given geography and a given set of demands to move people and goods between given locations. As we have seen in chapter 2, locational responses to transport improvements may change the geographical pattern of needs to move and transport demand. If we are to take account of such possibilities, then the objective of transport policy must obviously be extended to seeking the most efficient combination of transport stock and arrangement of land uses and activity locations. We can envisage this in terms of adding another dimension to the optimization problem of figure 16. We can picture this in figure 17 in terms of the relationship between capacity and movement costs and the geography of urban settlement. The geographical dimension is measured along the horizontal axis as the dispersion of manufacturing and service activities. This increases from complete concentration at the origin towards the uniform distribution of urban activities over the face of the country, which would be the maximum state of dispersal. If we presume that the market for manufacturers and services is distributed pretty much as the urban population, then the movement costs of distributing final products will not vary much with the degree of dispersal. When we consider the assembly of raw materials from mining and agriculture, however, then clearly movement costs will be greater for concentrated production than for more dispersed production. On the other hand, as production is dispersed the potential for larger-scale production and integration of processes, diminishing the amount of intermediate goods movement, will be dissipated, leading to an attenuation of the decrease of costs with dispersal and an upward-concave movement cost function. The cost of providing routes and terminals will increase as dispersal necessitates greater network coverage and dissolves the economies of mass movement on high-performance media in meeting the same production schedule. Since some minimal set of facilities will always be necessary no matter how concentrated production, in order to gather unavoidably dispersed agricultural products and minerals, the capacity cost function will have a positive intercept value. This function will have a fixed upper bound where production and services are uni-

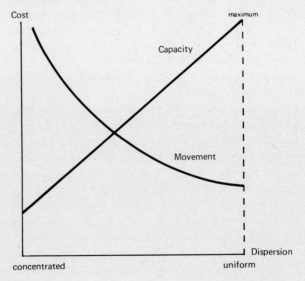

Figure 17

formly distributed. Between these two limits we may draw it as a straight line for want of a logical alternative.

If we combine the functions in figures 16 and 17 in a three-dimensional graph in figure 18, we can picture the total social cost of the stock of transport facilities and the settlement pattern. Given our surmises about the relationships of capacity and movement costs in terms of dispersion and the amount of transport facilities, the total social cost of transport and settlement will be a bowl-like surface with a unique determinable minimum point. This will indicate the most efficient combination of settlement structure and transport networks. We can view the governmental task as steering the economy's geography towards the combination of activity locations and transport facilities which minimizes the friction of distance.

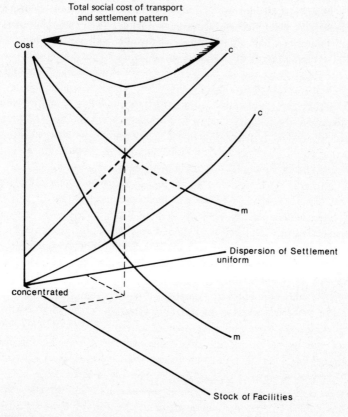

Figure 18

Given the historical short-term stability of locational patterns, the problem is usually attacked in practice as one of assuring adequate transport capacity and efficient, stable operations to meet the needs generated by the nation's geographical array of activities. This task is largely seen in terms of controlling competition and capacity. In addition to directly providing the innately collective elements of the system, such as roadways, governments allegedly seek efficiency by inhibiting the creation of artificial monopoly; controlling natural monopoly; internalizing or arranging compensation for externalities; correcting undesirable distributional effects and nurturing stability in the provision of services. What spurs politicians to these high-sounding objectives is frequently the more mundane objective of avoiding political discontent and retaining office, which is a tangible, trustworthy and effective motive.

The general ground justifying government intervention in the workings of the economy at the microeconomic level is that the market process fails to drive prices and quantities to levels consistent with the efficient equation of the cost and social utility of the goods and services in question. Such market failures take three usual forms in connection with transport.

In the first place, some goods, such as road space, are inherently collective in nature. It is extremely difficult if not impossible to ration their allocation by pricing their use. The costs of policing their use so as to exclude non-payers from their enjoyment would be prohibitive. Private enterprise could not recoup revenue sufficient to justify providing them, yet it is plain that the benefits they generate are real and great. Thus it falls to government, which can coerce revenue in the form of general taxation, to provide such facilities to a socially desirable level. The problem then is to decide on the socially desirable level in the absence of a stream of revenue signalling utility. A source of controversy on this kind of failure is whether the good in question really cannot be marketed in the usual fashion. For defence expenditure there is little argument, but over roads this is a serious question.

The second kind of market failure arises when the costs and benefits associated with the enjoyment of certain goods and services spill over and accrue to people other than the users. As an example of external cost, traffic noise and fumes from vehicles on roads impose themselves as costs of avoidance or pain on pedestrians, workers or residents alongside them. Political pressure may induce the government to internalize such externalities. This can be done by forcing those who cause the cost to compensate those who bear it innocently.

Since this can be difficult to administer a frequent recourse is to the imposition of standards on the design of goods, requiring suppression of excessive levels of nuisance, as in the case of catalytic convertors in car engines. In the case of vehicle nuisance, its incidence on others can be muted by more costly route-way designs, such as sunken or walled-off roads, so that taxpayers in general bear the cost. As an example of an external benefit we can consider the way a high-standard road draws traffic out of residential streets, reducing accidents and nuisance. This improvement in well being to residents is not registered in price terms — though it may reflect itself in the value of their property. Such benefits, however, can usually only be bought by collective action.

The third kind of market failure results from the potential for monopoly in the provision of some good or service. This can arise because of some collusive or individual effort at suppressing competition by institutional means. Monopolies granted by government licensing of entry to a business are of this kind. Governments have been persuaded to offer such protection from competition by the prospect of some generally beneficial outcome, such as the assured, steady provision of service. In other cases monopoly arises naturally when the cost of providing a service by one producer falls continually over the range of the market in question. Decreasing costs mean that two producers serving the same market would be producing at a higher cost than one. In this case the first in the business can always exclude a new entrant from competition. Such decreasing costs usually arise from the existence of massive start-up costs which are then spread ever more thinly over an expanding output. A railway system comes to mind as an obvious example. The problem with either natural or artificial monopoly is that the profit-maximizing strategy of the producer does not coincide with the best interests of the consumer. Being in effect faced with a downward-sloping demand curve, as the only supplier in the game, the monopolist can determine either the price charged or the quantity supplied. Profits will be largest if the price or quantity is fixed so that the extra revenue brought in by the last unit sold, the marginal revenue, just equals the extra cost involved. At this level the price will be greater than the cost of provision and total revenue will be far in excess of total cost, the difference being monopoly profits. It would clearly be in the interests of consumers to have more of the good, to have output expand to the point where the price they pay, the average revenue, just equals the cost of the good or service. The spur of competition is not available to expand supply and there is no incentive for the existing supplier to provide more.

In the case of licensed monopoly, the role of government must be to judge from time to time whether the supposed advantages of controlled entry are indeed worth the limitation of supply and the monopoly profits allowed. The instance of natural monopoly occasions government intervention in the form of utility regulation or outright public ownership, either by local or national government. Either by regulation or management directive, the objective of control should be to ensure that the price of the good or service involved, and thus the amount supplied, is such that utility and cost are equated. This can present the difficulty that charging marginal cost prices may not cover the total cost of service. If marginal cost decreases over the potential range of output, then it will always be less than average cost. Total cost is average cost multiplied by the number of units sold. Obviously, marginal cost times number of units sold will be less than this. Possible remedies for this defect include average cost pricing or discriminating among consumers on the basis of demand elasticity or subsidizing production out of the general exchequer. We shall return to these matters when we discuss railway policy in particular.

If the three above instances are the legitimate occasions of government intervention in the interest of providing the right amount of transport services, there are two other general reasons for influencing the price and quality of transport in the economy. Motivated by prudence and compassion the state acts so as to even out large disparities of well being between groups of the population distinguished by social or geographical position. As an indirect means of redistributing wealth in favour of the poorer, some goods, regarded as necessities, are subsidized, encouraging more consumption than would be warranted by a price reflecting the cost of provision. Since the target groups are seen as disadvantaged in terms of accessibility in many instances, being old, or too poor to buy cars, or in peripheral regional constituencies, then public transport subsidy or road building are undertaken with redistributional intent in many instances. Such indirect efforts to achieve greater equity are not always effective and they invoke a paternalistic attitude. The selection of necessary goods presumes on the preferences of the groups to be helped, artificially encouraging their consumption of certain things, such as transport. A blanket subsidy of a certain transport service with the aim of a progressive evening-out of welfare can also go awry and prove regressive in its outcome. There is nothing to exclude the better-off from enjoying the subsidized service to a greater extent than those for whom the benefits were intended. Public transport subsidies accrue to white-collar workers to a large extent and roads in the further reaches of the nation serve middle-class tourists from the central areas as well as local interests.

Under some stratagems the dictates of macroeconomic management require a control on the level of investment by government to avoid excessive swings of production and prices. Collective goods, such as roads, bridges and docks, provide suitable public works which may be committed or omitted to raise or lower the level of investment and counter destabilizing perturbations. This is done as macroeconomic considerations require, regardless of the intrinsic worth of these facilities to society. Road programmes are particularly prone to such manipulation, indeed they were frequently generated as counter-recessionary measures in the first place.

The force and nature of these political interventions and their outcomes do depend very much on the level of geographical resolution at which the service in question operates. Transport policy does have some natural divisions of effect according to geographical scale. We can distinguish international, internal long-distance and local levels of interest in policy. As we progress from the more far-flung to the immediate scope we also move from more remote questions for most of us to those in which we are intensely involved. Questions about international transport facilities are mostly concerned with terminals, airports, docks and international routes. The next band of the transport spectrum relates to longer-distance internal trade and travel, the connections from hinterlands to regional centres and between these — the flows up and down the central place hierarchy. The final range of concern on transport matters is that which encompasses the scope of our daily round — the provision for movement to work, shop, school, friends and to collect and deliver goods. The questions arising differ in intensity and accent between rural and urban areas but not in nature, being concerned with catering for private as opposed to public transport. In country areas, apart from those attracting large numbers of weekend and seasonal visitors, there is little call for the expansion of road capacity or parking space and the issue is largely one of how best to provide public transport for those without cars. The urban transport problem concerns the best combination of facilities for car users and public transport, the resolution of which extends itself into questions of urban locational structure.

International transport

For most of us the impacts of international transport which gain our attention are generated by its terminals. The location of waterside facilities and airports and the approaches to them do impinge largely on both users and innocent parties. In addition to congestion costs visited on users and those trying to cut across their paths, there is the unsolicited intrusion of the noise and fumes of planes, trains, road traffic and ships, congregating at the limited number of junctions between nations. Above and beyond these immediate effects, there are longer-run ones, as the locations of these terminals help to shape the comparative advantage of different regions and their attraction for industry. This in turn influences the geography of employment and the market for housing and services. Two major questions on international transport in the UK in recent years raised all of these issues and remain unresolved. One was where to build a third London airport. The other was whether the government should guarantee the financing of the Channel Tunnel (Chunnel), undertaken by a private consortium of investors. The two matters lurk in the background, set aside in the face of doubt and a need for austerity.

The report of the Royal Commission on the Third London Airport (1971) presents an object lesson in how not to ask the right question in seeking an answer to a particular problem. The commissioners chose to interpret their charge narrowly and ignore the basic option of not building a new airport at a specified date in the future, which is the outcome which has come to pass in the face of the realities of political and economic circumstances. The late Anthony Crosland, as the minister who briefed the commission, stated that this course was left open to them. A broader perspective might have produced more concern with timing than location. As it was the conclusion on location was not all that clear cut and has left the question open, and subject to continuing controversy. The majority opinion of the report distilled the vast amount of information and cost benefit analysis involved into the choice of building an airport at Cublington, which lies between the London and Midlands markets. Lord Rothschild, whose estate stands near by, was not amused. A member of the commission prominent is the transport planning field, Sir Colin Buchanan, had a 'gut-feeling' which caused him to demur with a minority opinion in favour of a site on the Thames estuary at Maplin. Since the proposal for this site would involve a joint port and airport development with the dredging for the docks providing the fill for the runways, there was a heavy weight of construction industry support behind it. The more muck that has to be shifted the happier the civil engineers. The report was presented during the period of the Heath government and Mr Heath was impressed by the case for Maplin. Evidence of a levelling off of the number of flights with wide-bodied aircraft and concern over the externalities associated with Maplin led to perhaps the first overt shows of opposition to the cabinet by senior civil servants in the UK. Data were leaked to newspapers and the campaign waged forced a review of the prime minister's choice of Maplin. At this juncture a change of government put Mr Wilson in the decisive position and he chose to shelve the issue, leaving it to rise Phoenix-like in 1980.

Extensive economic analysis of the prospects for investment in the Chunnel came to the conclusion that it was marginally viable. The decider in the issue was the judgement of the Wilson cabinet that the project lacked political sex appeal and even government guarantees were unwarranted extensions of potential public expenditure when all the signs read that this should be curtailed wherever politically possible. The circumstances of this project were so speculative as to be prone to disastrous miscalculation in terms of both benefits to users and indirect developmental impacts. The most sensitive assumptions involved the substitute services which might emerge. It is possible that the more widespread development of ferries, Hovercraft and roll-on roll-off services, requiring relatively little fixed capital, and an improvement in European air services will reduce the need for concentration of overland traffic, provide a more widespread improvement of accessibility to the continent and avoid a bridgehead congregation of activities among the prosperous acres of Kent. For the French, a growth pole near the declining coalfield and mills of the Nord with its excess supply of labour is politically attractive. To set up a focus for development in the southeast of England would not provide the same political payoff.

It seems axiomatic that in the face of a host of future unknowns, rigid solutions should be avoided and the greatest leeway for dealing with unforseen circumstances should be sought. Commitment to a few chief points of egress to international markets builds a potentially costly rigidity into the economy's geography. New technology would appear to allow for greater flexibility. The advantage of container ships is in their rapid turnaround which means that, given adequate machinery for loading and offloading and an abundance of natural harbours, there is a reduction in the need for elaborate docks and the intense concentration of port activity. The development of pontoon docks for roll-on roll-off loading at any state of the tide, and of barge-shedding ships, implies a minimum of waterfront capital investment and, thus, wider discretion on where goods pass over the shore. This allows for easier response to changes in the pattern of demand. More widely spread competition for traffic might well prove a spur to efficiency, with only a small attendant risk of creating sunk, excess dock capacity. Container ship loading gear can be moved from place to place, which dock excavations cannot. More widespread access to sea routes will obviously reduce overland traffic and its convergence on a limited number of ports, giving rise to road and rail congestion. This must be counted in favour of any more decentralized solution. The absence of central control over these matters in the USA means that a more diffuse and competitive solution is bound to prevail there, carrying with it some danger of a wasteful excess of port facilities. In the UK such a solution will meet heavy opposition from the dock unions, since it means the erosion of their wage bargaining leverage in the shape of a paralysing strike threat. Thus the Labour party's transport manifesto remains in favour of state monopoly and concentration of port capacity (*Socialist Commentary* 1975).

Interregional transport

Political controversy over long-distance, internal trade and travel focuses on competition between the various means available and on the extent of geographical coverage of the networks of these services. In the USA, since most of the intercity highway system is in place the latter question is mostly a matter of how far the rail network should be cut back and airlines be allowed to prune lightly patronized branches of their schedules. The question of the extent to which competition should be allowed to allocate traffic between trucks, trains, pipes and barges is a major issue of economic policy for the penultimate decade of the century. This is not merely a matter of dismantling the federal cartel arrangement of the Interstate Commerce Commission (ICC) but also of adjusting all the hidden subsidies and costs imposed by government which distort the clarity of competition in seeking efficient use of resources. Whether and to what extent the rail passenger system should be subsidized as an item of national prestige or potential energy savings and whether the ailing structure of northeastern railways can be put on a viable footing remain as issues.

In the UK, the belt-tightening found necessary in the late 1970s has temporarily put a damper on the construction of high standard, intercity roads, to the joy of those who opposed road building for the changes it would wreak on community and scenery. The concentration of what funds remain for road building on routes bypassing crucial points of conflict may reduce the unpleasant impact of truck traffic in particular on homes and living spaces, to everyone's satisfaction. When we examine the results of the spate of road building of the 1950s and 1960s there are clear indicators of politically induced, geographical misallocation of investment. In the USA, rural over-representation finds concrete expression in the interstate system. In the UK, areas where the local political organization has strong national influence, especially Northumbria, have been compensated by both Labour and Conservative governments for the industrial stagnation and unemployment they suffer by road building far in excess of any foreseeable demand. Hopefully the impotence of this remedy has been recognized. Quite apart from considerations of geographical equity, it has proved impossible to assess whether the total investment on roads is adequate in terms of the improved efficiency of the entire national economy which it brings about. No sound measurements exist to judge the matter on. In practice the question is tackled at the margin of growth of the network, by requiring that each additional piece of road, or improvement to an existing road, achieve a satisfactory rate of return of benefits generated over cost of construction and maintenance. The benefits are measured in social terms of the time and accident savings projected to result from the scheme. This generates a controversy over the way in which time and life and limb are valued, calling in practice for ministerial pronouncements. The other question raised concerns the lower limit of 'satisfactory' for a rate of return. This is usually set by some administrative ruling by the budgetary authority, but does not necessarily make economic sense.

The question of road versus rail competition has reached a greater degree of resolution in the UK and the railway question is simpler to explore where the industry is unified and nationalized and its only significant competition is with road haulage. It is, thus, possibly more enlightening to consider the general problem in the British context.

Intervention in the structure of the road freight sector in the UK was resolved in favour of competition by the Tories deliberately neglecting to execute the quality licensing provisions of Labour's 1968 Transport Act. Although pressure for nationalization of road haulage persists from the Left, on the grounds of faith in Clause Four, since no obvious scale economies can be detected in road haulage and since other proclaimed advantages of direct government control are essentially police and safety matters not requiring ownership, most interested parties seem happy to leave well enough alone and regard the competitive condition of the industry as satisfactory.

The state of the railways and what to do about it remains a prime puzzle in transport policy. British Rail (BR) is seemingly a perpetual commercial failure. Yet railway management and unions and conservationists of various kinds defend every mile of track and indeed press for extension or upgrading of the system. Annual deficits in excess of £1 billion and subsidies in excess of revenues become harder to swallow as a recurrent government expenditure.

Given the little that is known about the cost and demand characteristics for intercity passenger services, it is not in the realms of fantasy to postulate that these could be made to break even by a combination of price rises and cost cuts — in terms of thinning out the frequency of services at least. Covering the current deficit of these operations out of the public purse is almost certainly shifting resources towards gratifying the needs of the richer and those on company expense accounts and away from those who cannot afford to travel by rail or at all. There seems no obvious reason why bigger, less frequent trains with the same reliability should not maintain custom and merely improve load factors, this since rail travel between cities is seldom done on impulse and usually involves some preparation and planning. The raising of prices might cause some patrons to scrutinize the value of their intended journey more closely and the other means of making it which includes the less costly bus. The result of fare increases would involve not only switches to cars and buses, of minuscule magnitude in terms of road capacity, but also a reduction in the numbers of trips made. The substitution of a phone call, telex message or letter for a rail journey might be no bad thing from the national viewpoint.

In rural areas it seems so evident as to swamp any contradiction that subsidizing a generous level of road service to those captive to public transport would be vastly less costly than providing stopping rail services. To defray either taxi or bus fares for the very few without cars is by far the most efficient solution. Yet the taxpayer continues to foot the bill for anachronistic stopping trains, allowing the rail fanatics to gratify their necrophilic nostalgia behind a smokescreen of social responsibility.

Rail freight operations were always expected to be paying propositions by both political parties and not seen as likely candidates for explicit subsidy. It has been generally accepted that the carriage of goods by rail should be on a commercially viable basis. During the 1970s BR management and the railwaymen's unions showed signs of discontent with this state of affairs. In their annual report for 1973 the Board of BR referred to a review of 'the future of the freight business in the constrained terms of its *present* wholly commercial remit' (my italics). As the case for rail freight subsidies is being insinuated into the political arena, then the arguments in its favour require close scrutiny. A similar campaign is being mounted in the US to justify continued support for Conrail.

The general case for subsidy of a good or service is that its production is subject to decreasing costs and, thus, that the price equating marginal cost and marginal revenue, which equation is necessary to ensure the efficient allocation of resources between various activities, would produce insufficient revenue to cover total costs. This, because simple arithmetic demonstrates that marginal costs (i.e. the increment to total cost as output expands) will always be less than average costs (i.e. total cost divided by output) if these decrease as output is expanded. Some parties to the debate hold that railways enjoy decreasing costs and thus deserve subsidies to ensure efficient resource use. This is bolstered by an argument on environmental grounds which boils down to procliaming that the balance of negative externalities, including the noise, smell, congestion and accidents involved in carrying the freight of the nation is in favour of rail rather than road haulage. It follows from this that the total cost of these collective burdens could be reduced by encouraging a transfer of goods to rail with a subsidy on rail rates. The case for rail freight subsidies finally rests on the track cost issue. Those in favour protest that road carriers are not required to cover the resource costs involved in the provision of its travelling way fully. This puts truck operators at an unfair competitive advantage over railways, which carry this burden in full. The correction of this imbalance calls for awarding rail operations a compensating subsidy.

Let us consider these arguments one at a time. Firstly, when the evidence on the decreasing cost industry case is examined closely, it is not indisputably clear that beneath the complexity of rail cost relationships the correlation between output and average cost is essentially negative. Cross-sectional and time series data from the USA, examining cost and output relationships for railroads of various sizes through the years, suggests that over the relevant range of output for mature systems, railway costs increase proportionally with increases in traffic (Meyer, Peck, Stenason and Zwick 1959, chapter 3). From this evidence the dense northeastern railroads of the manufacturing belt, which are closest in nature to the British network in extent and traffic, exhibited no substantial economies of scale. Stewart Joy (1973), a former BR chief economist writing on its maladies, insisted that railways were not subject to increasing returns to scale, especially when one investigates the way costs vary with decreasing output, which is not necessarily symmetric with the way they change as output expands. He contended that track and signalling costs can be pared so as to maintain adequate safety margins, thus tailoring the capacity of a route to the expected volume and mix of traffic. With traffic reductions, surplus capacity and its costs are avoidable. This, of course, puts a hole in the decreasing cost case for subsidy.

In practice the gap between the sum of average costs and total revenue has been covered by charging what the traffic will bear. Discriminating in price between customers according to their elasticities of demand, by means of ad valorem rates for example, has allowed railways to provide service to a wider market than otherwise. The railway can provide service to customers as long as they can afford to pay a rate which covers the variable costs which can unequivocally be assigned to carrying their goods and makes some small contribution to the large portion of costs which cannot be assigned to any particular customer. Unassignable costs are recovered by charging as much as possible to those whose demand is somewhat more inelastic. If some substitutes for rail services exist to inhibit the gathering of monopoly profits by this means, then a case that such price discrimination is socially beneficial can be made. In the case of BR there is evidence that their deficit on freight arose partly from an unwillingness to indulge in such discrimination, even when given complete commercial freedom by legislation. In 1963 the Prices and Incomes Board reported that there was widespread underpricing of rail freight traffic. Following this report, BR raised china clay and gasworks coal rates and suffered none of the loss of traffic to road and water carriers they had feared. To a degree the difficulties of BR in the latter half of the 1970s were a matter of government counter-inflationary price restraints. Nevertheless, the suspicion that railway management, supported by railway workers, is most strongly motivated to maintain the railways' market share and run a lot of trains on a lot of track rather than a business, is not without foundation.

Proposed subsidies for rail freight also come up against the hard fact of an evident inelasticity of demand with respect to rail rates or the rates of competitors. It does seem that total demand for freight movement and demand for a particular form of transport is more strongly determined by structural and quality considerations than by price. The demands of an emerging component of the economy have often arisen and fostered the development of transport facilities for their particular needs. In addition there is not a homogeneous product 'transport' whereby a rail ton mile equals a road ton mile. There is instead a diversity of facilities to meet time-, place- and quality-specific requirements for movement. The adjustment process to changes in the price of transport relative to other inputs for many forms of production is a locational one, with an accordingly long elapsed time for its completion. This is also true for some switches between means of transport. If the construction industry wants to receive gravel delivered to a metropolitan market by sea rather than by rail, then coastal rather then inland sources will have to exploited. Switching between different means of transport may require a firm to invest in new loading and off-loading facilities. Often the production process is geared to a batch size determined by the form of transport it customarily uses to assemble raw materials and distribute products. These constitute strong inhibitions to price responsiveness. Given this inelasticity of demand, then a subsidy to rail freight services will merely transfer funds from taxpayers to existing rail users with no guarantee of improved national well being or greater equity in its distribution.

The scope of active competition between road and rail is not very great according to what evidence there is. In the UK rail nearly monopolizes iron ore and limestone traffic, while road hauliers are predominant in carrying manufactures, food, chemicals and building materials. Coal, coke, scrap, steel, oil, sand and gravel are contested for. The merry-go-round movement of coal from pithead to power station using Coal Board loading facilities accounts for half the rail tonnage and is not likely to be captured by road. Another 25% are train load movements which are pretty invulnerable. The remaining wagon load traffic might be susceptible to road competition. Oil is carried by the railways under long-term, inflation-indexed, contractual prices, and shifts in this seem unlikely. The traffic most sensitive to rate differences is sand and gravel. BR has tried to expand its market share in this, at the cost of offering fixed contracts subject only to an inflation index increase, which would generate a loss if any cost increase outstrips the general rate of inflation. What little concrete evidence there is on the demand for rail freight services suggests that, even where there is active competition, own price and cross elasticities for rail are less than unity. Demand is not strongly perturbed by changes in rail freight rates or road haulage rates. When we bring this fact to bear on both the question of externalities and compensating track cost adjustments, it seems probable that the insensitivity of demand to price would result in subsidies causing little transfer between modes of transport and, thus, little reduction in the social costs cited. Direct charges to road haulage, with the revenue to be applied in amelioration of the damage caused, would be more efficacious than rail subsidies in achieving a welfare improvement. The 1968 White Paper on Road Track Costs (Ministry of Transport 1968) suggested that the imposition of such a charge would result in a negligible transfer of traffic to rail. Concerning road traffic externalities it has been calculated that if half of BR's freight were diverted to road carriage, road traffic would be increased by only 2%, generating only a similar increase in external costs. The rail network does not have the capacity to reduce the volume of road traffic significantly. The railways carry only 9% of total tonnage and 18% of total ton mileage in the UK. Many of the primary routes are running close to capacity as it is. It must also be realized that the environmentally deleterious effects of trucks are mostly felt in built-up areas and, given that many rail services require local road delivery and that any expansion of rail services to those without sidings certainly would, then transfer to rail would tend to redistribute the nuisance of moving goods by road. With intercity trucking the nuisance is dispersed on the periphery of cities where main arteries penetrate the fringes. If the same amount of goods was carried by rail for the line haul leg of the journey to rail terminals near the centre of the city, the widespread, peripheral impact would be reduced. However, the local distribution by road vehicles from these terminals would shift the incidence of nuisance towards the centre and concentrate it.

Seeking a resolution to the persistent failure of railways in advanced economies, it is evident from even a cursory inspection that their networks are overblown. Service and track is provided where it is not used at great expense in terms of the neglect of the sections of the system which can and do pay. Some factions in railway management persist in a nineteenth-century frame of mind which eschews financial soundness in favour of maintaining coverage and market share. The hope may be that the competition will eventually cut its own throat and the cream of the traffic will flood on to the railways, heralding a new golden age when increasing traffic will yield increasing returns to scale and healthy profits. Whatever the reasoning, the tendency to defend the network's extent is reinforced by the railway unions. Their chief objective is the short-term protection of jobs and enhancement of wage bargaining power. Thus, they are unlikely to concur readily with any solution to the railways' plight which insists on commercial viability and attempts to cure the impecunity of railways by clearly cutting them off from assistance from fiscal largesse while relaxing any restrictions on the closing of branch lines and reduction of services. If, as a result of such pressures, there is no straightforward motive of commercial viability laid upon railway management, allowing for specific public payment for socially desirable subsidized services, with penalties attached to failure, then preservation of the status quo or plant-amassing motives take hold. Nonsense like trying to invest your way out of a situation of market stagnation or decline in the face of fierce competition is given credence. Just as the professional accreditation criteria for civil engineers encourages the pouring of as much concrete as possible, so the rewards and punishments for railway management have failed to curb the inclination to play railways with as much track and as many power units as possible. The attitudes and aptitudes required for the graceful management of contraction of an industry are not very highly developed as yet, and railways need such talent badly. This picture of management is compounded by union officials' desire to maintain or expand their membership. Among the public there is a powerful coterie of rail enthusiasts and preservationists whose nostalgic conservatism can be counted on to oppose volubly any contraction. For them the national heritage, represented by the arbitrary present extent of the rail network, must be defended at all cost. To declare my own feelings in this matter of passionate involvement, I cannot work up a glow for the romance of the rails. As a child I had to endure the miseries of the boat train from Paddington to Fishguard and then the discomfort of Coras Iompair Eireann from Rosslare to Tralee. Experience persuades me that many enthusiasts' ardour must have sprung from unrequited longing or travelling first class.

Local transport

In deciding how to provide and govern mobility for the daily round of work, business and leisure, it is necessary to pay regard to the whereabouts and arrangements of the buildings and spaces people occupy for their various employment. The problem of planning our habitat is how best to adapt, delete and augment an arrangement of structures, spaces and transport connections, a very palimpsest of centuries of evolving technology, market conditions and politics, to serve a continuously changing social and economic texture.

It is plain that man, his tools, social arrangements and aspirations are in symbiosis. Faced with a new element to adapt the fabric to, such as the car, it is no good pouring scorn on the ravages caused by the machine without reference to the motives of the man. Not only do the personal ordering of life and mores increasingly reflect the mobility which car use bestows, but the extension of car use reflects a desire to be rid of the limitations of the past. The local identity, solidarity and collectivism of the past, for the majority, was enforced by restrained ability to travel. Necessity is not totally virtuous. There is an aspiration to a greater degree of individual self-determination. The car has done much to fulfil this desire and change our behaviour and views of one another. The process of change is most advanced in the USA, where the largest number of adults have at their behest the means of getting up and going where and when they will. In terms of perception of the world this has unbound the limited personal geography of the many, restricted to the way between home and work and shops and a walking radius thereabout, or a few well-known spots connected by corridors of rail, throwing open a vision more closely approaching the continuity of the real surface. Unfortunately total dependence on the car blurs the fine-grained detail of the land. The growth of car ownership reinforces the egalitarian closure of the distinction between cavalier and villein. However, it also atomizes the sense of community. The advent of two-car households erodes the mobility dependence of women. At the same time it relaxes the bonds of the family, our chief focus of social stability. Although we may rail at the evils of this creature and the result of its use, there is little prospect of a reversal of what appears to be a universal desire for the freedom which car ownership confers. A set of wheels stands foremost on the list of the trappings of modernity and affluence.

Road investment

In the early 1960s the realization of this trend, and the demand for road space it implied, led in the UK to Sir Colin Buchanan's analysis of the situation (1963) and prescription in favour of a massive road building programme to accommodate growing demand for car travel to existing town structures. This solution has been discarded now in a confusion of purposes and emotions. The flaw in it has not been objectively articulated as yet, so that the course of events may be corrected more precisely for its error. There has been an over-reaction against road building.

Given the inertial force of the arrangement of homes, jobs, shops, etc., in the major cities in the UK, with a strongly centripetal tendency and a monocentric radial structure, which has for the most part evolved in accord with the economics and use of public transport facilities, then road building proposals which seek to complement this structure are in competition with high-density uses of land. High land costs, constituting one-third of construction costs for primary network schemes, seem to have been the principal cause of the low social returns which have been calculated for such investments in new urban areas. This is quite apart from the political dissension they aroused. This fact does not exclude the possibility that, in less concentrated and smaller towns and in the conurbation periphery with scattered focuses of travel demand, no practical form of public transport could compare with provision for car travel on even the most stringent social and environmental evaluation. The need in these circumstances is not for channelling flows into a limited-access, high-performance road network superimposed on the urban landscape, but for the easier movement of a more diffuse pattern of flows with a multiplicity of local concentrations — essentially for a higher-quality main road network. This is for the most part in place already, and primarily requires modest improvement of its junctions and the removal of parked vehicles to improve its quality to a satisfactory level. This may be achieved with quite small expenditures on signalling, addition of queueing lanes, clearway designation and the provision of safe crossing and protection for pedestrians. The only form of public transport likely to attain solvency in such circumstances must use the road network in the form of bus and taxi services. The density of development required to sustain fixed-track mass transport facilities is seldom to be found and unlikely to be fostered by land-use planning of anything but the most paternalistic and Draconian nature. Possibly the best form of government intervention in this situation would be to relax the institutional constraints on entry and pricing which the Traffic Commissioners impose on competition in the bus industry, maintaining control with respect to safety and financial and technical eligibility to run a service. And this is the course which the latest transport minister (Mr Fowler) has embarked upon, at least, as far as entry control to long distance service is concerned.

Public transport

Considering movements to and within the denser core of cities, only the world's biggest cities seem capable of supporting viable rail commuter services. Of employees in inner London, for example, a quarter travel by rail and less than 18% by car. It is more than possible that the current losses of rail passenger and Underground services in London could be met by fare rises. The nature of demand for these is such that a high price is not likely to reduce custom to the extent that revenue can never meet outgoings. Long-distance rail commuters are to a large extent owner-occupiers, in management, administrative and clerical occupations, with above average incomes and more secure employment, who are not going to change home or work places readily. 38% of professional workers, 25% of employers and managers and 33% of non-manual workers travel to work by rail in London, as opposed to 18% of skilled manual workers, 14% of the semi-skilled and 14% of the unskilled. Given little or no spare road or parking capacity in the centre, the main impact of prices more in line with cost of services would be little reduction in rail commuting, a reduction in demand and price for suburban housing and a rise in the price of dwellings closer in. In geographical terms the whole effect might be pressure towards a reversal of the 'hollow centre" distribution of residences and curtailment of growth along the rail radii. Housing competition for land and the increased cost of gathering a working force might lead to a greater tendency to disperse certain more routine office and manufacturing activities along with retailing and services to several peripheral nodes. Subsidy of the current losses of commuter rail services smells suspiciously of a regressive redistribution of the national output subsidizing the life-style of the suburbanite in marginal con-stituencies with funds drawn from all taxpayers according to their incomes and purchases.

Traffic congestion

Despite the small amount of road building in major city central areas over the last decade, the chaos and seizure feared have not come to pass. Even without traffic management and restraint on parking space available to end journeys in the centre, the equilibrium between cap-acity and use which has arisen is not unbearable. This is the queueing solution to the allocation of a fixed supply. Physical management measures which can improve speeds without an offsetting increase in journey distance or extra efforts imposed on pedestrians by severing their usual paths are obviously desirable. It does seem that pinches and bottlenecks in the road network are limited in time and spatial extent and capacities are greater than had been thought. The cost of doing little or nothing where road space is in fixed supply, and not worthwhile expanding in economic and political terms, is not heart failure for the city but is the gap between some socially optimal level of use, where the utility derived by the last user equates the objective costs borne by himself and others as a result of his joining the existing traffic, and the current queueing solution. The theoretically desirable situations would be achieved by a set of prices specific to time and place for use of the network. Although the technology is available to achieve this (Ministry of Transport 1969), the cost and possible bitterness engendered by administering it would probably be in excess of the improvement in welfare produced. The system of selling supplementary licences, without which one cannot use central area roads, also appears expensive to operate and police, except when the central area has a limited number of entry points. The notion that a subsidy to public transport, compensating for the unperceived and collective costs of road congestion, will produce a significant effect seems far fetched.

The major determinant of car use is car availability. Availability is determined more by a secular trend of income increase than in response to changes in the cost differentials between modes of transport. The advantages of the car for more diffuse circumstances seem so far in excess of anything that public transport can offer that even free public transport will not cause a return to the bus or train. Price reductions and service improvements mostly attract people who would otherwise have walked or stayed put. The thing which strikes home in motorists' perception of the relative advantages of the car and other means of travel is the availability and price of parking. Parking charges which represent the opportunity cost of the land and buildings used would in most central areas bring about a level of demand and network performance not far removed from the socially desirable optimum.

The option of inaction, apart from some minor adjustments to the present system, is sadly denigrated. It frequently comes about from political paralysis, yet it can be an explicit, reasoned response to the given situation. Being invisible and an admission of humility, it takes political courage in the face of 'crisis' panic. It has the great advantage of maintaining the maximum flexibility of response to changing circumstances and making the least ridiculous calls on our powers of foresight. If we sensibly hesitate to hazard a projection of total national population and GNP, never mind levels of various activities and the distribution of population, 20 years hence, then it would appear foolish to go into the details of how an unknown total is housed and carried. And yet this is what concrete plans to restructure cities radically require. Cautious incrementalism has much to recommend it as a strategy for urban transport planning.

Some would hold that the conurbations of the world have achieved congestion equilibria at tolerable speed levels and certainly without utter chaos. Whether this situation results from the degree of parking restraint and management exercised or would have arisen in any case is contentious. In judging between the present situation and the possible results of more stringent restraint, such as road pricing or supplementary licensing, the income distributional implications must be taken into account. It can be argued that rationing of a fixed supply by a queue results in a progressive redistribution of welfare, whereas price rationing is regressive — the poorer valuing time less highly in terms of money than the rich. In addition, putting the allocative bite on in terms of time rather than money may be more effective in spreading the peakedness of demand, inasmuch as it will more strongly influence those with a higher value of time, who for the most part have a greater degree of discretion as to how they dispose their day, not being governed by fixed work hours.

The planning and finance of local transport

The centralized nature of the British polity, and some recent experiments in legislation in the UK, again make its case the most appropriate basis for a general discussion of transport finance.

Along with the reorganization of the Local Government Act of 1972 in the UK, there was a new dispensation for the planning and finance of local transport facilities. This came into effect in 1975-6. Former specific grants for roads, public transport infrastructure, rural bus services, rail service subsidies and the purchase of new buses, were replaced by a unified grant from central government. This encompasses current as well as capital expenditure, public transport as well as roads. Some part of this payment is absorbed in the needs element of the rate support grant. Any transport expenditure above a threshold level, defined by a general formula in terms of population and type of area, is met by a supplementary grant. In the early years of operation this covered 70-75% of the expenditure by local authorities, but will be reduced to 50% by 1980. To obtain the supplementary grant and also sanction for any loans they wish to float, county councils must submit Transport Policies and Programme (TPP) statements to the transport minister every year. This annual package, including road, public transport infrastructure, vehicle purchase and operating subsidy outlays along with traffic and parking management schemes, is framed in a five-year expenditure rolling programme for the county. This in turn must be geared to a local transport policy strategy with a 10- to 15-year horizon. The whole should, of course, bear some resemblance to the intentions stated in the county's land use structure plan. This constitution certainly conveys the notion of the opportunity cost of various transport expenditures to county councils in a most telling fashion. The long-run benefits of investment must be weighed against the immediate relief of subsidies. Traffic restraint and management became clear alternatives to pouring concrete. Inasmuch as the procedure decentralizes local transport policy, it alows for a better adjustment to unique local needs and circumstances. Policy formulated at the national level can trample roughshod over these. After the first several rounds of this procedure, however, central administrators still appear in a quandary as to how much detailed control can safely be relinquished to local sovereignty.

All in all this set of more immediate and down-to-earth instruments of government appears as a healthy antidote to the thinking which the transportation/land use planning scheme, with its grand strategy for 20 years time, engendered. They encourage the good husbandry of what we have rather than neglectful dreaming of great days to come.

Equity and environment

It may be objected that thus far I have addressed the issues in terms of demands and not needs, and thus ignored specific questions of equity between parents and children, men and women, workers and pensioners, the healthy and the disabled, as far as ability to travel is concerned. The provision of transport facilities is not a keen enough weapon to wreak a prescribed change in family arrangements, even if one accepts the presumption of wrongness in what exists. Outside of this, the chief drawback under which people suffer is a lack of wealth. It would be more efficacious and in accord with the dignity of those deemed deprived to tackle that directly and leave it to them to choose whether and how they travel.

A further objection which might be levelled at the coverage is that insufficient attention has been paid to the depredations that certain forms of transport wreak on the environment. 'The environment' can be defined as the world as it exists in isolation from man, and therefore, all of man's activities and artifacts may be seen as undesirable blemishes on the face of nature. On the other hand, the definition of the environment might include man, and thus all of his acts and creations are in some way 'natural' and cannot be decried on these grounds.

Obviously the word is not a very useful category of existence, and we shall get into a philosophical tangle if we personify it in our deliberations — talking of harm to the environment. What we are concerned with in evaluating the relative merits of various transport proposals are direct and indirect, specific impacts on the well being of the various members of society, including those who will use the facility and those who will not, now and in the future. In response to an increase in popular sensitivity to noise, smell, dirt and danger, every effort is being made to incorporate the external effects on non-users in cost benefit analyses of transport projects. The physical measurement of noise, air pollutants and visual intrusion and the prediction of levels of these associated with various traffic volumes on roads of different configurations, say, is fairly well developed. Thus, it is possible to judge between different transport proposals to meet the same need for movement, for example, a sunken or elevated profile for a particular piece of road. The alternatives can be compared in terms of the numbers of people affected by undesirable levels of the various intrusive effects, for instance, within a certain noise contour line about the road. Any difference in costs between options examined can be judged against the external effects one at a time. A value judgement can be made of the relative importance of the various effects and their values can be turned into standardized scores, weighted and summed to produce a composite environmental score for each option. But only a politician has the credentials to do this and impose decisions made on that basis on society. Even this exercise falls short when the decision concerns different projects in different places. In such cases values in common units, i.e. in terms of money, have to be applied to the measures of intrusion, the benefits to users and the cost involved, if a comparable trade-off or rate of return is to be estimated. This implies putting a money value on external impacts. This is the stumbling block. One possible recourse is to look at the preference which people reveal in the market, for example, the difference in house prices which can be attributed solely to their degree of shelter from noise. It is very difficult to separate one attribute like this in the housing market, especially when, by definition nearly, it relates inversely to access to main roads. Observations of house price differences often suggest private reactions to noise quite at odds with the current conventional wisdom on the value of quiet. Results gleaned by asking people how important peace and quiet is to them are of little use either. Those in quiet locales proclaim it very valuable and those near major roads register indifference. The gap between perception and substance presents additional confusion. The main pollutant from motor vehicles which has a deleterious effect on health is carbon monoxide, which is imperceptible, while the diesel fumes and smoke from lorries, which are the occasion of much public outcry, have been considered relatively innocuous by medical opinion up till recently. It does seem that the difficulties in arriving at sensible and generally acceptable prices for peace, quiet and clean air will preclude their mechanical inclusion in cost benefit calculations. The evaluation of the physical measures of the undesirable external effects of transport operations must remain a matter of political judgement, and in some cases the question has been or will be resolved by the legislation of minimum acceptable standards for design of vehicles and routes, hopefully made with the cost of achieving these clearly in mind. There is as yet no theory or method available to social science enabling such questions to bypass the political process.

CHAPTER· 5

Kinds of Solutions to Transport Problems

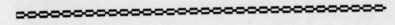

If we set aside the macroeconomic and distributional goals of transport policy, then the objective of government action is to relieve any political economic or social stress generated by the need for mobility and access. From the particular issues discussed in the last chapter it is possible to generalize four kinds of remedy to apply in seeking a solution. These are (i) constitutional, (ii) regulatory, (iii) operational and (iv) structural means. As a first step in elaborating on the process and methods of transport planning it seems appropriate to investigate the nature of these categories of palliative.

Constitutional remedies

By 'constitutional' I mean to imply a solution embedded in the laws and customs of the nation, involving a redrawing of the lines of responsibility and control over services and resource allocation.

Nationalization is one of the more obvious forms of constitutional intervention. For whatever reason, if it is deemed politically necessary that ownership and disposal of transport assets be vested in the state rather than in private persons or corporations, then the transfer of ownership rights in return for compensation can be accomplished by law. In some instances transport systems were matters of state enterprise from the outset and have always been government controlled. British Rail was created out of the remnant regional monopolies in 1948, joining its continental counterparts, and in the late 1970s some parts of the US system have been shuffled into de facto public ownership. This widely anathematized fate worse than death for private enterprise has at times been sought eagerly by owners anxious to convert the failing yield of an ailing enterprise into the secure return of government bonds offered in compensation for their ancient property.

The avoidance of impending losses motivated US railroad management to divest themselves of their passenger operations with great
alacrity. They most certainly encouraged the Federal government to
create Amtrak to relieve them of this burden and pass it on to the
nation as a whole. A similar means was employed in an attempt to
clear up the mess of the New York Central and Pennsylvania Railroads
in the northeast with the creation of Conrail. In this case the first
draft of the governing legislation was written by lawyers for the Union
Pacific Railroad. It is rumoured that the underlying motive was the
exclusion of the Burlington Northern from purchasing parts of a dis-
membered Penn Central network to create a coast-to-coast railroad.
Whatever the motive and the legalese involved, the net effect was to
nationalize the northeastern railroad network and make its losses a
charge on the federal exchequer.

In principle public ownership should reduce any disparity between
private and public good. With ownership goes total public control,
supposedly. The motives of the enterprise and the nation should then
become as one. Any gap between entrepreneurial and collective objectives should be eradicated. In practice the management of large complex systems requires more tangible and limited objectives than the
manifestation of the national will. Managers do not have the same
mandate as politicians to determine what this is. Politicians, quite
sensibly, are reluctant to enumerate and evaluate the components of
the national well being. Thus the translation of the will of the nation
into managerial objectives for a nationalized corporation usually takes
the form of a simple financial brief, such as making a specified rate
of return on assets or breaking even subject to a limited subsidy to
achieve certain specified social objectives. This is the source of the
departures between ownership and control which dog this form of
solution. In order to remove the operation of the system from the
machinations and temptations of partisan politics and to achieve a
degree of efficiency, a simple, recognizable and measurable optimand
must be set for management. Efficiency and resource allocation considerations require that this objective be comparable with measures
employed in the private sector. The management of the public corporation must then be given some stated degree of independent hegemony over the shape and operation of the system, protected from
political and bureaucratic intrusion in both the day-to-day operation
and longer-term planning of the enterprise. The attainment of non-
financial goals must be translated into specific contracts for service
and explicitly subsidized, so as not to confuse comparisons in effic-

iency terms with private enterprise. Management and the requirement for efficiency demand judgement in terms of financial performance. Success in this may not coincide with changing public sensibilities and the politician's changing views of the public good. In the last resort the only remarkable effect of national ownership is the cushioning of managerial failure and the power it gives to wage negotiators, who may pile on the pressure for rises without fear of causing bankruptcy and failure. Even in this, governments of various persuasions have extended these privileges beyond the nationalized realm, bailing out limping businesses in order to sustain employment. For activities which are not innately collective, it is difficult to see what advantage public ownership confers in terms of control that could not be obtained in some less committed fashion. The national ownership of nationwide, infrastructural systems might have some egalitarian and patriotic appeal but the security of ownership achieves little more in terms of equity and efficiency than can be got by some less drastic means.

Some transport facilities cannot be marketed in the usual fashion and in such cases public ownership is essential to economic efficiency. The roadway is an example of such a collective good which is nearly everywhere publicly owned. We explored the rationale for such collective provision in the last chapter. Such services are subject to joint consumption, such that once the facility is established to serve someone, the incremental cost of serving more customers is zero. When the marginal cost of a good is zero, the welfare maximizing price of that good is also zero. Optimality in this case is defined as a state from which it is not possible to depart by making some people better off without at the same time making others worse off: this is the Pareto criterion of optimality. Obviously a private interest cannot make a profit at zero price. Thus, the good can only be made available in efficient amounts by government, which finances it out of the general exchequer while charging zero or nominal prices. Another feature justifying collective supply is the difficulty of excluding non-payers from enjoyment of the good. We may view these difficulties of policing use as high transaction costs which make it impossible for entrepreneurs to capture sufficient of the value of the benefits involved to cover costs. In the case of roads, the manner in which their public nature is embedded in tradition and institutions makes the political and social cost of appropriating the resource cost for their use directly from users potentially high. Reductions in the administrative and technical cost of pricing and exclusion by electronic means, however, have brought the collective treatment of this good into question. The departures between private perception of the cost of using the system and the real resource costs involved which manifest themselves under collective provision, are an incentive to institute marginal cost pricing. Although this would require considerable change in the legal apparatus governing the use of roads, it is not contemplated that the state would divest itself of ownership of the network and give it over to a modern version of the turnpike trusts. Rather, what would be involved is a change in regulatory and operating practices under the same management.

One circumstance in which all transport services and facilities are subject to collective control is in the employment of the *ultima ratio regum* — war. In addition there is one aspect of transport services which is treated collectively everywhere so as to transcend ownership as grounds for control and that is safety. The police power of the state is used to enforce rules to limit the loss of life and limb to a minimum on both public and private properties. The motive for such control may be wider, as in the case of the 55 m.p.h. speed limit instituted in the USA in 1973 in the face of a panic over fuel. This institutional change has not, however, become an uncontested part of the social milieu. The policing of safety obviously spills over into engineering. Design standards and codes for vehicles and civil engineering works are set, monitored and enforced by the state. Economic judgements on the value of collective facilities are swayed by questions of life and limb, and these considerations are written into administrative decision procedures if not made instrumental as legal requirements.

Government control of transport may of course be constituted by less drastic means than ownership or the exercise of police powers. Laws may be enacted setting up bodies regulating entry and prices, enabling new forms of taxation or subsidy and authorizing government purchases as new budget line items. All other means of intervention depend initially on some legal provision. Regulatory, operational and structural actions are taken within a framework set by constitutional decisions. We can thus move on from the political choices which establish and change the laws and institutions to a consideration of practice within this framework.

Regulatory control

Economic regulation of the transport sector involves the day-to-day control of entry and pricing by a body with governmental authority. What this usually entails is both the general and individual interpretation of the vague legal formulas in which such authority is usually couched. The usual justification for regulatory agencies is market failure. It is held that competition will not bring about socially desirable quantities of service and prices. Founded on notions of 'excessive' or 'chaotic' competition for road haulage and 'undue discrimination' for railways, the charge to regulators is usually broad. The Transport Tribunal in the UK had a brief to decide matters 'in the interests of the public generally, including those of persons requiring as well as those of persons providing facilities for travel'. The Interstate Commerce Commission's objective in the USA is 'public convenience and necessity'. Such charges are open to interpretation, and regulation becomes a quasi-legal procedure. The results, therefore, often tilt towards those who can afford the best lawyers, which is usually the big, established carriers. These of course are the interests which the legislation and regulatory bodies were established to protect. The regulatory apparatus was constructed during the depression of the 1930s when small operators were cutting into the markets of big hauliers. The regulatory agencies do have many of the characteristics of cartels. Competition is stifled and the market shared out among the existing operators who, in return for their excess profits, promise stable service and some degree of cross subsidy to socially meritorious but commercially unprofitable markets. In theory regulation should operate so as to ensure socially optimal levels of service and compensation to suppliers. It is, of course, unclear how restricting entry and competition can work for the customer's good — but that is in practice a major element of regulatory activity. One justification which is offered comes by way of confusing police and safety functions with economic regulation. Regulatory licensing, it is held, keeps out reckless, small operators who would not only indulge in cut-throat competition but also cut safety corners and raise the social cost of accidents. Clearly if the police are doing their job this should not occur under any circumstances. Licensing in terms of vehicle and driver fitness is a separate matter from economic considerations. What theory we have about attitude to risk suggests that small operators will be more careful. Empirical evidence of past performance supports this. Questions of safety and competition can be separated out quite satisfactorily, and safety should not be used as an excuse for restricting competition.

If we agree that regulation of entry for the good of the community is a nonsense, and there is an increasing body of this opinion which has generated the appropriate constitutional changes in some places and promotes them elsewhere, we are left with the case of price regulation as a serious consideration. Faced with a decreasing cost industry with the potential for monopoly profits, the regulatory body operates to ensure a satisfactory level of service and adequate compensation to the enterprise involved. If a railway has a monopoly on transport in a region, what is the appropriate price for its services? In other areas of utility regulation, such as power and pipeline operation, rates are calculated so as to provide a 'fair rate of return' on capital. Railway price setting has usually taken the form of cost allocation to particular commodities over particular routes. This runs into the difficulty of the large element of railway costs which are not assignable to specific units of output, such as track and terminal costs, signalling costs and administrative costs. These do not in essence vary as a function of volume of traffic in the short run and when varied over the long run in response to demand variations, cannot be ascribed to particular services rendered. Given the lumpiness of railway capital, the notion of marginality becomes strained. The formulas devised, inasmuch as they assign the unassignable, are an absurdity and can have undesirable effects on the provision of service. Traffic for which close substitute carriers exist or which is only just worthwhile at a price covering short-run marginal costs, may be driven to others or out of existence. The longstanding commercial practice of discriminating in prices between customers according to their demand elasticities may well be more generally beneficial. There is much to be said for a pricing scheme which appropriates sufficient to cover short-term marginal costs from all traffic and covers the unassignable elements of cost by discriminating among customers according to their demand elasticities. Traffic is accepted as long as it makes some small contribution to overheads, and the excess is covered by charging what the traffic will bear. This is obviously not something a regulatory agency can successfully determine on a day-to-day basis, it is a matter of commercial acumen and judgement based on intimate knowledge of local circumstances. If charging what the traffic will bear is permitted, as it was to British Railways by the Transport Act of 1962, the only role for regulators is to adjudicate complaints of 'undue discrimination' and 'predatory' pricing. Since there are few instances where actual or latent competition will not protect customers from being nailed for every penny of their consumer surplus, there seems little point to economic regulation on these grounds. Predatory pricing, driving competitors from a market by undercutting, is only relevant if start-up costs are high. Since railways characteristically face road haulier competition for which start-up costs on any particular route are negligible, it is hard to justify losing sleep on this issue either.

Aside from questions of competition, there are clearly grounds for government regulation of safety standards of vehicles, tracks and operating procedures. On roads this is traditionally a matter for the police. In the UK there is a railway inspectorate parallel to the factory inspectorate. Recent evidence suggests that although the Rail Safety Act of 1970 gave the Department of Transportation jurisdiction over all matters of railway safety, including track, roadbed, freight car standards, and employee qualification standards in the USA, that agency is inadequate for the task. It is obviously either undermanned, incompetent or impotent to maintain a reasonable level of safety for the public from railway accidents involving toxic chemicals and bad track. These are exceptionally dangerous in a country where little concession has been made to separating rail operations from people's homes and the roads they travel. The point is that authority requires power. To impose control it is necessary to have sanctions against offenders and to monitor the state and operation of the system in question thoroughly.

Operational control

Discussion of policing the transport system for safety purposes brings us to another kind of way in which public stress generated by its functioning can be overcome. Given an institutional framework as a set of regulatory rules, the real-time running of the system can be manipulated to improve its performance. Operational control can be exercised to induce a more satisfactory configuration in, say, a road network's traffic flows. A policeman directing traffic at an intersection supposedly allocates road space so as to reduce the loss of time resulting from vehicular conflict. Given that British police regard this as a demanding chore, the outcome is not a guaranteed success. The monitoring and control of the system can be automated, and this can vastly improve performance. Traffic signalling direction is the most successful form of operational control in transport. It can, of course, be put to longer-term ends. The Nottingham 'ring and collar' scheme used traffic signal settings to deter traffic from the centre of town to a greater extent than warranted by road capacity considerations. The levels of tolls charged or, indeed, the prices of public goods could be used as such operational controls. We could look upon the subsidy of public transport fares as such an exercise. If variable road pricing were introduced, this could obviously be employed as an operational control device — if the price of using a piece of road at a particular time could be registered with the driver immediately.

Structural control

Beyond the more immediate manipulation of use, price and competition and the revamping of institutional arrangements, tension and failure in the transport system can be ameliorated with the longer-term adjustment of its balance by the provision of facilities and building of infrastructure. The successful exercise of such structural control is the objective of investment decision making. The building of new links, terminals and control systems for a network and the acquisition of improved vehicles, expands capacity to provide service and/or improves service performance. Given economic and political signals of lack of performance, if operational, regulatory or constitutional means will not suffice to meet existing and expected requirements, then it may be necessary to allocate resources to future better and greater provision at a cost in terms of the current consumption of resources forgone. The guiding principles behind the selection of new components for a system are slightly different according to whether the choice is made within the limitation of a budget or not. Without budgetary constraints all those components for which the capitalized value of the excess of benefit over cost is positive are worthwhile. When there is a limit on expenditure then all projects are ranked according to their capitalized net worth and a cut-off is made at the juncture down the list which can be afforded with the budget. The same principles apply to the creation of a new network from scratch or to the enhancement of an existing set of facilities.

If constitutional, regulatory and operational solutions to transport problems require political, jurisprudential or economic nous for their successful application, structural solutions require engineering and design talent also. The structural solution is fundamentally a matter of engineering. But this solution must be embedded in the legal framework defining standards and permissible options and be guided by an economic calculation of the balance of advantage. Legal and economic choices are governed by what is possible in engineering terms, and technical imagination and flair are held in check by the reins of political and economic feasibility. At its simplest we could view the problem as one of providing capacity to carry a given demand at given performance standards from a fixed construction budget. This represents an excessively artificial partitioning of the design process for structural improve-

ment in either the public or private sectors. It can seldom be separated
out into such a free-standing task with given and fixed relations to the
politics and economics of the issue, without doing damage to the final
value of the outcome. Demand will likely respond to design, and there
is usually a trade-off between performance standards and construction
costs to be balanced in the engineering calculations. Future events,
in terms of demand and performance, must be predicted in relation to
the engineering characteristics of the system in which they occur. This
involves the formulation of a model, using mathematical processes to
represent the events of the real world so that the solution to a mathematical problem, such as the solution of a set of simultaneous equations or the establishment of an extreme (maximum or minimum)
value for a mathematical function, determines the best structural
design. Prediction, problem solving and decision making are all intimately intertwined in this pursuit. To meet the needs of such circumstances, out of an amalgam of the institutional practices of commercial and political decision making and scientific method there has
arisen a commonsense rubric for setting about problems which has
been given the pretentious title of systems analysis. The abstractness
of the words is off-putting. In fact, the substance is not a rigid rule
book for problem solving but rather a set of reasonable research ideas,
procedures and techniques developed by investigators who have been
involved in the formulation of policy concerning massive and costly
investments (Thomas and Schofer 1966). Systems analysis provides a
framework promoting order and clarity within which the investigators'
creativity and imagination are given their head in a more efficient
manner.

The systems-analysis strategy as applied to design and investment
problems is given in figure 19. The first step, that of clearly stating
the problem, is obvious but deserves comment because it is so frequently
mishandled. If it is not done explicitly and rigorously there is a great
danger of accepting one possible answer to a problem as the problem.
In the case of designing cities, the problem could be taken to be the
more efficient, economical and safe movement of a large volume of
traffic. However, at a more fundamental level we might see the problem as how to reduce the friction of distance between persons wishing
to communicate and interact with others. The solution to this deeper
statement of the problem might involve reducing the need for physical
movement by some people by improving other media of communication, rather than providing for more movement.

After the objective of the exercise has been stated, the next move

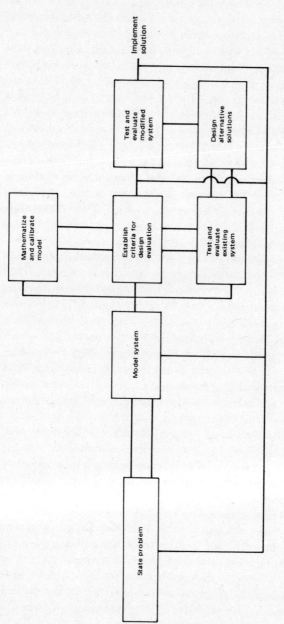

(after Thomas and Schofer 1966)

Figure 19

is to establish the nature of the thing being studied as an explicit model-building activity. The relationships between the various members of the system in hand are thought out so that no important elements or connections are left out of the picture. In doing this the harsh cost realities of the availability of information, difficulties of measurement and computation are ignored and a model unconstrained by practical difficulties is developed. An important task in this modelling process is deciding where to cut off consideration of possible relationships — the problem of bounding the system. Everything is related to everything else, but to make life manageable we have to do some partitioning of existence. Our objective in doing this must, of course, be to ensure that the boundaries we draw follow lines of weak connections and do not cut any important contacts. These boundaries are both geographical and functional. We shall return to geographical partitioning in Chapter 9.

In simplest form, a model of a system might take the form of a flow diagram with elements of the complex in boxes, their important relationships with one another indicated by arrows and their causal sequence by position. Whenever possible the nature of the relationships should be specified mathematically. But inability to do this at present should not inhibit the indication of an hypothesized linkage. The exertion of modelling the system may well bring to light a new conception of the problem, so there is a possible feedback from modelling to problem definition and the two activities will affect each other until there seems little to be gained from expanding or deepening the scope of the study. The model is then mathematized and calibrated, which involves devising measuring instruments, collecting data on the various relationships specified in the model and estimating the parameters of these relationships — their precise quantitative form. As these activities are carried out, results are fed back into the statement of the problem and the basic system model and, if necessary, modifications are carried out.

At the same time consideration should be given to establishing criteria by which the performance of the present and any proposed new designs can be evaluated. These criteria for design evaluation are also fed back, perhaps throwing new light on to the problem in hand or the basic model. When these criteria are established, in terms of what the system should or could do, we can evaluate the effectiveness of things as they stand. The next step is to devise alternatives to the present set-up which may improve any shortcomings it may have. The blemishes of the present system should suggest where innovations could be made. Proposed new systems are obviously costed as part of the design process. The performance of each solution to the problem is compared with that of others and with the existing system. It is at this stage that mathematical models pay dividends. Mathematical simulation of the operation of the system is the cheapest method of evaluating designs and often the only alternative to actually building them. The strategy of evaluation can take two forms. Depending on the mandate of the decision maker involved, it may be appropriate to ask which option gives the best performance and falls within the cost limits of a given budget, *or* which is the least-cost option which reaches a required standard of performance. Having selected a satisfactory solution to the problem the formidable political task of implementation presents itself.

The geographical dimension

Although they may have geographically differential effects, institutional and regulatory remedies must by their nature be universal in their applicability. Operational interventions are very fine-tuned in their geographical specifics, but are mostly attuned to the microgeography of their referent system's operational efficiency. As we suggested they can be used for more long-term ends, but this is unusual. It is with structural selections that the geographical arrangement of people and their activities and how these change become a premier consideration in making choices. We have seen in chapters 2 and 3 how, in attempting to predict changes in human geography, we are faced with a tremendously complex set of simultaneous and lagged interrelationships in time and space. The elements of the system are connected by a mesh of links of mutual causality. Transport network structure influences the disposition of economic activity and resident population which affects the geography of demand for the use of the network, and thus the way the network is developed. MacKinnon (1970) has pointed out the three approaches which have been used or mooted to tease out these relationships in a planning context. The crudest method is to assume simple cause-effect relationships starting from some given element in the system as prime mover. For example, an exogenous prediction of the pattern of land uses is made and a transport system most appropriate to its needs is planned. The flaw in this lies in assuming that the distribution of land uses can be predicted independently of the structure of the transport network. Some first steps in overcoming this have been made by transport planners. They have attempted to incorporate iterative procedures in their models so that results from subsequent forecasts of variables are fed back to modify former forecasts of other variables. In traffic planning this takes the form of accepting an initial independent land-use forecast; estimating traffic generated by this pattern; distributing traffic flows between origins and destinations; assigning traffic to a given network; reforming the transport network to accord better with these flows and then feeding back to the start to adjust the original landuse forecast according to the changed pattern of accessibility on the modified network. This iterative procedure continues until some kind of stability is achieved. The iterations do not represent real world processes but are merely a balancing-up procedure, ensuring that the various forecasts bear some sensible and steady relationships to one another. The best modelling style would consist of the specification of the social goals of the planning process as an explicit objective function. Forecasting would then consist of seeking the combination of transport system, flows and activity disposition which simultaneously optimize the objective. Especially in the sphere of urban planning, this ideal situation, where the optimum plan is the forecast, lies beyond our present mensural, computational and political capacity. Now we can only stumble towards an approximation to a hazily specified optimum with the methods of 'eyeball', intuition and iteration. This stumbling is done largely in terms of predicting future geographical outcomes of several possible policy and investment strategies.

Transport structures have to be planned for particular geographical settings, and once in place they are there as an outline for people's activities for a very long time. Components of transport networks, links, junctions and terminals, are required to meet specifically geographical stresses and shortcomings in the provision of access and mobility. Laying down track or carriageways, and placing points of egress to these, determines the focal points for the evolution of the human landscape. The design and choice of what and where to build cannot be made in isolation from each other. The elaboration of a transport system structure should be informed by, at least, intuition as to its geographical outcomes.

The exercise of operational controls depends upon a similar but more short-term appreciation of explicitly geographical processes. The setting of a traffic signal requires the prediction of the number of people who will use particular routes and cross particular junctions. With forecasts of the conflicting traffic streams and their characteristics, total waiting time can be used as an objective to minimize in making the setting, or the difference in waiting time with or without the signal can be used as a measure of benefit to set against the cost of installation. Inasmuch as waiting time at a junction may affect the choice of a driver's route, and even means of travel, destination and whether to travel at all over the longer haul, then the ramifications need tracing over a wider geographical scope. At least route choice and volumes on particular links will be influenced over some range from the site of the proposed change. In recognition of this, traffic control is being extended to significantly interrelated parts of a network in area control schemes. The monitoring and measuring of effectiveness for use in the operational adjustment of the system needs some fairly broad extent of geographical coverage.

Even though they may not be intended, legal and regulatory solutions to transport problems may have spatially specific effects. Restrictions on entry combined with route-specific licensing may disadvantage smaller, isolated communities and rapidly growing parts of the economy. On the contrary, regulation is sometimes justified in terms of the inducement it can bring to bear on natural monopolists to cross-subsidize service to isolated settlements from the lucrative carriage of main line traffic. This question of geographical equity in service is a prime consideration in the debate over the necessity for regulation or nationalization and the managerial objectives of public corporations.

We might conclude, thus, that no kind of solution to reducing the burden of distance friction on society can be found properly without careful scrutiny of its likely geographical ramifications.

CHAPTER·6

Measurement of Costs and Benefits

Whatever the decision-making rubric applied to constitutional, regulatory, operational or structural controls on the means of movement in seeking to guide the geographical array of our lives along a desired track, 'desirability' needs definition and measurement. We commenced chapter 4 with a definition of 'efficiency' as the objective, where the maximization of this was translated into the minimization of social costs of transport by assuming the locations of activities and demands for movement to be given. Relaxing that assumption leads to a more all-embracing definition of efficiency in terms of seeking the combination of settlement and land use pattern and transport facilities which will reduce the cost of distance friction to society to a minimum. Efficiency can, of course, be construed dynamically to incorporate the general desire for economic growth. A dynamic definition would have the most efficient evolution of transport system and locational structure as that which sustained society on a trajectory of increased well being at the least social cost. It was evident in our discussion of transport policy that efficiency is not the sole objective. The desire for efficiency is tempered by the coveting of other ends, such as a more even distribution of well being among the people and the stability of prices and employment. Efficient growth, equity and stability are not necessarily compatible aims, indeed they may be contradictory in their implication for transport policy. Frequently more of one must be bought with less of another. At the level of the national economy, the general standard of living is raised most rapidly by the efficient maximization of the rate of growth. A growth rate of 3% per annum will raise everyone's income, including the poorest in society, by 10% in just over three years. This would not reduce the differentials between people, of course, and much of the irritation is a matter of envy, stemming from the perception of relative not absolute measures of well being. The reduction of differentials by redistribution involves reducing the incomes of the richer to increase the incomes of the poorer. Since those with above average incomes have votes as well as those with below average incomes, to remain within the bounds of political feasibility the most that could be achieved is a once-off increase of income for the poorest by 10%. In reducing the incomes of the better off, who can save more of their incomes, this would reduce investment and halt the growth of the economy. Greater equity is achieved at the price of slower growth and reducing the circumstances of some of the population, which generates political dissension. Causing some people an absolute loss may be more dangerous politically than allowing a relative difference to remain while everybody's income increases absolutely. There is a political balance to be struck. In terms of transport facilities these motives are incorporated in decisions on the geographical coverage of a network. It is clear that in the USA, in order to get some road construction in major cities where it would pay off handsomely in terms of reducing accidents and congestion, it was necessary to provide the wide expanse of the interstate system, often at inefficiently high standards, to satisfy the political requirement of geographical equity. Questions of stability and anti-inflationary and anti-recessionary manipulations affect transport inasmuch as public sector expenditure is curtailed or extended for these purposes. They do have a geographical effect, determining which bits of the network will or will not be built. But these are unintended and treated as irrelevant in the larger context. As we have seen, there are instances in which efficiency in transport is sacrificed consciously in the name of stability. The regulation of competition, in circumstances where natural monopoly is not likely to emerge, is usually justified in terms of assuring steady provision of service and avoiding 'chaotic' competition with violent surges of bankruptcy and commercial failure and of prices cut below marginal cost only to be driven up with the attenuation of numbers. These effects are imaginative propaganda rather than dreadful realities, and thus the sacrifice is for nought.

To govern the use of various instruments and means in guiding the geographical array of transport facilities and services, the general goals of efficiency, equity and stability have to be translated into comprehensible criteria and related by some combination rule or trade-off relationship. Some of these criteria may be measurable, others may be less tangible, but not less important for that reason. To make bureaucratic, managerial and planning decisions in the public sector, without the mandate and obligation of election, it is more comfortable to seek numerical values for criteria and their relative worth and let decisions fall out of the arithmetic. The decision process can be seen as involving the analysis, measurement and prediction of the needs, performance and values which comprise and weight the politically given objective. Having achieved the capability to measure and predict a reasonable facsimile of the goal of general welfare, the optimization of this objective has to be translated into a tractable formula for making specific decisions and an efficient algorithm for calculating the solution to this mathematical problem must be devised.

That such a procedure is not open to the play of arbitrary whim or unwarranted discretion and is an explicitly repeatable process of choice, are laudable results of quantification. Judgement and the opportunity for corrupt preferment are reduced to a minimum. The results of the choices in question are usually manifest as quantities, either in an engineering design and miles of concrete slab, or in amounts of goods and prices charged. To determine particular values for these as a practical matter requires that the specifications fed into their selection be in numerical form. All of this should not blind us to the simplifications involved in such a rubric and the potential for departure between the social good and planning decisions that it opens up. Having said that, I will continue to elaborate on the requirements of a temporarily useful, quantitative decision calculus. The practice of the UK bureaucracy for road building is a rule of thumb which appeals to common sense. It is understood that a positive balance in terms of tangible measures of worth is a minimum requirement. A scheme is deemed permissible only if it can pass muster in terms of measurable value. Beyond this minimum threshold, the gap between permission and commission is available to weigh the intangibles. The measurable utility of a project is used as a first screening to riddle out those proposals which are not worthy of closer scrutiny. For those which make the grade through this coarse filter, the subtler questions not amenable to enumeration may weigh in the balance of choice. In the first place, then, the weighing of advantage and disadvantage is done in terms of measures of the benefits and costs which will accompany a proposed change in the transport sector. Thus, we need to consider how these measurements may be made.

The utility of transport improvements

For those forms of transport which are priced in a market, if we presume that what people are willing to pay for various goods reveals their preference among goods, then revenue generated provides a measure of utility. In this case a financial analysis of streams of revenue and costs will suffice to judge the worth of a proposition. To estimate a future stream of revenue it is necessary to determine the nature of demand and the response of buyers to various prices, and to determine the appropriate price to charge. The proper price must reflect the resources used up in the provision of facilities. For the economist the long-run marginal cost is the relevant measure of this. The most efficient price will be that which equates marginal revenue and long-run marginal costs. Thus, the revenue calculations cannot be done in isolation from the cost calculations. Since costs vary in the provision of transport according to the places being served and the time of operation, what will come out of this is a pattern of prices differentiated geographically and temporally. If competition prevails in the sector in question, this will operate to drive prices to efficient levels everywhere and there will be no need for government planning and public efforts to forecast revenues and costs.

The proper and most difficult task for public planners is the measurement of the utility of collective goods and the collective aspects of priced goods. Even though rail services are priced in the market and generate revenue, some of their worth is considered by some to be socially desirable in excess of what people are willing to pay form them, and thus warranting government subsidy. Roads, on the other hand, are a wholly collective good for which no revenue estimate of utility is available. We examined the time-honoured measurement of the benefits of micro adjustments in facilities and prices, consumer surplus, in chapter 2. At that juncture we considered its composition in terms of the behaviour of drivers in a road network and mentioned the translation of time and out-of-pocket expenses into a common price called generalized cost via the establishment of a value of time.

The generalized cost of travel to which drivers respond in their use of roads or public transport includes their own time and vehicle running costs and any charges involved such as tolls or fares or parking charges. The sum of these can be measured from two viewpoints depending on the purpose we have in mind. On the one hand they can be seen as 'behavioural' costs, reflecting the revealed preferences and perceptions of travellers. On the assumption that people simply add up the weighted components involved we could write generalized cost as:

$$c = a_1 \, t_1 + a_2 \, t_2 + a_3 \, p,$$

where t_1 = in-vehicle time

t_2 = walking and waiting time

and p = monetary outlays.

As we suggested in chapter 2, the values of the parameters a_1, a_2 and a_3 can be estimated from travellers' choices between different means of travel of routes having different times and costs. Mode or route choice models produce estimates of the value placed on time in various uses. In the UK the average value gleaned from many studies indicates that non-working time spent travelling is valued at 40% of the average wage rate and that the ratio of walking and waiting time to time spent travelling in a vehicle is of the order of 2 : 1. Such a behaviourally estimated function is quite obviously what should be extrapolated to predict changes in demand expected in response to proposed actions.

Economic evaluation of a policy or investment, however, is concerned with estimating the real resources consumed in travel and transport. For this purpose it is necessary to measure costs from another viewpoint. We need estimates of 'resource' costs which summarize the value of the resources used up by travel. These may diverge from behavioural costs because of the imperfect perception of consumers. It is evident that people seriously underestimate the cost of running a car, for example. The mileage cost induced from statistically examining people's travel behaviour is far lower than an engineer's instrumental assessment of cost per mile would produce. In addition to this, the prices to which people respond in making their choices of routes or means of travel may not reflect the resources consumed by the service. Taxation of fuel, for example, does not represent resources employed (unless one subscribes to the clumsy view of taxes as the price of the good offices of government) but clearly influences behaviour. Subsidized fares on public transport or regulated freight cross-subsidies represent similar departures. If we take the linear version of the incremental consumer surplus expression from chapter 2, $\Delta cs = \frac{1}{2}(T_1 + T_2)(C_2 - C_1)$, and consider this to be couched in behavioural cost terms, then some part of the behaviour represented in response to a change of cost from C_1 to C_2 does not reflect consumption of resources. The prices paid may include taxes, or public transport fares or parking charges and may not reflect the cost of provision or operation. What they reflect is an additional surplus transferred to the community in the case of a tax, or to or from an operator, depending upon whether prices are over or under marginal costs. In figure 20, the appropriate 'non-resource' correction to consumer surplus measured in behavioural terms is given by $(T_2 N_2 - T_1 N_1)$ where N is, in this case, an excess over marginal cost such as a tax. This gives a total charge in consumer surplus of:

$$\Delta CS = \tfrac{1}{2} \; (T_1 + T_2) \; (C_2 - C_1) \; + \; (T_2 N_2 - T_1 N_1).$$

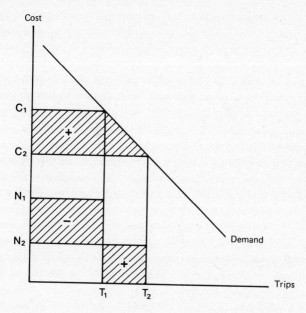

Figure 20

It follows from all of this that in order to measure the increased benefit generated by an improvement in transport, we need to know levels of use and costs before and after the change envisaged. Since cost is related to the level of use, our prediction must allow for the interaction of use and performance. The theoretical notions we have of the processes involved were paraded in chapter 2. In the last chapter a general procedure within which such theories may be employed was introduced under the name of systems analysis. We will reserve the details of the models and methods in current use for forecasting transport use and performance for design and appraisal purposes till chapter 8. If we provisionally accept that such prophetic exercises can succeed within admissible limits of error, we are left with the fundamental question of the resemblance of the proposed measure of value to reality and its theoretical soundness.

The measure does depend crucially on the premise that the benefits to each person in society can be added up without regard to precisely who gets them. The value of a pound's worth of benefit is taken to be the same no matter who benefits. A pound to a poor man must be worth the same as a pound to a rich man. This requirement that the marginal utility of money must be constant, strains against our experience even when we consider measuring benefits to a single person. An extra pound at a cost of £1 may not be worth as much as an extra pound at £100. Because of this assumption that a pound is a pound, several theorists have dismissed the measure as meaningless. Samuelson (1947) derived the conditions under which the marginal utility of money would remain constant for an individual. These are the necessary and sufficient circumstances for the area under a demand curve to measure well being. If investment decreases the cost of transport for a particular trip, all of the purchasing power released must be used to consume more trips on this route. It cannot be used for other goods or journeys, all cross-elasticities of demand must be zero. Hicks (1956) who allowed that consumer surplus was a reasonable measure of welfare for small changes in price and quantity, specified the measurements which avoid the possible pitfall of money not having constant value. There are two measures, depending on whether you view things in terms of the benefits of introducing a change or the cost of withdrawing the improvement once made. What he called 'compensating variation' is the amount of money which can be taken from an individual yet leave his level of satisfaction with life the same at the new lower cost of transport. The other measure, 'equivalent variation', is the amount of money which would be necessary to give a person the same level of satisfaction as a reduction in transport costs if it were not made available. For normal goods, equivalent variation will be greater than the area under the demand curve and compensating variations will be less, in principle. We cannot measure these quantities in practice because they depend upon a notional map of satisfaction and contours of indifference between goods and money. Although some proclaim that they can measure utility, which is the notion mapped with indifference curves (Louviere 1977), it is best conceived of as a handy abstraction for theorizing rather than as a real substance. Since the two theoretically acceptable quantities bracket the practically measurable one, should consumer surplus not be a reasonable index of benefit? It has been demonstrated that the observable consumer surplus will not necessarily move in the same direction as compensating or equivalent variation in measuring the welfare associated with different courses of action (Foster and Neuberger 1974). However, Willig (1976) has shown that it is a good approximation in most circumstances. From a more practical stance, he showed that the most extreme departures can be estimated from knowledge of the consumer's income and income elasticities of demand, and that these upper and lower bounds on the errors involved indicate that the errors will be slight, especially if we accept economics as the one-decimal-place, crude science von Neumann proclaimed it to be.

The theoretical arguments on the validity of this measure are all in terms of an individual's calculus of satisfaction. Even if we accept the consumer surplus measure as reasonable we are left facing the prospect of having to rationalize a measurement made and summed over a large number of potentially very different people. The obvious appeal is to the law of large numbers and the assertion that the values observed from the behaviour of a large number of individuals will reflect a strong central tendency in a population where divergences in preference and satisfaction are normally distributed.

The question that the total consumer surplus arising from a particular project does not address is the desirability of the distribution of benefits among people. For political judgement it is essential to know whether the investment or policy involved increases welfare uniformly or tilts to the rich or poor, or benefits the residents of some areas more than others, or helps some non-geographical constituencies or deserving groups. A distributional requirement may be imposed formally on the evaluation process as a constraint that projects must be at least distributionally neutral and preferably progressive, shifting income towards the poorer. To operate such a ruling it is necessary to disaggregate the measurement by income categories, or whatever designnation of the deserving is appropriate. Retired people and children may be singled out for preference, as may the crippled or blind or a racial minority whose former disadvantages call for redress. Almost all polities are based on geographical power bases if not on areal representation. Politicians have geographical constituencies, either in electoral or influential terms. There is in many nations an unwritten law of fair shares among geographical constituencies. This is sometimes modified by specific provisions favouring particular regions — the Mezzogiorno in Italy, beyond the Urals in the Soviet Union, the older industrial areas of northern and western Britain, the Appalachians of the USA, for example. The law of fair shares at the pork barrel is fuelled and enforced in representative governments by the need of politicians to be elected. Transport facilities are often provided by local governments with money raised within their jurisdiction by taxation. Thus the geographical incidence of benefits is of considerable significance and consumer surplus must be mapped according to the place of its recipients. For transport facilities, where the origins and destinations of users are known, this presents no great difficulty as surplus is usually measured. The usual summation can simply be done for each origin and destination individually. The issue which does arise is whether the final incidence of benefits resides with the users of the transport system or is passed on to their customers or the owners of the land they occupy as producers or residents. We have seen in chapter 2 that theoretically the surplus generated by transport improvements ultimately may be captured as the economic rent of land. Given the imperfections and institutional lags in the land market, much of the value may fall to the user, depending on the length of their lease and the fixity of the rental payment. In aggregate terms, if we assume that a pound is a pound is a pound, the final incidence does not matter and the measurement of consumer surplus in the market for transport services summarizes all other land value and price effects (Harrison and Holtermann 1973). To make distributional judgements, clearly the ultimate incidence is what matters, and this implies trying to trace effects through the complexities of imperfect commodity and land markets. This has never been accomplished in practice and is most likely to be gauged judgementally.

Another means by which equity judgements are introduced into the measure of transport scheme benefits is in the selection of a value of time to use in determining the generalized cost of travel. The selection of the mean value from behavioural observations across a spectrum of income groups, rather than using a weighted set of values according to income categories, will tend not to favour schemes which redistribute well being towards the rich, for seen from their perspective it will undervalue their time. The time of the poor will be overvalued and the net effect of the mean 'equity' valuation of time will be progressive.

The cost of transport improvements

We have seen that it is necessary to calculate the generalized cost of travel before and after a change in the system and put this in resource cost terms to estimate consumer surplus for economic appraisal. This implies the prediction of equilibrium volumes of use and performance levels given the engineering specification of network characteristics. In effect this is computing the movement costs associated with the use of the present and improved networks. If we view the planning problem as a matter of optimizing the transport system, then the optimand we come up with will involve these movement costs one way or another. Thus, movement costs appear on the benefit side of the equation, either in the generalized cost element of consumer surplus or in the objective function of an optimizing procedure. What they are weighed against is capacity costs. These include the costs of building and maintaining the parts of the network involved. Since performance and, thus, movement costs derive from the balance of use and the engineered characteristics of the system, it is sensible to treat system characteristics and capacity costs first before considering performance and movement costs.

A transport network quite naturally lends itself to representation as a graph consisting of lines for links of the network and nodes for points of access and egress or mere intersections of links. This is usually given in the form of a directed graph with the lines indicating direction of travel, so that there will usually, though not necessarily, be two lines between each pair of adjacent nodes. A one-way traffic system would only have single lines. From this map a network can then be characterized by a list of its links, giving their physical nature, use and performance. Each link is identified by two end point nodes. Its length, surface or track type, design speed, gradient, width and number of tracks or lanes can be specified and used to determine construction costs. The cost of civil engineering works can be calculated by using long profile, cross-section and construction standards in terms of surface type and width to get the cost of the track or wearing surface, the roadbed, foundation, earthworks, bridge building and culverting and right of way. For rail or road construction there are well-established standards of width and type according to expected volume of traffic. So on rural roads, for example, for 100 vehicles a day 3.5 metres of gravel surface is adequate, for 100-1000 vehicles 6 metres of seal coat will do, for 1,000-2,000 vehicles 6 metres and for over 2,000 vehicles 7 metres of ashphalt concrete will do. Most usually the decisions to be made cover not only new construction but also rehabilitation or upgrading of existing links. Rehabilitation cost will depend on the state of disrepair the travelled way has been allowed to sink to. Upgrading costs can be calculated as the differences in construction costs or cost of additional requirements between two classes of road. Maintenance costs are often treated under a separate budget heading than construction costs and do not enter into the planning process. This is an unfortunate institutional hangover which has misinformed many decisions. Clearly maintenance costs are a significant element of capacity costs, and may exceed construction costs over the life of a road. The size of the annual road maintenance bill exceeds the yearly construction outlay in many countries. The discounted value of maintenance costs should figure in the appraisal of transport system economic worth.

Given the physical characteristics of a link it is possible to determine speed in terms of any legal limit, grade, alignment, surface conditions, traffic volume and width. Link use given in terms of the number of people or volume of goods passing over a link must be translated into vehicle numbers by the application of an average load factor. Known speed flow relationships, such as that we treated in general in chapter 2, for roads of different capacities, can be used to determine the speed associated with an expected volume of vehicles. Performance is measured in terms of the travel time and cost implied by the capacity, speed and volume on a link. Speed, the characteristics of the link and the volume can be used to calculate fuel and lubricant costs, tyre wear and depreciation costs, vehicle maintenance costs and travellers' time costs on the link. These can then be summed over all travellers or goods on a link or over the sequence of links in a route to give origin to destination movement costs. Terminal costs can be added on at the nodes at which movement starts and finishes. If journey involves more than one means of transport, transfer links between separate modal networks can be designated, in effect linking a node to itself by signifying the cost of switching bottoms and moving off the road and on to rail, for example. If such complementarity or competition is an important consideration for the investment or policy in question, the effects may need tracing over the several networks involved. Separately described modal networks will be related via their common origin and destination nodes and the transfer links joining them. The planning proposals under consideration enter into the calculations of performance and cost as improved link or terminal characteristics, or new links in the system, or as changes in systemwide cost or performance parameters, in the case of institutional, regulatory or technical improvements.

For a detailed exposition on the relationships and methods used for the figuring of transport costs a civil engineering text should be consulted. The latest and clearest of these is by Morlok (1978),

Externalities

Besides those costs and benefits which fall to the users and providers of transport, a collective judgement on the worth of a particular bridge, road or service, or a general policy governing transport operations, must weigh the advantages and nuisances that touch those not participating in the transport market. We have already dismissed as double counting the 'developmental' benefits which are sometimes proclaimed for transport projects. The reduction of transport costs enables a growth of production which sends ripples of increased income reverberating through the local economy. If demand has been forecast accurately, these generated benefits, arising from greater access and reflected in increased land values, are incorporated in transport market consumer surplus.

Indeed, many claims of developmental effects evaporate when the perspective from which they are viewed is broad enough. The effect of a new route may be merely to redistribute geographically what exists or would have emerged anyway. If we employ Walters' (1968) simple static model of road investment effects, to push a road into an agricultural interior from a point on the coast will merely rearrange the location of a given amount of production if demand for the product is perfectly inelastic at the port. This is illustrated in figure 21.

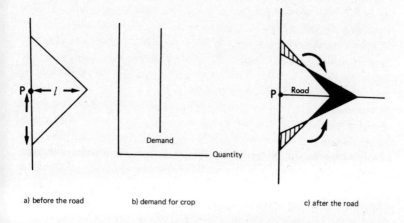

a) before the road   b) demand for crop   c) after the road

Figure 21

If before the road is built transport by footpath takes a dense square lattice of routes between fields, the limit of commerical cultivation will be given by the locus at which the price at *P* is eroded to nought by transport and production costs, with subsidence production prevailing beyond this. For orthogonal paths of travel the limit of cultivation will extend to a maximum *l* in both directions along the coast and straight inland. These three extremes will be joined by straight lines to give a triangular area as in 21*a*. If a road is built inland from *P* along which haulage is cheaper, then the reduced transport costs along this alignment will attract a relocation of the same total production, with a shrinking of the margin of cultivation closer to the port to meet the same fixed demand. In a more complex economy the building of a road in one part of the country may simply draw to it industries which would have located elsewhere in any case. The only effect has been on the geographical distribution of output, not on its total amount, and this may or may not be desirable depending on the denuded alternative locations. To lay claim to developmental effects it is necessary to prove that the activities in question were only made possible by the increases in accessibility in the particular locales afforded by the project under investigation. This can be very difficult. There is a grave danger in retrospective economic appraisal of falling prey to the *post hoc ergo propter hoc* fallacy. That certain developments occur in certain places after some improvement in transport facilities is not proof of the necessity or sufficiency of this as a generator of growth. The chronological order of events is not proof of causality. For both historical investigation and prescriptive prediction the question must be whether or not the same changes could have occurred in the absence of the transport improvement in question. If not, then the developmental benefits do not exist. The cost of transport associated with it will be less than it might have been and this will be beneficial and to the credit of the project.

The externalities more often remarked are the negative ones introduced at the end of chapter 4. Although it is possible to argue that some modern roads and particularly their intersections are the finest examples of monumental architecture of recent decades, and that airports and railways by their visible displays of unity of purpose and power, are aesthetically appealing, these are minority views. The general feeling seems to be that the unintended effects of transport are a nuisance to be counted against the merit of any proposal. The inclusion of these factors in any formal procedure for appraisal requires the identification of the relevant items and plaintiffs; the prediction and measurement of the impacts and their evaluation for weighing up the balance. Since these issues mostly arise over road building proposals now, the germane particulars are concerned with traffic noise, pollutants and danger, the visual intrusion of the structures involved, the geographical disjunction of existing communities and social interaction. The population at risk from these consequences includes pedestrians and occupants of nearby buildings as residents, workers and trades-persons. One item of damage is the possible conflict of a well-engineered road alignment with a unique natural or manmade feature of the land-scape, the Chilterns escarpment or a time-honoured church, for example. In such a case the market price of land-take required to build the road may not reflect the national, collective value of a widely cherished feature of the scenery, and statemanship may have to be invoked to settle the choice. The details of scaling, forecasting and valuing the various 'environmental' externalities are treated fully by Lassiere (1976). It will be sufficient here to highlight the procedures involved and the problems associated with them.

Noise is undesirable sound and thus a subjective notion. There is, however, a consensus of reaction and experience that makes it possi-ble to translate the physical sensing of the pressure and frequency of sound waves into a standardized measurement of noise. The pressure measure, the decibel (dB) is weighted according to its frequency pattern to produce a good correlation between sensed values and judged annoy-ance, yielding the dBA. It is evident that traffic noise measured in dBAs will not emanate from a particular piece of road at a constant rate over the day but will fluctuate with the flow of vehicles. Thus, to characterize a stretch of highway simply with one number, a statistic L_n has been devised indicating the percentage of the time over which a certain dBA level is exceeded. Such an index was employed in the 1973 Land Compensation Act in the UK and L_{10} was specified as a limiting value for annoyance, this being a pattern in which the average hourly level is exceeded for 10% of the 18-hour period from 6 p.m. to midnight.

For prediction it is necessary to derive these measures from the expected traffic pattern of the project in question and model the process of propagation from the noise source so that the numbers afflicted by attenuating levels of noise can be counted. The pattern and magnitude of noise at its source on the road is related to the vehicle mix in a stream of traffic, its volume, speed and the road gradient and surface type. The map of propagation and attenuation, the contours of noise about a road, will vary according to the cross-section of the road, whether it is in a cut, at grade or raised, the texture of the sur-rounding terrain and the arrangement and stuff of the buildings which people inhabit. To sink a road sends the noise pretty much straight up in the air, while to elevate it maximizes its impact on the surroundings. These attenuation relationships give clear indication of the remedies which might be applied by way of design to reduce the deleterious effects of noise. The appropriate set-back to avoid undue noise can be calculated. It has been demonstrated that double glazing has a significant effect in reducing noise and that trees and hedges, not being continuous, are not much use as a barrier. The cost of more elaborate construction, more land for set-back or double glazing, can be offset against the reduction in the number of people afflicted with disturbing levels of noise. The value to ascribe to a reduction in noise levels is not, however, readily come by. It is difficult to tease out of the bundle of goods that constitutes real estate that part of the value of a site which measures the amenity of quiet. Often the effect of reduced transport costs from greater access to a facility will overwhelm any difference in the other direction due to noise. The individual's rational response when asked hypothetically about the value of a collective disamenity is to push the cost to infinity, in the hope that public action, thus informed, will collectively provide shelter from the nuisance. Spontaneous responses to questionnaires, however, have suggested that people adjust within a considerable range and can filter out road traffic noise in most circumstances. Willingness to pay for private protection in the form of double glazing may provide a suitable market value. Starkie and Johnson (1974) induced a value from such data, but this was for a combination of road and aircraft noise and it was difficult to isolate the amenity of the noise barrier from the insulation benefit.

The dirt, dust, smell, particles and gases which vehicles generate are another source of irritation if not danger. Equations have been established between concentrations of carbon monoxide, nitrogen oxides, hydrocarbons, smoke and lead and traffic flow parameters, but they have not proven worthy of sufficient confidence to employ in forecasting. The divergence between perception and harm we alluded to in chapter 4 over carbon monoxide and diesel fumes means that expert opinion would be required to advise on a suitable measure of cost. Expert opinion is still divided on many issues and is not available as dogma. There is now a suggestion that the diesel fumes which people dislike but were not deemed dangerous by experts, may contain carcinogens, but this is surmise. These matters are likely to weigh in the balance of choices affecting the commitment to, or control of, motor vehicles on the whole, rather than in selecting between bits of road building for their specific use. They may sway judgements on the total budget, the emission standards to apply to trucks and cars or the subsidies to apply to railways.

Where the geographical specifics of transport interference with people's lives are important is in the matter of visual and physical intrusion. Lassiere (1976) has proposed as a measure of visual intrusion the 'solid angle' blocked in a field of vision and describes instruments to use in prediction from design drawings. This begs the fundamental aesthetic question. Many working-class people might well find a piece of well-designed and executed road and its furniture more appealing than a canal or railway and deem its presence a benefit. As a symbol of modernity it provides an avenue of escape from a past replete with the artifacts of industrial slavery. To the middle and upper classes it may signify the instrusion of hoi polloi upon their privilege of privacy. It would be difficult to come up with an objective, singular measure of the cost of such purely visual significance. The more readily measurable intrusion of a new piece of limited access road, or the designation of a one-way street, or any such barrier, is its sundering of the customary circulation of a community. This applies to local vehicular and pedestrian traffic and may be measured as the increased circuitry of journey and delays. Since it can be gauged in time lost it can be put in money terms. Local community is not chiefly an ethereal, common feeling of identity embodied in a shared sense of territory. Evidence suggests that the boundaries of the territory are not coincident for large numbers and shift with the place of residence of the person describing them. Local community is much more concrete and is the sum of a complex of social and commercial interaction and movement. The result of truncating people's usual paths to visit, shop, learn and work is in principle quite discernible and quantifiable. The material cost of severance, then, can certainly be included in the costs of a project. In calculating the cost of the land take, the market price at which people would voluntarily leave their houses or businesses along a proposed right of way would include their estimation of the cost of disruption of communal ties or commercial goodwill and of relocation. Since compulsory purchase is usually involved and compensation is a 'fair' price in the light of current transactions for similar properties, these items may not be adequately accounted for.

One of the premier benefits advanced to justify road building and improvement is the reduction in loss of life and limbs through accidents. I suppose this might be classed as an internal cost saving for drivers and passengers and credited in the generalized cost of travel, but the danger of accidents is certainly an externally imposed burden on pedestrians in historical terms and as the danger to walkers is an unintended and unmarketable by-product of motoring. Much of the cost of injury and death is borne by society in general, certainly where there is a national health system. Vehicular accidents can be predicted fairly well as a function of traffic flow conditions, and reductions in these as a result of improved road geometry and design are usually credited as operating benefits along with savings in drivers' time and expense. Pedestrian injury and death are also presumed to decrease as higher-quality roads have the separation of those on foot and in vehicles as a design criterion. The causes and occasion of pedestrian accidents are more uniquely determined by circumstances of road layout, the mixture of persons crossing and the type of traffic, the lighting and weather conditions. They are not understood sufficiently to provide a general relationship to predict the injuries and fatalities associated with a particular design. This must be a matter for local judgement. Clearly, one way or another the phenomenon involved can be quantified. If the probable number of deaths or injuries of various kinds which can be avoided by a certain expenditure can be established, the problem reduces to one of valuing life and limb.

Individually and in combination we habitually put our own and others' lives and health at risk in order to gain some satisfaction, be it in the form of cheaper coal, fish, buildings or farm products, in sporting victory, or in a saving of time in crossing a road or making a turning. It is evident that we do not put an infinite price on human life. But at the same time resources are expended to reduce risk, so the price of life is not zero. Although there is no reputable market to signal the going price of life and good health, if we demand consistency in public action, this would require that the amount we are willing to spend collectively to save an additional life should be the same whether it be spent on grade-separated junctions or more police. If we could deduce the additional cost involved, this could be used for valuing lives saved. To require consistency and the public utterance of such a price is evidently too much to ask of ourselves as citizens and politicians. Failing this, we can turn to a materialistic, accounting approach in which we regard ourselves for the sake of these decisions primarily as producers and consumers. The costs of property damage, insurance, police, ambulances, hospitals, and time out of work for the injured can be estimated. The difficulty arises with deaths. By saving a life we save the discounted value of what the person involved would produce over the rest of his or her expected lifetime. Death, however, not only puts an end to production, but also to consumption. How do we treat the discounted sum of consumption forgone due to accidental death? Clearly it will depend on how we view the potential victims of accidents, which must include ourselves. Are people who die in accidents a part of society? If so, their loss of consumption must be counted a loss. On the other hand, if we exclude them from our definition of society, the loss of consumption will be deducted from production. Obviously, then, the value of a life on this basis varies according to the stage of life at which you die and how productive you are. If we deduct consumption, in the extreme it would be economically disadvantageous to incur costs which save the lives of the old and the very young. The old can be expected to consume more than they produce over the rest of their lives if uninterrupted by accidental death. The effect of discounting the value of future goods will overwhelm the later productivity of the young by the earlier weight of sheer consumption so that their net production will be negative. Treating the prospective loss of consumption as a loss to society will at least value every life positively if not equally. The decision of the House of Lords in Pickett v. British Rail Engineering in 1978 gives judicial authority to this position. The dependants of a construction worker, whose life was cut short by a job which brought him in contact with asbestos dust, were ruled to be entitled to compensation for the earnings he might reasonably have expected if he had not died from work-related illness. The Lords opinion was that 'the interest which such a man has in the earnings he might hope to make over a normal life, if not saleable in a market has a value which can be assessed'. This reverses the 1962 ruling in Oliver v. Ashman which denied such compensation on the grounds that 'what is lost is an expectation, not the thing itself'. This made it financially better for employers to ensure that all on-the-job accidents were fatal.

Efforts have been made to incorporate some value for the emotional losses to both injured parties and the friends and relatives of the dead in cost-benefit calculations. Judicial settlements are invoked as evidence of the social value of grief. This raises the prospect of the disentangling the punitive and compensatory elements of such decisions, since the purpose of the law is to deter as well as to recompense. Distinguishing judgements on the basis of mere responsibility or actual carelessness may separate out the components of awards to reveal the appropriate compensation for life determined through legal wisdom.

With the basic question of how we value our vitality and health we complete a survey of the main categories of cost and benefits which bear upon transport policy and decision making and the problems of their evaluation.

CHAPTER· 7

Transport Planning in Theory

Characteristic decision circumstances

We can ascribe the doubts which haunt planning decisions to two general sources. There is the doubt which stems from lack of knowledge about the causal relations of the world and consequent lack of ability to predict the outcomes of possible actions. If Heisenberg's principle holds for social phenomena as well as in quantum mechanics, then we must accept that an ineradicable residuum of uncertainty will always persist in our affairs. The other doubt arises from an inability to comprehend present and future preference orderings among different possible outcomes of any proposed action for large numbers of people. The fluctuating fortunes of politics indicate a lack of definition about the present state of these preferences. The electorate can be persuaded to bring about a fairly radical switch in government personnel and programme. For planning purposes we must compound this doubt by projecting it into the future, adding uncertainty about how the tastes of the constituency for any public decision will change over time, especially since the constituency will itself change in composition.

The doubt we entertain about these two questions is a matter of degree. For convenience of expression we can distinguish three points from a continuum of states of knowledge. At one end of the spectrum 'certainty' can be taken to mean that we can put odds of varying degrees of precision on the likelihood of a particular outcome. The condition where any such numerical grading of possible states of the world would be spuriously exact we designate 'ignorance'.

Falling out of these categories of sources and types of uncertainty there are sets of circumstances under which different approaches to the decision-making problem will be appropriate.

If there is certainty about the outcomes of various courses of action open and certainty about the value of the outcomes and costs involved, then the decision process becomes a purely computational one. For all that we know of the existence of a unique best solution to such a problem, it may still be a cumbersome matter to calculate which it is from a vast array of possibilities.

If out knowledge of causal structure and outcomes is limited but we are certain of the preferences among the various goods produced and employed of the clientele of the action, then the decision involves professional judgement of the trajectory of events and relations governing the outcome.

Certainty about the results of various actions coupled with uncertainty as to the preference structure of their constituency, makes choice a search for compromise among the unarticulated goals of various factions which are party to the decision.

When both causality and the ranking of preferences are matters of ignorance, then what is called for is inspirational leadership or random groping.

Cutting across these distinctions based on uncertainty, decision problems can be distinguished by the degree of partiality which circumstances allow us to indulge in as far as the substance of what we are planning is involved. At one extreme it is possible that the effects of whatever action we intend will be confined narrowly in both geographic and sectoral terms so that we can readily assume its independence of the rest of the economic system. If the price and quantity changes engendered by any proposed investment or price change will be sufficiently small and cross-cancel in their net effect on the rest of the system, we can treat that decision as an independent project and indulge in a partial cost-benefit analysis for its appraisal. Based, however, on the article of economic faith that 'everything is related to everything else' our expectation is that there will be some degree of interaction with the rest of the system. Some of these effects can be incorporated in the partial appraisal. Budgetary interdependence, for example, is the usual state of affairs and can readily be taken account of. The operational interdependence which characterizes transport networks does, however, spread the realm of influence of an improvement in one part of the system far and wide. As long as the effects can be captured within narrow geographical confines, then a more elaborate form of cost-benefit analysis, taking local systems effects into account, will suffice. Once the network we are planning improvements to takes on a modest degree of complexity and extent, then the true decision space we are facing becomes enormous. The possible combinations of improvements and additions that could be achieved with any budget expand exponentially as the number of links in the network increases. Instead of evaluating a few obvious potential additions to the system a vast array of possible arrangements must be searched for the combination which meets the objective of the exercise best. Evaluation becomes optimization. Such an operation obviously involves treating the relevant network and the activities it serves as an integrated system and seeking its general equilibrium for many possible actions and determining those which produce the most desirable state of rest.

In chapter 9 we shall examine the prospects for narrowing the geographical definition of the extent of the effects of network changes and partitioning independent regions of a network from the point of view of evaluation or optimization so as to reduce the burden of calculation involved.

To simplify matters for the present we can characterize decisions as being concerned with independent projects or with interacting systems. If we take this distinction along with the categories of doubt about our knowledge of causality and utility, we have a framework with which to examine theoretical formulations of the transport network planning problem. In the first place we can consider the evaluation of independent projects when certainty is allowed in respect of both states of the world and preferences. This will be followed by a treatment of adjustments for various degrees of conviction about values and processes and a relaxation of the partiality assumptions, moving towards a more general representation of the problem.

Independent projects

Suppose that additions to a transport network can be taken to be independent of the existing system of links and of each other in their outcomes. In effect we assume that the benefits generated by putting new or improved lengths of way in place accrue entirely to potential or existing users of that alignment without influencing the performance and use of other links at all. If this were the case, a straightforward investment rule could be applied, given a measurement and value for net benefits (B), knowledge of construction or improvement costs (K) and a discount rate (r), trading future consumption off against current consumption. If the construction cost for a project were the same regardless of when it was executed and if the stream of net benefits were endless, then projects should be selected for action if the present value of the benefits they generate exceeds the cost of construction:

$$\int\limits_{t}^{\infty} B(t)\, e^{rt}\, dt > K.$$

Marglin (1963) showed how this static formulation of the investment problem can be extended to deal with the question of when to build a project. If, for simplicity, we assume that the project produces output at a constant rate from its opening into the future, then this can in general be set equal to unity so that the expression for net present value becomes:

$$Y(t) = \int\limits_{t}^{\infty} B(t)\, e^{-rt}\, dt + rKe^{-rt}.$$

Equating the first derivative of this to zero determines the best time to get the project in operation. What Marglin called the marginal net present value of postponing construction is:

$$\frac{dY}{dt} = -B(t)e^{-rt} + rKe^{-rt}.$$

Setting this equal to zero we obtain:

$$B(t) = rK.$$

To ensure that this maximizes net present value we check that the second derivative is less than zero:

$$\frac{d^2Y}{dt^2} = -r\frac{dY}{dt} - \frac{dB}{dt}e^{-rt} < 0.$$

This will be the case as long as:

$$\frac{dB}{dt} > 0.$$

i.e., provided that the benefit rate is increasing when $\frac{dY}{dt} = 0$.

These conditions for maximization of net present value imply that the best date for construction is when the value of a scheme's output (B_t) catches up with its interest cost (rK).

If benefits continue to increase indefinitely into the future so that:

$$\frac{dB}{dt} > 0 \quad \text{for all } t,$$

then the first-order condition may be applied as a rule for investment decision making and be repeated year after year to obtain the optimal starting date for building. Rearraging $B(t) = rK$ we obtain:

$$\frac{B(t)}{r} - K = 0.$$

From this it is clear that a scheme should be scheduled for opening when its net present value is non-negative for the first time.

Interdependence due to budget

Investment decisions are frequently made within the confines of an exogenously given budget which dictates a limit of expenditure over a year or quinquennium or some discrete period. This is especially the case for government spending, organized on a line item basis or, indeed, one of its newer variants. The limit on expenditure forces the decision maker into comparing all the projects which are up for judgement. They can no longer be considered on their independent merits. This budgetary interdependence among projects can be formalized into a programme for choice. Supposing that the line item sum for, say, roads in any year t is K_t and that the net present value of the nth project in the tth period Y_{nt} can be determined, then the problem of selecting investments is to determine the values of a binary decision variable δ_{nt} so as to maximize total net present value:

$$\sum_{n=1}^{N} \sum_{t=1}^{T} Y_{nt}\, \delta_{nt}.$$

This is subject to the budget constraint:

$$\sum_{n=1}^{N} K_{nt}\, \delta_{nt} \le Kt.$$

The decision variable takes the value zero if a scheme is rejected and unity if it is to be built, thus:

$$\delta_{nt} = 0 \text{ or } 1.$$

These three expressions form a soluble integer programme which may be used to allocate a fixed budget among many operationally independent schemes.

Uncertainty of project outcomes

Thus far we have assumed the ability to determine the outcome of any investment precisely. If we know the returns to each of two projects exactly, then the best of the two can be selected unambiguously and for any larger number a rank order of preference can be established. If, however, some risk attaches to the benefits of an investment, we will only be able to put odds on the likelihood of a particular outcome. The probabilities specified will be of varying degrees of precision, dependent on our state of knowledge. We can picture the spread of density of possible returns to a number of schemes as probability distributions as in figure 22.

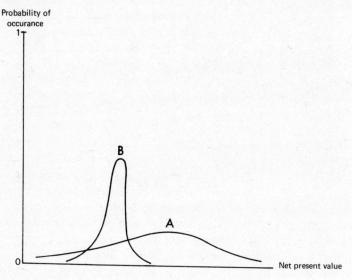

Figure 22

It can be seen that a shadow of ambiguity over the relative merits of the schemes now arises. The probability distributions of their associated returns overlap. There is a distinct possibility that scheme *A*, for example, may do worse than scheme *B*, whereas if we knew that the outcome of investment would be precisely the means of these distributions, we could declare *A* better with certainty. The choice of the better scheme now must be resolved in terms of the trade-off between a mean expectation of high net present value and the greater security of a low variance about the expected value. It depends then upon the attitude towards risk of the decision maker. The best choice may vary according to whether the choice is made by one who is neutral to risk, a gambler or averse to taking chances. In the example in figure 22, project A has a higher mean net present value, but also a higher dispersion of possible outcomes. The lower returns associated with project B are a much surer thing. There is no prospect of pathetic performance. If the degree of risk aversion of the person making the choice can be specified as a trade-off function between the mean and variance of the outcomes then this can be incorporated formally in a decision procedure. Someone with a strong aversion to risk might select project B despite its lower mean return because its outcome is much surer than that of project A, for which there is a well-defined chance of very poor performance, giving a lower return than B would achieve under any circumstances. Putting the requisite trade-off between mean and variance of outcomes as the coefficient of a negative expotential utility function, we can embody it in the choice mechanism quite readily (Roberts 1971). The utility associated with particular outcomes of decision A, U_i, with probabilities p_i can be established and set against those for decision B, U_j, the possible outcomes of which have probabilities p_j. Then A is chosen if:

$$U_A = \sum_i U_i p_i > U_B = \sum_i U_j p_j.$$

Limited foresight

The above statements of the transport investment problem assume that enough is known of the circumstances involved to compute the probability of various configurations of demand and performance associated with particular courses of action. In many instances this is far beyond our capabilities and it would be better to plead ignorance honestly. For the state lying between exact knowledge of probability density functions of outcomes and the admission of complete ignorance, Pearman (1976) has proposed a procedure where there is sufficient information to permit a ranking of the likelihood of future states of the world. If the pay-offs, in this case the net present values of transport network investments, associated with certain choices under given future states of the world, are known, then it is possible to calculate the minimum and maximum expected pay-offs for any single investment strategy consistent with known pay-offs and a subjective, ordinal ranking of the probabilities of states of nature. Should the mean tendencies of pay-offs be insufficient evidence for judgements, the analysis may be extended to find the extreme values of the variance of pay-offs. The employment of such measures in making choices would only apply to a set of independent investment projects. They do also depend on an assumed, certain knowledge of the pay-offs of combinations of choices and states of the world.

Ignorance

When it is impossible or dishonest to mark the likelihood of future circumstances on any cardinal or ordinal scale, but when we know the pay-off associated with each possible combination of action and state of the world, then there are several stratagems open to us. Figure 23 gives a table of values of net present value for four projects, A, B, C and D, under four possible futures. The pay-off associated with project i and state of the world j, c_{ij}, we know with certainty. We thus have a pay-off matrix (c_{ij}) for the various choices available under possible futures. Assigning equal probabilities p to each possible future state on the basis of insufficient knowledge, and computing the expected value of each project, we can select the scheme which maximizes expected pay-off:

$$\text{maximize} \quad E\Pi_i = \sum_j pc_{ij}.$$

This is the Bayes or Laplace strategy. The outcome of its application does obviously depend on the number of equally likely states identified in the first place.

If this seems inappropriate we can turn to the minimax criterion. This goes to the extreme of timidity by determining the worst possible outcome for each course of action and selecting the network with the highest minimum pay-off, i.e. project B. For the more adventurous it might suit to go for the biggest possible return. The maximax strategy heroically selects the project with the highest maximum pay-off, i.e. scheme C.

Another criterion is Savage's (1951) measure of regret. The decision process can be seen in terms of finding the scheme which minimizes the maximum regret associated with it. Regret can be viewed as the opportunity cost associated with a decision turning out wrong. This is measured as the difference in pay-off between pairs of action—state couples. For each state of the world j, let c_j be the highest attainable return under that state among all the projects, i.e. $c_j{}' = \min_i c_{ij}$. Regret, then, is the difference between the highest return under any state of the world and the return to some particular project in that state, i.e. $r_{ij} =$

c_j ' $-$ c_{ij}. Thus we can construct the matrix (r_{ij}) in figure 23 with entries expressing the regret associated with each action—state combination. This matrix registers what is forgone for any action—state representation by the action chosen. If the action chosen turns out to be the best then the regret is zero. The minimax strategy can be applied to this regret matrix to select the choice with the minimum value of its maximal regret. In this case, project D is clearly superior. Again, the focus with this strategy is on extreme values of pay-off.

It is evident that the application of these different ignorance criteria can yield completely different best choices among possible actions. This was first pointed out in general by Milnor (1954). It all depends on the attitude expressed in the choice criterion. If you are cowardly, which may be very sensible, your best choice may differ from that of the plunger.

These various criteria can be imployed so as to embody several objectives in the choice calculus, if the rate of exchange between the objective is known. Roy (1971) has shown that if only a ranking of preferences among objectives is meaningful, it is still possible to use an 'outranking' relationship to delineate an inner 'kernel' of actions none of which is clearly preferable to the others. Having defined this kernel, closer scrutiny of the schemes within it may serve to reduce uncertainty and the incomparability of objectives.

Interdependence in operation

To this point we have assumed independence of the outcome of various projects. Putting questions of uncertainty aside once more, we need now to explore the interaction between parts of a transport system, examine how this translates into interdependence of project outcomes and determine how this can be handled in making choices. In chapter 6 we discussed the measurement of the welfare associated with the use of transport facilities. In chapter 2 we analysed the composition of this measurement in the operation of a transport network, taking into account the effects on other parts of the network than the proposed improvement and the consequent effects on travel demand. In general form the benefit of a scheme for improvement is given by:

$$\sum_i \sum_j \int_{C_{ij}}^{C_{ij}^2} T_{ij}\,(C_{ij})\,dC \quad \text{for all relevant } i, j.$$

Relevance in this case is an empirical matter of where the ripples of effects set up by changing a component of the network die out. This will be the subject matter of chapter 9.

This designation of the quantity which the transport investment decision-making process seeks to maximize, obviously makes it a much more ponderous exercise than it appeared heretofore. The frenzy of analysis, theorizing and modelling of the uses of land and the demand for travel which have occupied such energy in the last quarter-century, were directed at understanding the relations of accessibility and activity locations so as to forecast and evaluate the outcomes of transport improvement. Despite the power of thought levelled at the problem it has not yielded completely to an elegant solution yet.

Systems optimization and transport planning

When the geographical scope of attention of transport planning is extended over a network where there is a strong interaction of demand and performance over its many links, it becomes clear that the simple, one at a time, cost-benefit evaluation of schemes is inappropriate. What is called for is the search for the best set of interrelated projects to build, and this involves determining the network equilibrium arising from each of an enormous number of possible combinations and finding which maximizes some desired objective. To establish the equilibria and execute the search efficiently requires formal computational procedures, and it is to these we turn now.

For this investigation we shall assume that politically acceptable and easily measured objective for transport planning desisions has been adduced. If this is the case, then the evaluation procedure can be inverted to become a method of searching for the best design. Rather than measuring the welfare associated with a limited number of projects we search more widely for the projects which maximize the measure of well being. It is possible to use numerical methods of optimization to compute the location and capacity of links of a network which will maximize some measure of social welfare. This involves some denials of reality in order to achieve tractability. The programming methods employed operate in discrete, not continuous space, and so the transport network must be represented as a graph of nodes and links. This is not too great a departure from the nature of transport operations. The solution produced by numerical methods specifies whether two nodes should be directly connected and what the capacity of that link should be. Given that we know little about the relation between the geography of activities and the array of accessibility structured by transport networks, such programming formulations of the transport planning problem have been driven to employ an assumption of given total demand for travel and a fixed matrix of trips between nodes which does not change in response to network improvements. This reduces the problem to manageable proportions and translates the maximization of the consumer surplus measure of welfare as an optimand into the minimization of social costs of travel.

The readiest demonstration of the simplifications which it is necessary to indulge in to employ mathematical optimization methods is given by following the evolution of these methods as applied to transport network planning.

Linear programming

Military logistic problems in World War II provided the forcing ground for the perfection of numerical methods to find the extreme value of a linear function within a domain of feasibility defined by linear constraints. With the advent of digital computers and the incredible increase in calculation speed they brought, these linear programming methods were extended to solving a wide range of production engineering, commercial and administrative planning problems. One of the fundamental logistic propositions was the transportation problem which we touched on in chapter 2. It was not a far cry from this matter of moving goods between fixed points to the design of telephone or transport networks. The transportation problem was extended by Quandt (1960) so as to solve not only for the best flows between origin and destination nodes but also for the optimal capacity of the network links joining them. From the movement of a homogeneous product the basic transportation problem given in chapter 2 is augmented as follows. The links between supply and demand nodes are construed to be capacitated with capacity U_{ij}. In addition to solving for the flows T_{ij} which minimize the total cost of shipments, the programme must determine the optimal increments to existing capacity, ΔU_{ij}. These are constrained by a fixed budget for link construction, K, which the sum of individual link building costs, K_{ij}, must not exceed. The driving force in this selection is still the minimization of the total cost of shipments. The augmentation takes the form of two additional sets of constraints ensuring firstly that link capacity is adequate to meet flow requirements:

$$T_{ij} - \Delta U_{ij} \leq U_{ij}$$

and, secondly, that the construction budget is not exceeded:

$$\sum_i \sum_j K_{ij} \, \Delta U_{ij} \leq K .$$

This simple extension was elaborated by Garrison and Marble (1958) so as to incorporate coefficients to express the effects of link capacity increments on the accessibility of nodes, and thus their potential as supply and demand points. Inserted as coefficients of a linear relationship to be determined empirically, the nature of these relationships remains in question in terms of their form, parameter values and stability over time. The fact that Garrison and Marble felt obliged to take a stab at incorporating such an effect does, however, display a shortcoming in the simple formulation of the problem. The structure of a network clearly does influence the location of production and consumption. How and in what fashion we do not know with any precision.

In addition to attempts at more fundamental modification, the network optimization problem has been generalized to deal with many commodities or types of vehicles, flowing over different modal networks allowing for transhipment between means of transport. The manner in which the network is represented can be transformed from a set of simple arcs of a non-planar graph joining its nodes to an arc-chain specification where chains of arcs trace paths between terminal points over intermediate junctions of the network.

Integer programming

Where the network optimization problem is formulated in linear terms, the solution value for link capacity increments is a real number with an infinity of possible values. Engineering and administrative practice usually deals in building a whole link between two junctions to one of a discrete set of standards. The practical problem is usually couched in terms of completing a new link or adding capacity to an existing one between terminals or junctions of the system in discrete increments. For road planning it is a matter of building a whole link to a given standard or upgrading an existing link from one standard to another, by the addition of a whole new traffic lane for example. The decision then reduces to the binary choice of whether or not to build a link between two nodes or improve its capacity by an incremental step by upgrading its quality to a higher standard. In the 1960s mathematical and computation methods were devised to find solutions to optimization problems in discrete, integer terms. These developments accommodated the lumpy conception of the problem of standard civil engineering practice.

The mathematical programmes arising from such a binary view of the investment decision process take a different form from the linear formulation. The nodes of the network, some of which are end points for traffic, others merely route-crossing points, are labelled i or j. Connecting these N nodes we have the set of links which are presently in place, R. The improvements of the network will involve a selection from a predetermined list of all possible improvements P, including new links, link rehabilitation or link upgrading. The optimand to be minimized is the social cost of travel, which we can express as:

$$\sum_i \sum_j T_{ij} \, C_{ij} + \sum_i \sum_j T_{ij}{}' \, C_{ij}{}'$$

where the unprimed variables refer to traffic volume and unit generalized cost on a link before some specific improvement and the primed variables refer to the same measures after the improvement. The selection of links from the set P so as to reduce this transport bill by the largest amount must be done in such a fashion that the balance of traffic is not upset. A set of node flow equilibrium conditions to ensure that the demands D_j and the supplies S_j available and required at terminal nodes are met and that all intersections are cleared of traffic are applied as constraints:

$$\sum_i T_{ij} + T_{ij}{}' - \sum_i T_{ji} + T_{ji}{}' = D_j - S_j.$$

The links of the unimproved network are subject to a set of capacity restraints:

$$T_{ij} + T_{ji} \leq U_{ij} \, (1 - \delta_{ij}) \qquad ij \, \epsilon R.$$

Similarly, the set of potential links improvements have capacity limits:

$$T_{ij}{}' + T_{ji}{}' \leq U_{ij}^{n} \, \delta_{ij} \qquad ij \, \epsilon P.$$

The decision variable δ_{ij} takes the value unity if the improvement is to be made and zero otherwise. Clearly the product of this binary choice and the construction costs for the relevant improvement when summed over all possible links must not be greater than the amount available in the construction budget:

$$\sum_{ij} \delta_{ij} K_{ij} \leq K .$$

Finally the flow solutions to the problem must be constrained to be zero or positive and not take a mathematically possible but realistically inconceivable negative value:

$$T_{ij} + T_{ij}' \geq 0.$$

As with the Quandt formulation, this schema does not allow for any response of total traffic or its terminal volumes to changes in network structure and improved accessibility.

Dynamic programming

The temporal conception of the problem embodied in the programming methods we have examined to this point is a static one. Problem and solution exist in some instant now or some instant future for which the variables defining the problem can be predicted. In reality planners are faced with adding small bits to a network with a limited annual budget. There is then a sequencing problem. Which pieces should be added to the network first and which later? If we can state the network planning problem in a tractable and acceptable fashion in a static context, then the ordering of additions through time is a relatively simple matter. Optimal sequencing in general is tackled with dynamic programming methods and these may be applied to the network problem.

To start with, the static problem is solved for some planning horizon year using predictions of demand and the construction budget summed over all the intervening years. This provides a fixed structure towards which final form the network should be built up. From this fixed point, dynamic programming works backwards through time towards the first year of planned construction. The process effectively deletes a sequence of links from the final network by solving the static problem for each earlier time period with the budget reduced appropriately, and the set of links which are up for selection limited to those which appear in the temporally subsequent network. This can be formally represented in the integer programme of the last section by subscripting the flow and decision variables for the year of their incidence and adding a set of constraints requiring that what is done in one period cannot be undone subsequently:

$$\delta_{ij},\, t-1 \leq \delta_{ij},\, t\ .$$

Since the dynamic programme is based on a commitment to the configuration of demand in the planning horizon year its solution does not necessarily describe the most efficient trajectory of road building. The focus on the requirements of the far future may lead to some mismatch of demand and the network structure in the near future. Effectively the configurations of demand in the shorter term do not determine which links are built but which of the finally optimal set of links are built first.

What should be evident from these mathematical statements of the transport network planning problem as the search for the extreme value of a function within well-defined limits, is how tenuous an exercise this is. So far it has been required that the values of all the variables and parameters involved be known with certainty. This is at odds with our realization of how little we truly know. We do not know sufficient about present demand for transport facilities, never mind understanding its causes so that we can predict its future path. The same is true for the costs both of construction and operation of transport systems, and thus their relative importance. We have not settled on a socially acceptable value to apply to travel time relative to other goods such as peace and quiet, the safety of life and limb and a slower depletion of world oil reserves. The popular preferences among the various amenities of life which sway politics, and are nurtured and mustered to gain power, may change radically and unpredictably. The blunt assumption of a known budget figure within which the selection is made is, to say the least, politically naïve. History would suggest that the uncertainty of the future amount budgeted for transport construction, especially road building, is the one certainty in the picture. This is a notoriously easy item to use for either Keynesian expansion of public investment or whiggish cutbacks to balance the budget. Large changes from current expectations in either direction will give rise to very different solutions.

Uncertainty and programming

If we can assume that the only significant connections between various proposed transport schemes arise because they are funded from the same budget, then uncertainty can be incorporated in programming procedures fairly readily. Roberts (1971) formulated the planning decision as a programme with some cardinal measure of utility as its optimand. The components of this index of utility and the benefits of possible projects are taken to be subject to chance and capable of representation by probability distributions. If it is presumed that the utility function is additive in nature, then the variance of the outcomes can be discarded and the mathematical programme may be solved simply with mean, expected values in the place of point estimates of costs and benefits. This implies neutrality to risk. It is possible to accommodate an aversion to risk in such a formula. This requires, as previously suggested, that decision makers be willing to express their degree of risk aversion, setting mean off against variance of project returns, as the coefficient, a, of a utility function which decreases exponentially with quantity. If we can determine the present value of known variances of project outcomes σ_i, their mean values μ_i, and covariances with other project outcomes σ_{ij}, all discounted at a given rate, the choice of schemes which generates the greatest expected utility within some budgetary limit K is made by maximizing:

$$\sum_j \delta_j \mu_j - \frac{1}{2} a \sum_i \sum_j \delta_i \sigma_{ij} \delta_j$$

subject to:

$$\sum_j K_j \delta_j \le K$$

$$0 \le \delta_j \le 1 .$$

The choice variable in the continuous case indicates the fraction of project j that should be built in the budget period. In the discrete case it signifies whether to build (1) or not (0). What is assumed in this design is that even if the value of predicted benefits is subject to chance, the construction costs, K_j, are known with certainty. In the continuous case this will mean that the budget constraint is met exactly. If it is conceded that costs are also stochastic, then chance-constrained programming is the appropriate method to use. This is formulated so that only projects for which the expectation of meeting the budget constraint exceeds a predetermined probability, α, are selected. To express this condition the budget constraint on an investment programme is written as:

$$P\,(K - \sum_j K_j\,\delta_j) \geq \alpha.$$

Operational and locational interactions

Even the superficial glances at theory and history with which this book begins offer convincing evidence of the intimate and intricate relations between the demands placed upon a transport network and its performance, and the strong effect of transport network structure on the development of our economic geography in the long-run train of events. Clearly the treatment of financial dependencies among schemes drawing on the same budget is not enough to comprehend the demand and performance interdependencies which characterize transport operations. The incorporation of an allowance for the interactions of network structure, the location of activities and the demand for movement present great difficulties. An attempt by Pecknold and Neumann (1971) sought the best trajectory for network growth allowing for the connections between structure, land use, performance and demand in a stochastic setting. In this the probability distributions of demands placed on the system at any stage in development are dependent on events and structures which precede them. It is evident that this domain of probabilistic relationships through space and time, which must be searched for the best expansionary path, distends at an explosive rate to achieve immense proportions for more than trivial cases. The expense of searching this extensive decision space can be reduced by use of a Bayesian scheme following a tree-like path through it. It is necessary to assume that the distributions describing states of the world at each stage are known exactly and that the demand curve for transport is given and constant through time. The prophetic powers and confidence required in these assumptions are somewhat daunting.

Robustness

When we considered decision making under 'ignorance' earlier in this chapter in the context of independent projects, the divergence of solutions produced by the different criteria employed pointed up the power of subjective differences in ascertaining what is optimal. To adapt a simple and singular objective and produce a solution with the

Pay-off = net present value

States of the world

Projects	1	2	3	4	
A	2	2	0	1	
B	1	1	1	1	
C	0	4	0	0	$= [C_{ij}]$
D	1	3	0	0	

Regret

	1	2	3	4	
	0	2	1	0	
	1	3	0	0	
	2	0	1	1	$= [R_{ij}] = [C_j^i - C_{ij}]$
	1	1	1	1	

Criteria

	$ET\!T_i$	min C_{ij}	max C_{ij}	min R_{ij}
A	1.25	0	2	2
B	1	1	1	3
C	1	0	4	2
D	1	0	3	1

Figure 23

mathematics which drive this quantity to an extreme is elegant. To do this, however, sometimes requires a contorting oversimplification of the real problem. It is evident that the attitudes which watch over and define rationality should be given expression in deciding on a course of action. And allowance should be made for these attitudes to change. In the four-scheme, four-states-of-the-world example of figure 23, clearly the attitudes reflected in the various ignorance choice strategies produced completely different solutions. There is ample historical evidence of changes in 'the mood of the time', which would parallel the attitudes of these criteria. Thus, it is obvious that the definition of 'best' can change drastically through time. This being the case, it would be appropriate to build a degree of flexibility into any system so that can respond to changing attitudes without an excessive strain. The choices to be made do occur as a stream of events through time. Transport networks are built up in a sequence of constructive actions and not as a spontaneously generated assembly of links. Some railway networks were laid down in decades but even that is far from instantaneous. In putting together a transport network through the years, there is an opportunity for modifying the geographical structure which develops in the light of increasing knowledge and changing attitudes. To shape the system unwaveringly towards some plan for a golden age in the future is foolish and unnecessary. Plans may be changed at will, since they are only transformed to irreversible facts by action. A plan is only a proposed decision and may be overturned at any time prior to its due date. In a world of uncertainty it would seem axiomatically desirable to strengthen that ability to reverse or revise plans as circumstances and understanding unfold through time.

To put this aim into operation, Gupta and Rosenhead (1968) devised a criterion of 'robustness' for making sequential decisions where probabilities cannot be assigned to outcomes of action. In many more instances than are admitted, the only reasonable treatment of the future is to describe a finite number of possible states of the world lying between the worst and best extremes. What we can hope for is that through time the nature of the desired future will become clearer to the decision maker. In these circumstances we would wish to be able to adapt those steps in the set of prospective dated decisions consti- tuting the plan, which are not yet pledged to action. It must be obvious that in order to contemplate this kind of intervention in response to the dawning of better comprehension of needs, goals and prospects, the possibility of such amendments must be built into the planning framework. If flexibility is not incorporated as a criterion of choice then there may not be enough give in the structure to adapt it. Any choice reduces the number of possible futures left open because it commits the present. The Gupta and Rosenhead criterion seeks to devise a plan so that the first decisions made limit the future as little as possible. The quality of flexibility is clearly 'an evolutionary advantage in an uncerain world' (Rosenhead, Elton and Gupta 1972). Robustness is a measure of the quality of useful flexibility. The familiar statistical use of the term 'robust' has the implication of insensitivity to assumptions. A robust decision then is one whose sturdiness will enable the network to perform satisfactorily no matter what transpires.

To investigate the measurement of this quality and its use in transport network planning we return to the example represented by figure 23. Suppose that the projects were in fact four network strategies consisting of various combinations of links connecting four towns as shown in figure 24. In this case the matrix in figure 23 gives the pay-off values associated with 16 maps combining actions and states of the world. Of this set of combinations M, one will be realized. The decision to build one of the possible links, which we label s, will reduce the available futures to a subset M_s of all the possibilities. Faced with uncertainty about the future state of the world and unsure of the proper attitude to adopt to the network planning problem, none of the ignorance criteria seems appropriate. It is not clear whether excessive caution or adventure is the best posture. Possibly there is a political squabble under way. This does not have to paralyse the planning process. In such a case we would wish to ensure that actions taken now leave the adoption of any of the ignorance strategies open to us as long as possible. When we make our minds up we would like to be able to go for the Bayesian, minimax, maximax or minimax regret solution. For any particular link s the robustness of deciding to build it now is given by the ratio M_s/M. In our example this ratio takes the value of unity for the diagonal link. Thus we would maximize robustness by selecting this link as the first step in a sequence of decisions, placing the emphasis on continuous planning rather than on the elaboration of a final plan.

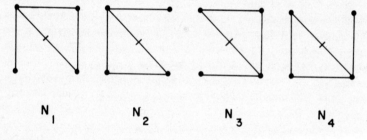

Figure 24

To generalize the procedure for the transport network planning problem we can say that at any time we are faced with a number of links of the network which could be built or improved. At any time budget limitations severely limit the number of links for which a positive decision is possible. The future is represented by a set M of possible action-state maps, of which one only will be realized. The decision now to build link s will reduce the futures available to us to a subset M_s of M. For some subset M^* of M which we now judge to be satisfactory final outcomes on the whole gamut of criteria of relevance, a subset M_s^* will still be potential after the present decision to build link s. The robustness of link s then can be measured by the ratio:

$$R_s = \frac{M_s^*}{M^*}.$$

The maximization of this quantity should be the criterion employed in immediate selections in a sequence of decisions.

Good builders have always incorporated robustness in successful designs for useful structures. Buildings were put up to meet unforseeable contingencies with minimal costs of adaptation and yet to meet immediate needs quite well. As with species so with our artifacts, the evolutionary process favours adaptability. Excessive specialization carries the seed of its own destruction. This extends beyond buildings, roads, tools and vehicles to our political and social institutions. To ensure long-term political stability it is better to avoid fragile over-specialization. Adaptability and resilience come from having robust components which can be flexed to accommodate to new circumstances.

Gupta and Rosenhead presented their criterion first with a factory location example. It does, however, lend itself admirably to the needs of transport network planning. An early application (Friend and Jessop 1969) used the criterion in the context of local government finance and planning where road investment was a significant item. In the UK the Local Government Operational Research Unit (1976) have built a development plan evaluation programme around this measurement. The criterion could have been conceived with the long-term sequential nature of transport network planning in mind, faced as it is with conflicting objectives and great uncertainties as to outcomes and the preferences involved. This led O'Sullivan, Holtzclaw and Barber (1979) to its advocacy. Transport network planning requires constant reappraisal of objectives and of the future, and ready adaptability. The robust planning strategy offers an honest recognition of the nature of the problem from the outset. It does more than merely allow that there are divergences from a deterministic ideal.

CHAPTER·8

Forecasting Transport Demand and System Performance

━━━━━━━━━━━━━━━━━━━━━━━━━━━━━━━━━━━

On forecasting

We have traced a path from controversial issues of transport policy to the kinds of solutions which might settle them. From these we moved on to the measurements required to judge the efficacy of proposed solutions and, finally, the decision rules employed to translate general objectives into specific choices of controls or investments. The measurements specified in chapter 6 require us to predict the geographical structure of society in the small or the large, in the event of certain actions and in their absence. The difference between the two yields the worth of the action. The delphic conceit involved in such an exercise is forced upon us as individuals, households, firms and governments by our ability to control some aspects of our existence. We can make choices about allocating our time, energy, enterprise and resources to particular activities in particular places. In the tight fabric of each level of our hierarchy of communities, the choice of any member sets up stresses and strains which cause others to adjust their behaviour geographically. In accounting the advantages and disadvantages of various options available to us, it is necessary to gauge how others will respond. Beyond achieving a better understanding of the world in which we live by producing theoretical statements which predict real events closely, we are involved in making decisions which require calculations of future states of the world so that desired goals can be achieved more nearly by what mastery we can exercise over circumstances.

The methods we use are a combination of extrapolation of past events and an understanding of the basic processes involved. Supposedly process-based models usually have some empirically determined and, hence, extrapolative elements, whilst most methods of extrapolation make or imply some assumption about the underlying process. No matter the method, conjectures have to be made. Our focus here is on current best practice in such reckoning.

Forecasting the geography of society and its means for mobility can be undertaken in a number of fashions. There is a spectrum of intended precision and rigour in the methods used. At one end of the range we find prophetic journalism. A man with a good 'feel for the system' and good 'judgement' of broad trends and political forces might be able to bring off a good prediction using the proximate calculus of the human imagination, which no mechanism has been contrived to reproduce. Must usually, however, this type of speculation merely underlines the prejudices of the speculator. The speculative process can be formalized and made more explicity in Herman Kahn's 'scenario' method or in the Rand Corporation 'delphi' format. These produce well-informed, normalized, quantitative guesses as to the future state of affairs. If, however, quantitative evidence exists of the sequence of behaviour of any phenomenon then more exact methods can be used. If we are willing to assume that the behaviour pattern underlying the object of our investigation will continue unchanged, or will change regularly over time, then 'curve-fitting' methods can be used to express past behaviour mathematically as a function of time and from the known terms of the series giving rise to the fitted curve, future terms beyond the current range can be calculated. This is extrapolation. Car ownership and air passengers have been treated in this fashion. One can take one step back from this and relate such demands to some variable for which reliable estimates of future values can be made, such as gross domestic product, perhaps. Demand can then be estimated for given values of the independent variable in future times.

These approaches have little to say about the behaviour of the subject under scrutiny over time, thus they cannot deal with the more volatile elements in the social fabric; for example, the impact of a new form of transport is beyond their comprehension. The most satisfying and demanding procedure for predicting events is the formulation of a model relating events to the system in which they occur in mathematical form. What we deduce to be the objective of the system's operation becomes a quantity to be maximized or minimized as an optimand, or a quality, such as simultaneous equality, to be solved for. The real problem is translated into a mathematical problem which we have tried and proven methods of solving. The solution of the mathematical problem becomes the prediction. So, to forecast the demand for transport we can put it in terms of finding the level of demand which maximizes private profit or social welfare for some future, quantitatively described state of the world.

Our discussion of uncertainty in the last chapter sounded a warning against excessive pretension over forecasting. It is evident that any forecast we can produce is conditional on some presuppositions. We must do all we can to make these and their implications clear in presenting 'expert' forecasts. To apply a model to predict quantitative outcomes in the world, we have to take certain determining factors as given. When time-series analysis is used for prediction, it can be said that the independent, determining variable, time, is known with certainty, barring *dies irae*. But even here, the assumption underlying curve-fitting and extrapolative methods is that past behaviour patterns will continue in the future.

Adopting a Laplacean stance, we can say that, even if we regard the behaviour of man as ultimately determined, our colossal ignorance enables us only to write theory and make forecasts in a tentative manner. Given the contingent nature of forecasts, the likelihood that the model builder has not identified all the important relationships involved, has made errors in measuring the variables of the relationships he has hypothesized and can specify many connections only in probabilistic terms, then clearly no forecast of man's behaviour is deterministic. All predictions contain errors and the analyst should make their existence and nature as explicit as possible. In quantitative terms this means expressing a forecast as a range of variance about a mean value, or as a probability distribution of outcomes, rather than as a point estimate, with some indication of the confidence that can be placed in the rectitude of the estimate produced. If this cannot be done then it should be avowed in all honesty, indicating that resort to the ignorance criteria discussed in chapter 8 is appropriate.

Forecasting is usually done with some objective — so that a decision may be made and implemented. The geographical and time scale of observation used; the degree of disaggregation of entities and sub-systems in the model; which variables are accepted as exogenous and which are estimated within the model; whether a continuous or discrete mathematical formulation is used; the required level of reliability and acceptable level of error, are all dependent on the purpose of the forecast. Thus, the objective of the exercise must be clearly understood and stated at the outset.

To make quantitative forecasts of man's geographical behaviour you can work either on the basis of historical, statistical records, or on that of assumptions concerning the objectives and decision-making process of the actors under consideration. The dangers in both approaches are evident. Predictions based on statistical evidence can only hold if the assumption that the underlying behavioural processes are immutable is sustained. A forecast based on assumed goals and decision-making processes can only be as good as their identification and specification.

Despite all the drawbacks and seemingly insurmountable limitations involved, it is worth striving to do better, mostly because it might improve our understanding of the human condition. By trying to model and forecast we may learn a little more. Out of the alternative, to do nothing, comes nothing.

The demand for transport

The quantity we are faced with forecasting is a somewhat complex matter. We are dealing with the most heterogeneous of goods, along with real estate. What the customer is selecting and the supplier is providing is the capacity to carry particular things between specific places at specific times. We cannot sensibly treat of lumps of homo-genized 'transport'. The demand for transport is also complicated inasmuch as the choices which have to be made in the long run involve interdependences between the kind and amount of transport to be used, the location of production and consumption, the input mix to be used in production and the product mix to be output, and the markets to be penetrated or the sources from which to buy. Fundamental transport demand decisions are made when a home is chosen or a factory is sited, when a job is taken or when production processes and markets are established. One of the premier considerations in siting is the minimization of costs of access to jobs and services or raw materials, factors of production and markets. The location decision may select a mode of transport by choosing a road-, rail- or water-accessible site. The production batch size and loading facility investment in a factory may lock it into a particular means of transport. Given the prevalence of such circumstances there is obviously a massive short-term stability about market shares between means of transport, and the choice of mode of transport is insensitive to small price changes. The same could be said for the split between car and public transport, the main determinant of which is ownership of a car. In the competitive portions of the transport sector, the short-run decisions on the kind and quantity of transport to purchase are closely interwoven with decisions on the timing of the activity at the end of the trip or the sale or purchase involved. In the last resort you will use a taxi to catch a plane or a car maker will charter a plane to get a bag of bolts without which the assembly line would stop.

What emerges from all of this is that when we specify the demand for transport we really have to get down to details and recognize different quantities for different purposes. If we were writing the demand for transport as a subscripted variable where each subscript indicates an essential characteristic, we should need to have at least T_{ijkmt}, where i is the origin of the demand, j the destination sought, k the commodity or purpose of the trip in the case of passengers, m the mode of transport and t the time. The time interval would in some cases need to be less than hourly, certainly with passenger travel and perhaps even with air freight. Obviously, the same is true for all the categories used in all the subscripts. Cities or regions might do as origins and destinations for some instances, but in other cases you would need to get down to the street.

Having said that the demand for transport is complex and inter-woven with a great many other considerations. the question is whether we can unravel this complexity and discern some predictable pattern to the relationships. The groundwork for this was laid in our review of theory in chapter 2. Theoretical notions must now be translated into operational forecasting methods.

As a framework upon which to drape this translation we can distinguish a hierarchy of levels of demand for transport, with decreasing levels of aggregation suited to different types of policy or investment decision. T_t for the total quantity of transport in ton-mile equivalents in the nation for any time interval, is the most aggregate measure and not particularly useful to anyone. T_{mt} would distinguish the quantity carried by different means of transport. For some national-level decisions on the allocation of resources such an estimate might be useful. To evaluate some methods of reducing energy consumption in the transport sector by technological or operational improvements, a do-nothing baseline has to be compared with the trajectories of energy consumption for the options available. To get the order-of-magnitude estimates, which are all that one could aspire to in such an endeavour, a projection of total ton miles by major modes of transport is sufficient. For transport sector planning the quantity must at least have a commodity label on it, T_{kt}, or T_{kmt} when it is distinguished by mode. These quantities for some future dates are pertinent to the fleet capacity planning of a large carrier, say the airlines where the commodity is passengers. The tonnage originating or terminating at a particular location i, T_{ikmt}, is appropriate to the planning of terminal facilities, for example in the installation of dock capacity. The UK

Ministry of Transport went to great lengths to estimate such quantities for various coastal cities to determine how much and where container port capacity should be allowed or fostered (Ministry of Transport 1966). We may further disassemble demand to the quantities which are sold over the counter, T_{ijkmt}, the origin-to-destination movement of particular commodities by particular means of transport. This is the quantity which is marketed and the relevant variable in service planning. If the system in question consists of a somewhat complex network, operational controls and capacity planning decisions require a final disaggregation describing the volume flowing on a particular link of the network l, T_{ijklm}.

Forecasting

National-level forecasts in broad categories of traffic may be of value for broad sectoral allocation questions and to vehicle manufacturers and large carriers making vehicle fleet size decisions. Past records of total tonnage or ton mileage of freight can be related to gross domestic product, allowing for any temporal lags in the relationship, using statistical estimation procedures such as regression to find the best fit. Then, by assuming a growth rate of gross domestic product, it is possible to compute the volume most likely to be associated with the given level of national output in any future year. There are two sources of possible error in this procedure: uncertainty about the stability of the relationship between national output and transport demand and uncertainty about the future level of gross domestic product. The compounding of these two means that very wide confidence intervals have to be put about any forecast of this type. A second method is to identify the major traffic-generating industries, form a view of their future expansion paths and predict the greater part of freight tonnage from these, knowing how much transport demand per unit output they generate now. To establish the shares of different modes at this level, one could simply extend current trends judgementally. Similar exercises are possible with passenger data, involving the translation between vehicle miles and numbers of passengers in the form of load factor assumptions.

In attempting to forecast geographically specific demands for transport we face the complex interdependences of choices of location, destination, means, and route. The usual procedure is to advance by a series of successive approximations, breaking the transport demand decision into a sequence of related but separate steps. This produces a set of nested estimates with some assurance of numerical consistency built into the procedures. This structure of modelling evolved in the pursuit of planning for the expansion of road capacity in cities in the 1950s and 1960s. Realizing the systematic interaction of flows in road traffic and the functional relationship between urban land use and traffic, urban analysts sought a means of prediction which respected and represented these affinities. After obtaining control totals of population and employment from linked demographic and economic appraisals of a city's future, these were allocated geographically as increments to residential land use and employment and service foci. At the outset this was a matter of the drawing-board allocation of land uses in the architectural tradition of planning by aesthetic instinct. With greater understanding of the course of events involved, the prescriptive component was reduced in favour of mathematical description of underlying processes. These extended from mere curve-fitting extrapolations of population density gradients, through more complicated gravity-model-based probabilistic projections of residential and service activities given the location of basic production activities, to linear programming or econometric representations of the urban land market. The details of these land use models along with the historical background to such endeavours are discussed in O'Sullivan, Holtzclaw and Barber (1979).

A map of the future land use of the city provides a basis for projecting trips generated or attracted by areas of the city. The relationship of trips taken for various purposes, during the peak or in the off peak, to the level of activity on various categories of land use can be established from current data by regression analysis in its stricter form or in the shape of category analysis. The latter involves the construction of contingency tables, cross-referencing categories of many independent variables with mean observed values of the dependent variable, trips. If the data are plentiful and the objective is forecasting rather than explanation, then this more precise shaping of a response surface avoids the strain of the limiting assumptions underlying estimating procedures such as least squares. This freedom is purchased at the expense of the inferential capabilities and precise measurements of association, error and confidence in the relationships established which regression affords.

Having projected where trips of various kinds will start and end, the next requirement is a means of allocating origins to destinations in a distribution of trips. Working with predicted numbers originating and terminating in zones of the city and a first-cut approximation to the cost of movement between them, the volume of travel can be forecast in either of three main ways. A growth factor can be applied to currently observed volumes based on some extrapolation of trends or a relationship to total city activity level. This works quite well over short periods with a stable structure but fails abysmally in growth areas, where demand is expanding most rapidly and which is precisely where planning and, thus, accurate forecasts are most needed. Secondly, the interaction process can be treated as a response to the attractive and generative capacities of zones and the friction of distance between them with a gravity model after the fashion suggested in chapter 2. The appropriate parameter governing the influence of generalized cost can be estimated from current flows using a maximum likelihood estimator. Assuming that this parameter remains constant over time, future values for trip-end volumes and generalized travel cost are used to generate an origin-destination matrix of trips which satisfy the row and column total restrictions on availabilities and requirements with an appropriate set of balancing factors. These are produced with an iterative procedure starting from some arbitrary designation of initial values and sequently calculating sets of A_i and B_j values which meet the constraints. As a result of the innate symmetry of the flow matrix the iterations converge to equilibrium sets of values quite rapidly. Finally, as an alternative to treating the friction of distance as an explicit determinant of travel behaviour, the geographical structuring can be seen as a matter of the potential opportunities for satisfying the purpose of a trip which intervene between any origin and destination zone as well as the attractive power of the zone itself. In general the intervention of other opportunities will increase with the distance between places, and so distance is implicit in this formulation. This intervening-opportunities model is again calibrated from existing data on movement, seeking a set of probability values for trips between zones which simulate the current trip-length-frequency distribution well. The same assumption of stability over time as for the gravity model parameter enables the use of these probabilities for forecasting from given trip-end estimates.

Although in some cases it is realistic to treat the generation and distribution of car and public transport traffic separately, viewing the latter as a captive clientele, there are instances where the policies or investments proposed are intended to disturb the balance. In this case it is necessary to predict the choice of mode simultaneously with that of destination. Taking the mode choice aspect on its own, the volume of travel beteen any pair of places can be viewed as splitting between the modes of travel available on the basis of their characteristics in time, cost and convenience terms and the characteristics of the travellers in terms of purpose, income, etc.. Quarmby (1967) put the choice in terms of the relative disutility of the modes, with the travellers making choices according to their perception of disutility. The relative disutility of one mode compared with another can be expressed as a linear combination of the weighted characteristics of the mode and travellers. On the assumption that travellers choose the mode which minimizes disutility, discriminant analysis can be used to find the best set of weights to explain the currently observed choices of a sample of travellers. Proposed system characteristics and predictions of traveller characteristics will then yield a forecast of mode choice. This model derives from biology, where it was devised to sort populations into two sub-categories on the basis of differences in their make-up, so as to minimize classification error. The other models of mode choice have a similar lineage. The binary choice of transport mode is treated in the same manner as placing a mathematical expectation on the responses of a population of plants to varying levels of a stimulus such as dosage of weedkiller. The proportion of the population dying with increasing dosage typically displays an S-shaped cumulative frequency such as that in figure 10. The distribution of the threshold of tolerance which tips the balance between life and death among the population which generates such a sigmoid accumulation can be assumed to be normal, and the mean and variance of this distribution of tolerances can be used to predict the response of any similar population. Probit analysis is used to estimate those parameters from the behaviour of an observed set of responses with a maximum likelihood estimator. If the assumption of normality of the tolerance distribution is strained, the more general logit analysis can be used to estimate the parameters of the generating equation for a similarly shaped logistic curve by the same means. In application to modal choice, the binary dependent variable becomes the choice of either of two modes such as bus and car, which summed over a population gives the percentage using one or the other, and the stimulus is differences in speed, price and so on between the modes.

With estimates of the volumes moving between zones split according to means of travel it remains to assign trips to particular routes and thus to specific links of the network. Summing these over all pairs of origins and destinations and all travellers loads the networks with traffic. Since the volume on a link affects its performance it is necessary to allow for some play between the choice of route and the build-up of traffic on particular links and thus their performance. A suitable formulation of the problem and a way of determining the solution to it for any configuration of demand was given in chapter 2, and this is representative of the assignment models used in transport planning.

The specifics and details of these components of what has come to be called the urban land use transportation model are treated extensively by Stopher and Meyburg (1975).

This same nesting of a sequence of increasingly disaggregated estimates, each stage taking the product of the last as its control total and independent variable, can with profit be applied to the forecasting of freight traffic when a comprehensive scope is important for the planning problem in hand.

The amounts of a commodity entering the transport system for carriage at originating points and the quantities used at destinations are clearly related to production, calls for raw materials and intermediate goods and consumption levels by area. If we have forecasts of production, population and income by regions of the economy, then it should be possible to establish some statistical relationship between current traffic generation and activity levels and employ this for forecasting. One difficulty involved is that transport data usually indicate where traffic joins a particular mode such as the railway. This is not necessarily its ultimate origin nor is the point where it exits inevitably its final destination. Even if we are dealing with one mode of transport, goods are often stored at intermediate locations, bulk loads are broken down for local distribution. If we had a comprehensive set of data such contingencies could be allowed for by having a multimodal representation of the network with transfer links between modes or legs of modes, such as line-haul and local collection, specified. To illustrate what is involved in traffic generation forecasting for freight in a simple setting consider an exercise undertaken for a province of Indonesia (Ahmed, O'Sullivan, Sujuno and Wilson 1976). As the basis of forecasts of consumption for the administrative units of the province of South Sulawesi, the population of each unit was projected. For lack of anything else the rate of change over the last censual period was applied as a compound growth rate. In an agrarian, undeveloped society a 'surplus–deficit' model is a suitably uncomplicated way of estimating traffic generation. Taking consumption first, growth rates of consumption which had been forecast for Indonesia as a whole were applied to current consumption by regional unit and projected to the target year so that multiplication by projected population yielded consumption by commodity. Turning to agricultural output, for this it is necessary to predict acreage and yields. Acreage under various crops for the target year was taken from an agricultural development plan. Rates of yield increase were based on those realized and observed most recently in the area, which were assumed to persist through the planning period. Production of various crops in the target year was got by multiplying yield by area with due allowance for field and milling losses. It was assumed that local consumption needs for these crops were met first and that trade between regions occurred to take up local surpluses to satisfy deficits where they arose. This then was a simple matter of subtracting local consumption from local production to generate surpluses and deficits. After allocating the surpluses to the deficits within the province, any net shortage would be made up by imports and any surplus exported to the rest of the Republic through the nearest port. The only manufacturing in the region was of paper and cement. The future level of production of these was specified in a national plan. Provincial consumption of these products was assumed to increase in line with population, with any surplus being exported to other islands. Consumption of imported fuel and manufactures was projected in line with industrial production, car ownership and population forecasts. To plan the build-up of a road network over 25 years, area cultivated, yield, population, imports and exports for 45 years hence were used to estimate production and consumption of commodities by areas and the differences yielded surpluses or deficits to be traded via the transport system.

Whatever the means of estimating tonnages originating or terminating in regions, the next decision to model concerns the distribution of traffic, i.e. which markets to serve from which sources. If we are dealing with a homogeneous commodity for which the market is strongly competitive, say an agricultural product such as rice, then we might assume that for fixed demands and supplies, demands will be met from various sources in such a fashion that the total transport bill is minimized. If we know the cost per ton of serving each origin from each destination then the transport bill for the whole system is the minimand of the transportation problem we examined in chapter 2. Thus we can employ one of the algorithms which finds a set of flows to minimize transport cost in such a fashion as to preserve the balances of supplies and demands in various locations. If we are dealing with either a strongly competitive market or a single firm's distribution problem, we should expect the solution of this optimization problem to be a forecast of the desired level of demand for movement between origins and destinations.

Nested within this distribution problem is the one of deciding which is the preferred mode of transport joining each origin and destination, and thus the appropriate per-ton cost of transport. In principle in freight forecasting this should be a fairly straightforward matter if there is no congestion problem in the transport systems involved. The preferred mode would be the one with the minimal transport cost. The question then is: with respect to what cost does the shipper make his decision? Is transport cost just the freight rate times the tonnage or cube? Increasingly shippers are conceiving of total assembly or distribution costs as the relevant item. The appropriate unit transport cost consists not only of the freight rate but also takes into account time and storage cost related components. Simplified, the transport cost equation for a shipper might consist of:

$$\text{UNIT TRANSPORT COST} = a_1 \text{ RATE} + a_2 \text{ IN-TRANSIT TIME} + a_3 \text{ INVENTORY COST}$$

The sum of these is the value to be matched against the difference in ex-works price and that achievable in any market in deciding to trade. In making a choice between modes the shipper has to establish his trade-offs between the various elements of his total transport cost function, the weights a_1, a_2 and a_3. To simplify further, suppose we can express the last two items in terms of time and add them together, then the shipper is involved in a trade-off between a cash price and a time price for transport. The final decision the shipper makes reveals the money value he places on speed, reliability and low inventory. That trade-off value, as we have seen in chapter 6, is a most important quantity to get a feel for in evaluating transport investments. It is necessary to know the sensitivity of demand not only to freight rates but also to the speed and reliability of service. Clearly the issue has been simplified for exposition. Time as such, or speed, might or might not be important. It obviously is with perishable goods. In some cases time is a handy proxy for exposure to damage and pilferage. However, for large shippers with a regular flow of traffic for whom a transport leg is a part of the production line, a transport element of whatever speed can be programmed in as long as the rate of delivery is reliable. Indeed, it may be advantageous to have part of their buffer stock in the pipeline rather than in costly warehouse space. Hartwig and Linton (1974) have conducted some preliminary investigations of shipper behaviour in this light, employing the discriminant, logit and probit models which have been applied to personal modal choice. Their results suggest that choices are made in terms of relative rates and reliability. Differences in transit time between road and rail were found not to be significant in explaining the choices surveyed. One other variable which proved of some significance was the value of the commodity. A plausible rationalization is that more valuable commodities are sent by the mode which minimizes exposure to loss and damage and evidently there is significant but unspecified difference between road and rail in this.

When the class of traffic being forecast displays a degree of heterogeneity, as is the case with parcels and especially with passengers, then it is difficult to formulate demand in the deterministic fashion of the transportation problem. Cross-hauling is prohibited in solutions to this problem. Mail, parcels or passengers obviously flow in both directions between pairs of places and do not obey such rules. For a single, homogeneous commodity it is defensible to formulate a simple motivating objective like satisfying demand from supply at a minimum transport cost. You obviously cannot capture the plethora of motives for personal travel or communication or a flow volume representing a whole myriad of goods with such simplicity. Where this is the case intrinsically, or because of the degree of aggregation of the data available describing the state of the world, we can resort to a probabilistic formulation of demand for transport. With observations of current flows and costs of travel we can calibrate a gravity model as in the case of urban personal travel, representing the most probable disposition of demand. The parameter so estimated can then be used along with forecasts of future terminal tonnages and costs to predict flows. Such gravity models have been fitted to volumes of some fairly heterogeneous classes of traffic by road and rail between regions of the UK with some degree of success (Chisholm and O'Sullivan 1973). For forecasting, an assumption of stability of the relationships over time is invoked. Some experiments testing the stability of gravity model coefficients with historical data have suggested some short-term constancy at least. Fitting a gravity model to the USA intercity distribution of food and animal products for 1963 and then for 1967, produced coefficients which were statistically indistinguishable. But, of course, four years is a brief spell in the life of transport policy or investment decisions (O'Sullivan and Ralston 1974).

The assignment of flows between end points to a freight transport network can be achieved by the methods employed for an urban road system. Indeed, in the case of road haulage in urban areas it is part and parcel of the same assignment. Such an assignment procedure may be a fundamental real-time instrument for the management of freight operations. In the case of freight and passenger carriers which operate in slugs of service, such as trains or planes, this becomes a scheduling problem involving not only assignment to routes but also the frequency and size of the transport unit. Operational economies encourage larger units with greater headways, while user costs in terms of waiting time increase with greater headways. The best schedule of departures must balance out these two considerations. For car travel the transport system can be represented as having continuity of service, allowing for variations according to time of day, and terminal circumstances need only enter into the picture as the parking charges component of generalized cost. For public transport and freight operations with intermittent services, terminal costs take on a major significance as waiting time. Assignment as a prescriptive tool must seek to minimize operational costs and waiting costs jointly. This involves modelling the formation and service of a queue. Since there is seldom sufficient evidence to predict the precise arrival times of passengers or shipments they can be presumed to arrive according to some probability density function, such as the Poisson. This probabilistic representation of arrivals can be meshed with a deterministic treatment of the service time, the availability of a vehicle and berth, the loading and unloading process and the time in transit, to generate the amount of waiting time involved. For some transport operations the amount of uncertainty about in-transit time is such as to warrant the stochastic treatment of the vehicle and berth availability components of the assignment. With ships and railway freight this would certainly be necessary. For sea and rail transport this question of terminal operations overwhelms in-transit considerations. Waiting time may be months for a transit time of hours by rail. The prediction of performance in terms of the assignment of traffic to the network should then concentrate its modelling precision on the operation of terminals. The elements to be modelled are the time spent by the vehicles waiting for a dock at both ends of the journey, the time of the shipment spent waiting for a departing vehicle and the loading and offloading time. The loading bits can be handled with deterministic calculations of work rates for men and equipment given the vehicle's configuration, the general character of the cargo and the amount in the queue. The other elements are essentially queues and are best treated as stochastic processes. The Poisson model gives the probability of n arrivals in any time interval t as:

$$p(n) = \frac{(\lambda t)^n e^{-\lambda t}}{n!} \qquad \text{for } n = 0, 1, 2 \ldots$$

where λ is the mean arrival rate, i.e. the total volume divided by the number of time intervals. For low volumes there is a high probability of no cargo or vehicle arriving in any time interval, but some probability of many arrivals. As volume increases there is a higher probability of more arrivals in any interval, there is still a non-zero probability, however, that there will be no arrivals. This model thus simulates the uncertainties of life.

With this we have reviewed the chief methods used to forecast the demands placed on transport systems and the performance of such systems under the strain.

CHAPTER·9

Transport Network Regionalization

□□

One expressly geographical contribution to the analysis of the work-ings of transport systems consists of the traditional exercise of dividing them into regions. The identification of distinct regions has great utility in the political arithmetic of transport. As we have seen in the last three chapters, to judge the social or financial worthiness of building or improving a road or track, the politician, administrator or entrepreneur needs predictions of its outcome. To do this for any one scheme implies a far-flung tracing of costs and benefits, for each piece of way is a potential substitute or complement for many other links in a network as far as those who do or may use it are concerned. The cost of travelling on a stretch of the network depends on the number of other vehicles using it. As numbers increase, headways decrease and so do safe speeds. As speeds are lowered, cost increases. As the cost on one link increases so does that on routes of which it is a component. By such effects an improvement in one strand of a mesh of roads may be spread over a wide circumference. In calculation this necessitates seeking a new balance of traffic volumes and speeds, which may occur over a large territory. Considering an addition to the roads of a city, the adjustment of traffic may be over its entire extent. Such calculations are costly, requiring much expensive information not to mention computational capacity, and imply commitment to assumptions about the future geography of living and working over a wide area. It should be evident that if regions with impervious boundaries can be distinguished, then the magnitude of calculation and presumption about the future involved in investment appraisal can be limited.

A more profound justification for seeking to partition parts of a whole geographically is that of understanding and explaining the nature of the phenomenon. Distinguishing unique parts of a system and their connections is a major step in comprehension.

Decomposition of large systems

The exploitation of structure plays a major role in the analysis of large systems. Be they military organizations, production processes, spatially separated suppliers and consumers, electrical circuits, or transport networks, complex, integrated systems become far more manageable if they can be decomposed into parts. An attempt to optimize system performance, or the search for stability conditions for the system's operation, is often only possible if advantage is taken of its structure to separate the overall problem into elements whose solution is within the range of available computing machinery.

A familiar example of the insight provided by decomposition concerns Leontief input-output systems. The Leontief model of the economy postulates fixed-proportion, constant-returns production functions, so that the solution of the system for equilibrium outputs consists of the inversion of a matrix of fixed intersectoral, input-output coefficients. With a large number of industries specified, this presented a hefty computational task. Given the somewhat arbitrary assignment of position to industries, the coefficient matrices presented seemingly random patterns of inter-industrial connections. Initially these matrices were manipulated to seek pattern purely for computational convenience. If they could be recast so that all the non-zero coefficients fell below the main diagonal (triangularized), then great computational advantages would accrue. In the course of these manipulations it became clear that discernible coefficient structures implied structured inter-industrial relationships. A homogeneously dense matrix reflected complete interdependence; triangularity indicated an hierarchical structure; diagonal blocks represented fairly autonomous sectors connected by one or two industries while sparse, scattered coefficients showed complete specialization. This qualitative input-output analysis has been applied to international comparisons and to tracing the course of development (Chenery and Watanabe 1958).

Prior to this, in electrical engineering, Kron (1963) had formalized the notion of tearing integrated systems into pieces which could be solved individually but with system coordination. He entitled this the art of diakoptics. For him the system parts were a series of electrical motors in some combination. In the same fashion Dantzig and Wolfe (1960) devised a decomposition principle for solving large-scale linear programmes characterizing a system consisting of separate managerial units. The system of equations describing such an operation can be arranged so that the coefficients form independent blocks linked by coupling equations. The solution algorithm works by iterating between solving the independent sub-problems and a 'master' problem. This process lent itself to interpretation as an economy in which a central director coordinates the independent solution of local allocation problems to achieve overall optimality by setting prices on the common resources used. The identification of structure and means of using it to solve optimization problems has burgeoned in the last decade and a half following these developments.

There has recently been a surge of efforts to reduce the task of tracing the geographical effects of social and economic disturbances to manageable proportions. Aggregation or decomposition procedures for sparse matrices have been applied to travel and residential relations (Batty and Masser 1975), and to population change and migration (Rogers 1976).

Network regionalization

In the transport geography literature there is an initial glimmer of concern with regional structure in Ullman's (1949) seminal work on railroads. Wallace (1958) referred specifically to 'regional railnets. . . separated by cols of low traffic density which approximate the hinterland boundaries of the focal cities'. Garrison and Marble (1962) applied factor analysis to regionalizing the airline networks of Argentina and Venezuela. This was followed by work by Hebert (1966) and the application of this technique to flow matrices by Berry (1966) and Goddard (1970). The objective of these studies was essentially parsimonious description. To aid the comprehension of a map of the network it was divided into regions whose integral coherence exceeded the variety between the parts distinguished.

Thus, geographers have struggled long with defining and delimiting regions of transport systems. Among these Haggett (1966) did offer an algorithm for decomposition of a network by analogy with river basin structure. This provides a descriptive simplification of physique which is not really adequate for structures with many potential sinks and consequently a greater interplay of route choices. Batty and Masser (1975) have approached the problem in the context of a demand forecasting and investment evaluation. Their concern was chiefly with the effect on the parameters of land use models of various levels of aggregation of urban zonal structures. Thus they were essentially looking at the pattern of desire-line flows rather than use of the network. They constructed an objective function for area partitioning based on an entropy statistic. It appears that the optimization of this criterion to determine a suitable aggregation of zones, constrained to avoid a singular answer, would result in a twofold division of the urban area. The statistic can be used to find the best combination of zones for any desired level of aggregation, but not the best level of aggregation. The statistic is applied to display the efficacy of the obvious partitioning of Merseyside into the Wirral and Liverpool. This hardly constitutes a convincing show of analytic power.

For more mundane purposes, transport networks have long been divided into managerial and administrative territories. Many national railroad networks have emerged from the operational linking of regional monopolies. In the case of British Rail, this linking is reflected in the managerial structure with its regional divisions, even after amalgamation into a national monopoly. In planning practice at both the intercity and intra-city level, corridors of influence have been taken as the limits of concern. In the famous North East Corridor in the United States, however, no formal justification of its extent exists.

Transport system characteristics

In most of the large systems which have been addressed with formal decomposition methods, the structure is fairly obvious. The analyst is faced with the several plants for a firm, a military hierarchy, or a sparsely connected circuit. Transport networks present no such ready partitions.

Because transport routes facilitate trade and travel, which drive the economy, one would expect any geographical organization which the economy evinces to be reflected in the arrangement of the transport system. The distinction between urban and rural areas is a fairly clear demarcation. We are happy to draw such a boundary around a city and treat the rest of the road network, for example, as a single, 'rest of the world' or as a few exogenous origins and destinations. Everyday and political usage distinguishes 'regions' of a country, and economic models have been constructed dealing with a local economy's functioning in detail. The definition of 'regional' economy is not as obious, however, as the urban—rural limit. In practice, arbitrary administrative aggregations have been strung together to delimit a locality.

The most difficult task of partitioning is encountered in treating relationships within the city. Here, where the investment questions are most serious and the repercussions of changes most powerful, the reality of independent parts and geographical limits is most questionable. Theorists have postulated annular, sectoral, and multinuclear arrangements of activities within the city. The debate over which of these is correct continues unresolved. If particular cities were found to have sectoral structure, this might well hold the key to breaking the transport network into separately operating enclaves. Sectoral structure would imply a pattern of interaction largely confined to a wedge focused on the centre of town.

The structure of a city is conditioned by the nature of its transport facilities. Locations for setting, production, and dwelling are responses to the accessibility afforded by the means of transport, and generate the surges of goods and people which employ their roads and tracks. It is, therefore, more valuable to examine the shape and use of the transport system directly rather than the land use structure which derives from it.

Economic theorists have usually presumed an extremely simple urban transport network structure of radial independence with one focus. This monocentric arrangement collapses readily to two-dimensional diagrams and solutions. If we take this theoretical abstraction with one focus and an infinity of radials between which there is no interaction, or a more realistic version with a finite number of radials, then there is no difficulty in breaking the net down into parts. Each sector associated with one radial operates independently of the others. The only coordination is via the downtown focus. This generates market effects impartially to all radii. Some actual networks, such as commuter railways, do on the face of it have strong radial components and may lend themselves to a simple dismemberment.

At the other abstract extreme to the radial network is a square grid network, serving a uniformly dense demand with random origin—destination pairings. If this network is not capacitated and if no penalties are associated with turning, then the effect of a change in any one member link will be broadcast throughout the entire network. Before a change is made, all paths that get farther from an origin and closer to a destination are of equal cost and thus will be used with equal likelihood. If the cost of traversing one link in such a set of paths is reduced then all trips will be diverted to it and its complements and away from its competitors. If we assume equiprobable interaction between all points in the network, then it is obvious that the diversionary effect will be felt everywhere. If congestion effects operate so that cost increases with volume, however, if additional costs are involved in turning, and if some distance friction effect is operating on the distribution of origin—destination pairings, then the effect will dampen out with distance and possibly disappear.

The significance of the congestion effect, at least, may be demon-

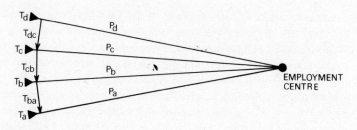

Figure 25

strated by considering the market for travel in a simplified geographical context. Suppose there are four routes (a, b, c and d in figure 25) of equal length and capacity which converge to join uniformly dense and separate residential areas into a single employment centre. The loading points for the arteries are equidistant and connected by local streets large enough for no capacity constraint to be likely to apply as a result of any transfer between the arterials; thus it costs a fixed amount in generalized travel cost (t). At the outset of the analysis, equal volumes of trips load at each of the termini and travel to the centre at identical generalized cost of travel, resulting in no transfer between the routes. The performance of the arteries is described by the same increasing relationship, S, between volume of travellers and cost of travel to the centre. As volume increases, so cost increases as a result of congestion. The demand to travel, D, increases in a similar fashion for all loading points as generalized cost decreases. We can motivate possible increases in total travellers by supposing the analysis to refer to the peak hour of

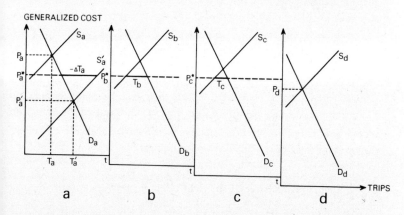

Figure 26

travel, when capacity constraints apply, and by postulating that more people will travel in the peak, rather than before or after, if more capacity is available and generalized cost is lower.

We now perturb the situation by investing in road a, adding new lanes, so that at each volume level generalized cost is lower. We can represent this as a rightward shift of the performance curve in figure 26 from S_a to S_a'. Taken in isolation, this would result in a drop of generalized cost to P_a' and an increase in volume from T_a to T_a'. If, however, the cost of transfer t does not exceed the generalized cost difference between a and b $(P_b - P_a')$, there would be an inducement for travellers to switch from b to a. The resulting drop in generalized cost in b as volume is reduced will induce travellers to switch to b from c as long as $P_c - P_b > t$. The incursions into a, the switches from and to b and the movements out of c, will continue until the generalized costs on the difference routes are separated only by the cost of switching, offering no incentive to further change:

$$P_a^* + t = P_b^* = P_c^* - t$$

and requirements and capacities are equated, taking switches into account by the 'trade balance'.

$$-T_{ab} = (+T_{ba} - T_{bc}) + T_{cb}$$

or

$$-\Delta T_a = \Delta T_b + \Delta T_c .$$

As drawn in this instance, $P_d - t$ is always less than any price P_c compatible with equilibrium in the first three markets; thus transfer will never occur from d to c. Cost and volume on d are left undisturbed by the change in a. In these special, though not unlikely, circumstances, the travel cost impacts, volume changes, and diversions between routes will diminish with increasing distance from the improved link, until arterial route cost differences are overwhelmed by transfer costs. At this juncture the ripple of effects will disappear.

Empirical evidence of the field effect of network change

Evidence of the traffic effects of improving individual roads in urban networks does conform with the above simple theoretical construction.

Effects have been shown to be geographically limited by simulations with traffic models for the city of Lincoln. In the course of a transportation study for the city, a strategy consisting of five schemes was evaluated. This strategy has ring and radial, outer and inner components. The city's network and the five schemes are mapped in figure 27*a*. Project 1 is an outer radial improvement, project 2 is a major new road combining radial and central area orbital functions, projects 3 and 4 are inner ring roads, and project 5 is a small piece of inner radial. Each of these schemes was added to a base network in turn. The departures from the base which the schemes generated were estimated with a transportation study model incorporating modal split, distribution and multi-route, capacity-restrained assignment. The fields of influence of schemes were established by comparing traffic flows on links for the base and when the subject link was added. An examination of the way the number of trips on links changed between iterations of the assignment algorithm used suggested that changes of less than $\pm$ 50 trips could not be counted as anything other than random noise. Since the average load on a link was 540 trips, this gives a confidence interval of about 10% as a threshold for significant differences. The differences in the traffic on links between the base and each scheme greater than $\pm$ 50 trips are mapped in figure 27 *b, c, d, e* and *f*. Other than in the case of project 2, the big effects of schemes are fairly localized. Most of the more widespread ramifications fall in a volume range where there must be some uncertainty about their precision. For the most part a compass of four or five nodes from their terminals contains the major source of the benefits and costs arising. Even in the case of the second scheme, which is a new alignment bypassing what was a congested river crossing, the chief effects are confined pretty much to the 180° sector which it bisects. For the other schemes the confinement is even more narrow. The extent of the reverberations of different schemes accords with engineering and geographical intuition and thus holds out some hope for a regionalization schema. Even in this small city the impulses dampen down in a limited orbit. In a larger, metropolitan network one would hope to identify regions of similarly limited extent. Similar evidence is available from US sources.

In Chicago, studies were undertaken of the effects of the Dan Ryan and Congress Expressways (Hinkle and Frye 1965, Frye 1962). In addition, there was an effort to establish the 'travel corridor' limits of the Gulf Freeway in Houston, Texas (McCasland 1964). This study concluded that, of the origins of all trips using the freeway in the morning peak, more than 90% fell within one mile on either side of the alignment. In Chicago the evidence pointed clearly to a tapering of diversionary effects, becoming negligible at two miles from the route. The studies show the percentage change in traffic before and after the opening of the expressways falling with distance from them. The significance of the precise relationships is dubious because the observations represented a reallocation of the rapidly growing total volume of the early 1960s.

In the more fully quantified Dan Ryan study, the extent of the change and its cause are blurred by the existence of the lake shore to the east and a marked social barrier in the urban fabric to the west. Damen Avenue, which coincides with the two-mile limit where effects become small, was also a longstanding boundary between black and white residents. That the area between Damen and the Dan Ryan was inhabited by blacks may well have inhibited whites from percolating through to gain access to the expressway.

To demonstrate the field effect of changes in a network more clearly O'Sullivan (1978) conducted an experiment with data from the most accurate of origin-destination surveys, for a town of reasonable size, in the possession of the Illinois Department of Transportation. These were

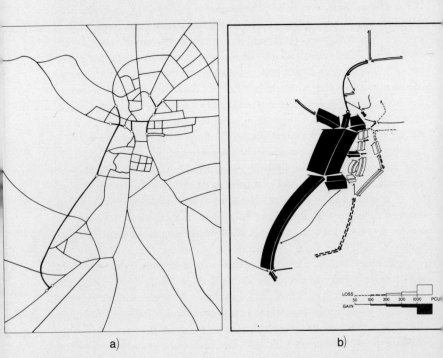

a)   b)

Figure 27

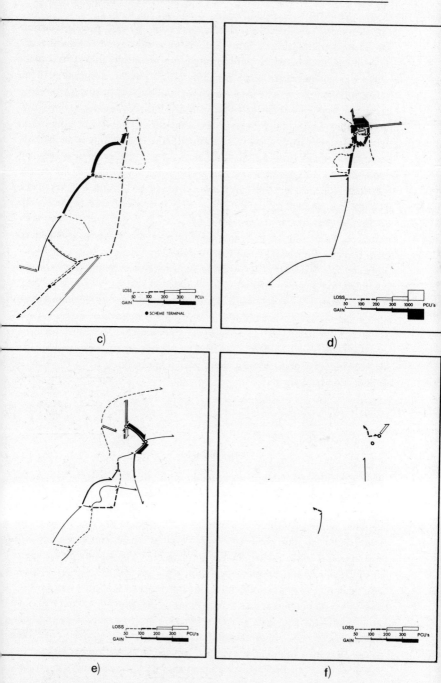

Figure 27 continued

for Bloomington-Normal, a twin city of some 67,000 people, forming the hub of the McLean County SMSA. Normal houses the Illinois State University campus, whereas Bloomington is a considerable central place with large manufacturing plants and the national headquarters of an insurance company. The base-year origin—destination matrix of daily trips for all purposes, from a transportation survey conducted in 1971, was loaded on to the base-year road network. This was accomplished with a deterministic, capacity-restrained, traffic assignment procedure. Free flow travel time on the link marked x in figure 28 was reduced from 1.9 to 1.5 minutes and the same matrix was reassigned to the network. The differences in network loadings before and after the change are shown in figure 28a. The procedure was repeated for further reductions in travel time on x to 1.0, 0.5 and finally, 0.01 minutes. Each reduction was a more unrealistic but stronger jolt to test for the limits of impact diffusion. The changes in traffic flows between the base situation and each improvement in the performance of link x are shown in figure 28b, c and d. There is, for the most part, a diminution of impacts with distance from the modified member of the network. As the magnitude of the time reduction is increased the impact intensifies, but large changes appear to be contained within a confined area, never penetrating the southern part of the network. The dampening of ripples is in accord with expectations from the simple theory we began with.

Partitioning networks

We have remarked on some breakpoints in the geography of the economy and noted their lack of sharpness at a close focus and especially within the city. It is difficult to partition an urban road network because of the fineness of its mesh. Streets and roads constitute about 40% of the land area and could well be conceived of as a continuous surface rather than a graph. Such a conception of the space involved presents fewer opportunities for *a priori* partitioning. Beckmann (1952) formulated a transportation problem continuously and showed that the solution for certain geographical configurations of supply and demand does indeed generate a discrete division of the flow field. This merely shows that independent regions may exist, and does not suggest how to get at them prior to solving allocation problems.

Apart from barriers of rail and water which are sparsely penetrated by roads, lines of discontinuity in the city are bound to be impermanent and fuzzy. The interactions of concern here are those which transmit the secondary and lesser effects of network changes. These interactions occur in competition for use of the network, not at the land uses from which trips originate, and do spread afield. The seemingly clear lines of land use and social demarcation become blurred when people seeking access to them compete for road space and routes. Because user costs are a function of the level of demand, the choice of activity locations as well as routes may be determined by the equilibrium which emerges from this competition for network capacity.

In order to make progress in the partial appraisal of transport network investments, we need to know more about structure in the use of transport networks. It is not sufficient to know the geometry of the network. In addition, we must be able to characterize the use to which it is put. In the assignment exercise with Bloomington-Normal data reported above, the objective was to find where the limit of the sphere of influence of an individual link lies. The problem may be attacked globally by seeking to determine whether a network can be divided into regions which encompass the effects of any internal change. Within these regions the internal interactions between parts of the network and its users should vastly overwhelm any exchange with the rest of the net. In effect, the latter problem is a more general statement of the former. In both cases the intent is to discover if there are indepently operating parts of a network. If one is evaluating a series of separate projects, then the partial, sphere-of-influence formulation of the question would seem more efficient, whereas for a network optimization effort the general regionalization approach is more appropriate. The empirical evidence presented thus far suggests that discontinuities of the regional boundary type may well be discernible in urban traffic fields, and it is to the potential for such partitioning that we turn next. In transport networks where the interstices between branches are broad enough to inhibit interplay, such as fixed rail systems, spheres of influence and regions could be expected to coincide. If the effect of any change on the rest of the system dampens out in a smooth fashion without a break, then the limit of influence could be treated as a template centred on the improved link.

The search for structure in a transport network, which can be exploited for computational purposes, may be pursued along two convergent paths. On the one hand, the limit of effects of a change in an individual link in a network can be traced by simulating the effects of changing the cost of travel on a link in a real network with a traffic

Figure 28 The Effect of Changing Travel Time on Link X of the Bloomington-Normal Network

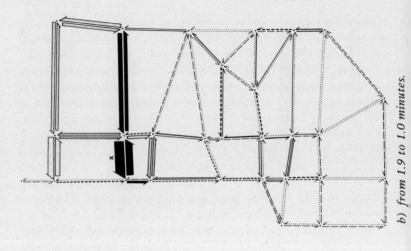

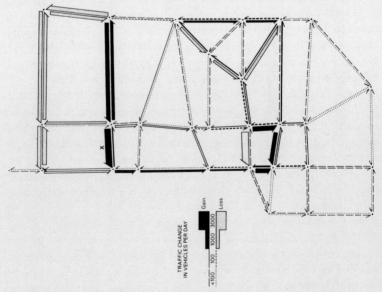

a) from 1.9 to 1.5 minutes.

b) from 1.9 to 1.0 minutes.

TRAFFIC CHANGE
IN VEHICLES PER DAY

Gain

Loss

<100 100 1000 3000

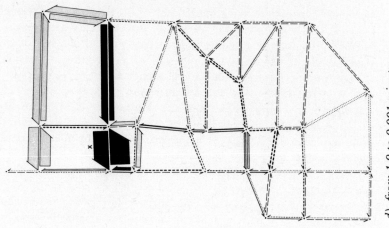

d) from 1.9 to 0.001 minutes.

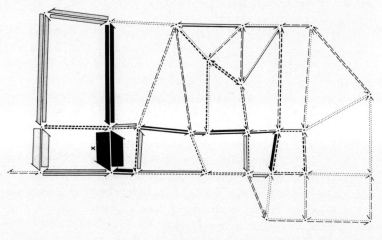

c) from 1.9 to 0.5 minutes.

assignment algorithm. Taking the efficacy of the assignment procedure as given, this would enable an assessment of the affinity between the magnitude of improvement of a link, its location, and the limit of its effects on the rest of the system, in terms of flows and travel time. It is enough for this purpose to trace the effects in route-choice and travel-cost terms only, assuming a fixed travel matrix, because longer-run adjustments in choices of locations and destinations will only arise if the short-run route and travel-cost changes are sufficiently large and widespread. Locational changes in one part of a town are unlikely to be causally related to speed and volume changes on links for which the occupied paths of their associated shortest distance trees are neither competitors nor complements.

The other line of attack on the problem is a general quest for structure in a transport system. Essentially this implies dividing a network into regions. One approach to this is to attempt to rearrange the rows and columns of an origin—destination matrix for some exemplary town. The desired configuration is one with the large positive elements arranged in diagonal blocks with small or zero volumes in the off-diagonal sectors, or some such shape, which would map into certain regional arrangements of zones. The connection between these two endeavours can be forged by applying the assignment procedure to the effects of a change in a link in one of the regions identified. This would test the efficiency of the regional delimitation by determining if effects are contained in an appropriate manner.

The practical genesis of this exercise is the quest for computationally efficient ways to estimate the economic welfare change associated with a network change. Whether one accepts the merit of the disputed consumer-surplus measure or not, it is evident that an important component of the worth of a road improvement will be gauged by some combination of traffic before and after the proposed change, and the speed and distance costs incurred. Thus significant network effects can be measured in terms of traffic volumes and speeds.

The Bloomington-Normal data were available as a 227^2 matrix of car trips for all purposes, surveyed over twenty-four hours with a 12% household sample. This was accompanied by a network of 2,140 nodes and 1,579 links. As one might expect with a smallish city, for which the continuous built-up area extends six miles north to south and four miles east to west, the flow matrix was oversparse. There were non-zero entries in 9,999 of the 51,529 cells (20%). Sparsity is, however, relative. Wilkinson (quoted in Bunch and Rose 1976) suggests that:

A matrix should be considered sparse whenever it has become

worthwhile (to whomsoever) to take advantage of the zeros in the matrix. Conversely, a matrix may be considered dense (by whomsoever) whenever it is not worthwhile (to him) to take advantage of the zeros in the matrix.

One can obviously read 'insignificantly small' for zero.

To make it easier to grasp, handle and present results, the network of the city was reduced to the main road network of 32 nodes and 54 links shown in figure 28. The flow matrix was aggregated up to movements between 30 of these nodes. Three of them operate merely as traffic junctions. The zones were arbitrarily, but in characteristic Midwestern fashion, numbered and arrayed in ranges from northwest to southwest. A visual impression of the structure of connections is given by figure 29*a*. Cells with more than the mean interzone trip volume are blocked in, whereas those with smaller volumes are left empty. In aggregating the data up to these 30 zones, it was assumed that the matrix was symmetric about the trace. This seems a reasonable postulate for aggregated zones and twenty-four-hour trip counts in a small city.

A mapping of desire lines between all zones with any trips between them for the complete 51,529-cell matrix, and examination of the numbers involved, was strongly suggestive of a Strassendorf strung out along Route 66. The initial arbitrary ranging of zones revealed a hint of a threefold division of the urban area into non-communicating northern and southern sectors with a common central focus. Some manual reordering of the rows and columns of the 30^2 matrix was done so as to maximize within-region coherence and the coincidence of zero and small flows in the off-diagonal sectors subject to a contiguity constraint. This produced the arrangement in figure 29*b*. Examination of the values in the northeast and southwest sectors of this matrix suggested that it would be feasible to assign them zero values and ignore them in treating interactions between parts of the city. A conservative definition of the northern suburb in favour of a larger central area, as shown by the broken dividing line in figure 29*b*, would result in a loss of only 5,010 trips of a total of 164,339 (3%) if the extreme sectors were disregarded. A more liberal definition of the northern region, the solid line in figure 29*b*, would eliminate only three sizeable connections if used as a basis for eradicating flows between north and south regions. The loss of information involved is still small. With this boundary, 10,758 trips (6.5% of the total) are lost. This is clearly within the bounds of a reasonable confidence interval one would place about such estimates in any event. The disregarded trips could conceivably have a strong focus on a limited number of destinations and

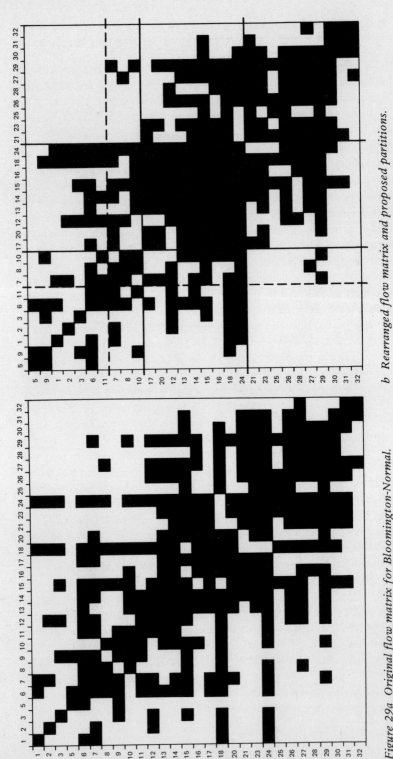

Figure 29a Original flow matrix for Bloomington-Normal.

b Rearranged flow matrix and proposed partitions.

thus constitute a significant contribution to loadings on particular links. On inspection, apart from the three connections noted, they appeared to constitute a fairly diffuse pattern of small numbers of trips. The numbers and percentages of total trips in the various partitions of the networks are given in figure 30. Figure 31 shows the desire-line maps from the matrix in figure 30 for each regional divison, if we adopt the more generous definition of the northern sector.

It is clear that an assumption of no interaction between the northern and southern sectors would reduce the computational burden of evaluating network changes considerably, at a very small sacrifice and risk of error. Even for the evaluation of a chae in the central region, it would be possible to ignore the cross-centre flows along with the flows internal to the northern and southern sectors, with little loss. A cruciform structure, with zeros in the extreme blocks as in figure 32, would be sufficient. The active parts of the whole matrix for evaluating projects in the northern and southern regions are also shown in this figure.

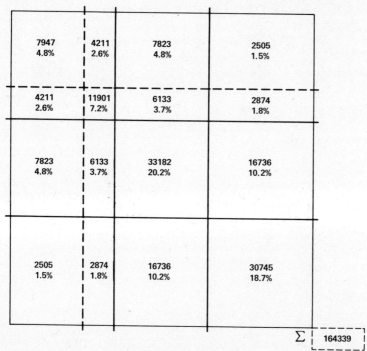

7947 4.8%	4211 2.6%	7823 4.8%	2505 1.5%
4211 2.6%	11901 7.2%	6133 3.7%	2874 1.8%
7823 4.8%	6133 3.7%	33182 20.2%	16736 10.2%
2505 1.5%	2874 1.8%	16736 10.2%	30745 18.7%

Σ 164339

Figure 30 Numbers of trips between the partitions of the network, with percentage of total trips.

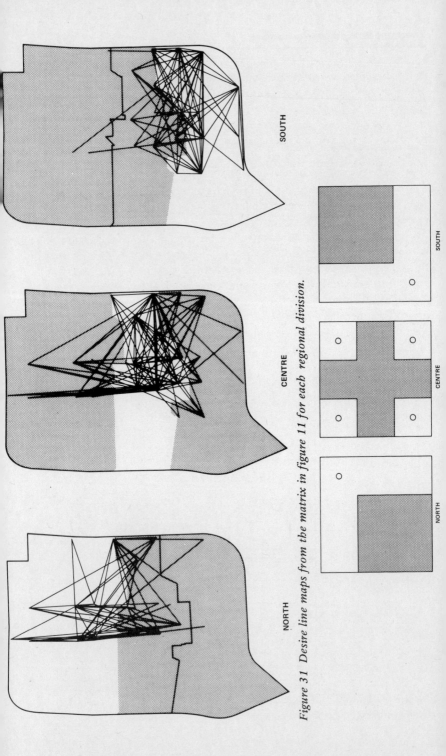

NORTH   CENTRE   SOUTH

Figure 31 Desire line maps from the matrix in figure 11 for each regional division.

A test of regional integrity

Regions delineated solely on the basis of movements between end points fail to acknowledge the interactions between transport demands which take place in vying for limited road space in a congested system. The roads and travel desires of the population of Bloomington-Normal were used to simulate the effects of changing the road network of a town. Rather than seeking a set of regions *ab ovo*, the regions produced from manipulation of an origin-destination matrix were tested. To do this it is not necessary to predict the spheres of influence of all links in the network but only those bordering a proposed partition. If the effects of changing a bordering link in the northern region, for example, do not penetrate through the central area in the south, then those for a link deeper in the north will hardly do so. To check this proposition

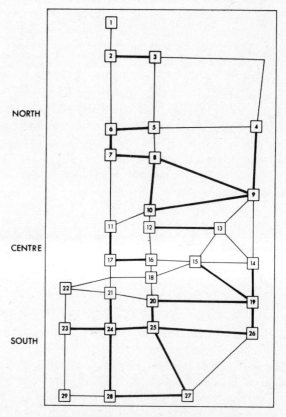

Figure 33 Regions of the Bloomington-Normal road network.

and achieve a geographically representative picture, a selection of non-border links were also put to the test. This test of the permeability of the regional structure proposed consisted of simulating the outcome of improving the links shown by heavier lines in figure 33.

In projecting new traffic equilibria as a response to improving pieces of the road network it was assumed that origins and destinations of travel remained unchanged as a result of road changes. Only path selection was affected. The proposition is that people do not change jobs or homes or where they shop but only the routes by which they reach their chosen journey ends. It seems reasonable to hold that if network changes were not broadcast beyond a certain limit as short-term speed and volume changes, then it is unlikely that they would translate into longer-run locational changes beyond that ambit. That a change is powerful enough to influence the choice of routes seems a prerequisite for its influencing choices of places between which to travel. Thus, the test of reassigning a fixed origin—destination matrix of trips to a modified network is sufficient to capture the sphere of influence of a road.

The computation of route choice responses to network improvements employed in this study assumed absolute travel-time-minimizing behaviour on the part of drivers. Drivers are presumed to select a path of travel between a given origin and destination so as to minimize their perceived, private cost of travel. In selecting a particular link as part of this path, a driver influences the travel speed of others using the link. This can be described by the general supply relationship between increasing vehicle numbers and decreasing travel speed. Such a change causes all other users to reappraise their choice of routes, thus possibly changing route volumes and speeds, and so on. By a series of convergent iterations such a market arrangement can be brought to a balance between the sum of individual desires to minimize travel time and the capacity of the road system. The results of putting in new capacity can be seen as the difference in traffic equilibrium volumes on roads before and after the improvement.

Road improvements were introduced to this representation of the market for road space as capacity increases. For elements of an urban network only drastic amendments of the city's fabric will change alignments sufficiently to reduce the time taken to move between two points. Improvement is more likely to take the form of adding lane capacity to a given alignment. The form of congestion function used to represent the supply characteristics of a road usually presumes that speed decreases slightly with increased traffic volume up to some critical limit of free flow. Beyond this congestion sets in, causing a drastic deterioration of speed. The Federal Highway Administration approximates this relationship with a fourth-order polynomial:

$$t_{ij} = t_{ij}^0 \quad (1 + 0.15 \, (T_{ij} \,/U_{ij})^4)$$

where

t_{ij} = travel time when the volume on link ij is T.
t_{ij}^0 = the free speed travel time on ij when volume is close to zero, and
U_{ij} = the practical capacity of link ij.

This form was used in the algorithm employed here. An improvement in a road can be represented by raising its practical capacity U. This has the effect of shifting the inflection of the congestion function between freely flowing and congested conditions to a higher volume. For the present exercise, the capacities of the chosen links were raised to a standard sufficient for 10,250 vehicles a day if they were non-arterial and to 13,600 for main roads. These were taken from current Federal Highway Administration design standards for such roads (US Department of Transportation 1973).

The algorithm used for this operation assigned the trip matrix to the road network in five iterations of 20% of the total (Burik and Ormancioglu 1977). Thus, the average increment of traffic distributed from any origin in an iteration was of the order of 1,000 trips, there being a total of 140,000 trips emanating from 29 origins. Clearly, an increase or decrease in traffic registered which is less than this number is below the level of resolution of the computational procedure and cannot be counted appreciably different from zero. This is a daily traffic volume and, given a ratio of 8 : 1 for daily to peak hour flows, translates to 125 vehicles per hour in the morning rush hour. Taking 1,000 vehicles as a lower bound of confidence in the precision of the model, the significant changes in volume were mapped in figure 34. The roads upon which a consequential increase or decrease of traffic occurred because of the increased capacity of the link under test (arrowed) are shown. This displays the fields of influence of these elements of the network.

The city structure and regional divisions construed from volumes of trips going between parts of the city, if not watertight, do largely contain the interactions of parts of the road network. The results of increasing the capacity of northern roads are mostly confined to the

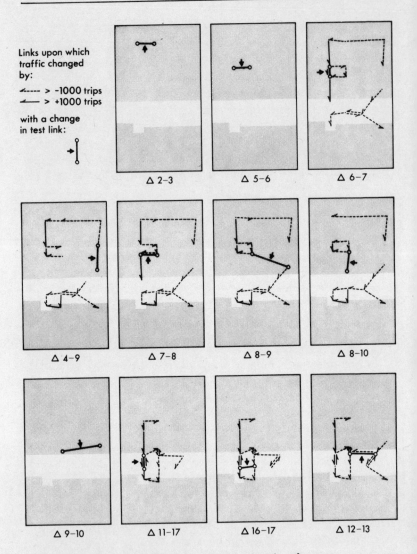

Figure 34 *Fields of traffic effects of link capacity changes.*

north and central regions, while southern perturbations seldom penetrate the north-central dividing line. Thus, the measurement of the benefit of improving a road in either extreme region could be adequately done without reference to the other extreme, but only the centre. The lines drawn are not impervious. The percolations which occur do suggest an underbounding of the central area. The circuits of

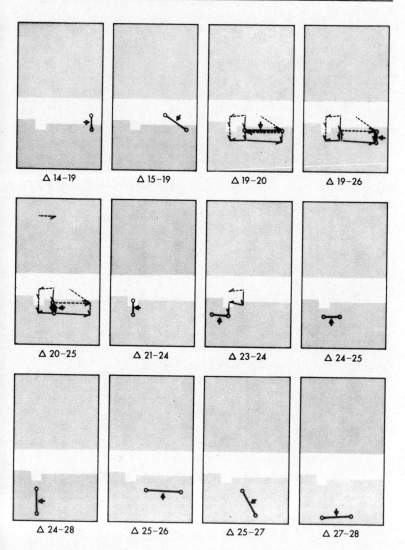

△ 14—19   △ 15—19   △ 19—20   △ 19—26

△ 20—25   △ 21—24   △ 23—24   △ 24—25

△ 24—28   △ 25—26   △ 25—27   △ 27—28

Figure 34 continued.

change around links 4—9, 7—8, 8—9, 8—10 and 20—25 call for the inclusion of node 20 and links 20—21 and 20—25 in the centre region.

In general it is quite plain that improvements to peripheral streets, such as 2—3, 5—6, 21—24, 24—28, 25—26, 25—27 and 27—28, generate benefit to their existing users alone and have little in the way of network effects. These roads serve as suburban feeders into the main channels. There is little competition for use of their capacity. Indeed, most of them are more than adequate in size for their function. The greater the bridging function of a road, carrying traffic not arising nearby and destined for far afield, the wider the ripples of a change in it go. The more median the position of a link in the web of roads, the greater its potential as a bridge and its field of effect on other links.

From evidence presented here, it seems that the fields of traffic change are not necessarily characterized by a regular waning with distance. In the cases of links 4−9, 8−9, 8−10, 16−17 and 23−24, no significant change registers on the link itself. Nevertheless, the small change which does occur has been sufficient to bring volume on adjacent or connected links beyond or behind the threshold of congestion and tip the balance. The case of link 20−25 especially indicates that large effects can show up very far afield with little seeming continuity over space. This tripping over a discontinuity is a reflection of the way in which the supply of road capacity is characterized. It is deemed to have a sharp inflection where a gently inclined, free-flow relation between speed and volume gives way to the steep build-up of congestion. Evidence suggests that this is a good reflection of the way in which traffic behaves. Even accepting the sharply bent capacity curve, there is still a conflict between the sharpness of its threshold and the coarseness of the interative steps employed here. A finer-grained specification of the assignment procedures would probably smooth out much of the seeming discontinuity.

To generalize, in the economist's patois we are in this exercise looking for where *ceteris* are *paribus* enough. We seek if and where we can draw lines on a map which isolate some local autonomies. When confronted with the complexity of people's use of land and movements, our instinct is to analyse − to resolve the thing into its component parts. We separate out and investigate the workings of individual elements exhibiting some independent distinction. If we can do that, we can have some confidence in putting the bits back together to confirm our understanding of the whole. For geographers analysis has largely consisted of defining regions. In essence, this embodies the assumption that the relations between localities are not so pervasive and strong as those contained within the boundaries drawn. It so happens that this theoretical search for geographical parts which sum to a whole with the smallest residuum of relatedness, has considerable practical value.

The mundane task which led us into this was the calculation of the returns to improving bits of road, The same need arises whether this is done for the investment appraisal of individual projects or in terms of network optimization. To do either job it is necessary to determine the balance of traffic and performance on the links of the network affected, before and after any change. With this information, the change in social welfare resulting from an improvement can be estimated. Such calculations are costly if they extend over the entire network. Urban travel demand matrices, however, do contain many zero entries. We have sought to arrange such a matrix so that the new equilibrium need only be established over a limited expanse of the network. The zero or insignificant flows may be disposed so that many potential but inactive relations may be ignored without noticeable loss of information.

The integrity of the regions distinguished was tested by computing the equilibria resulting from increasing the capacity of a selection of the network's links, one at a time. A fixed matrix of trips was reassigned to the network for each modification and the changes in volume on links were recorded. The traffic changes which resulted were, indeed, largely contained by the structure described. Changes in the northern or southern regions impinged on the central area but did not infiltrate to the other extreme to any significant degree. Thus the threefold decomposition may be employed to calculate the benefits of investment in network capacity with very little loss of information.

Bloomington-Normal is a small place, 67,000 people in a town six miles north to south by three miles wide. That some simple structure and the possibility of separating the network into independent parts exists here is encouraging. Once you go below this size it is unlikely that a strong structure can be uncovered. Looking at some similar data and the effects of perturbing the road network of Sioux City, Iowa, suggested that at such a scale people make all of their trips within some threshold of indifference with respect to distance. The travel demand matrix for such a city exhibits a full set of connections, and a change in the network registers on every link in the system.

The lines of demarcation drawn for Bloomington-Normal do make sense on the ground. Travelling south on Route 66 there is a lull of development between the college town of Normal and downtown Bloomington. The core of Bloomington does give way quite abruptly at Oakland Avenue to low-density southern suburbs.

What can be done in this small place should be possible in larger more differentiated places. The fact that a semicircular city 150 miles north of Normal spawned the sectoral theory in the hands of Homer Hoyt raises expectations that it would fall into some useful divisions if treated in similar fashion.

Formally what we are dealing with here is the manipulation of sparse matrices. To determine when it is worthwhile 'to take advantage of the zeros in the matrix', we need some geographical theory about where things are and how this generates flows, which transcends the fixed focus symmetries of urban theory. What has been developed in the way of analytics of late are spatially non-specific representations of the process of flowing, given the geography. We need some theory of geographic structures. It is time that we revisited sectors, zones and nuclei with, hopefully, a better idea of what we are looking for and why we are looking for it.

CHAPTER 10

International Transport

In the next three chapters the efficacy of constitutional, regulatory, operational and structural solutions to transport problems will be viewed in the stream of current events. This will be done at three levels of geographical resolution. Firstly, in this chapter, the problems of trade and travel between nations will be explored. In chapter 11 the state of affairs surrounding longer-distance movement within nations comes under scrutiny. Finally, chapter 12 focuses on the questions of local travel, which all of us are directly involved with. The material for these three chapters is recent history and is drawn from news sources. My chief informant, providing facts and opinions, has been *The Economist*. It would be tedious to cite every item. I hope it is sufficient acknowledgement of my debt that I claim to have placed most pieces on transport from this magazine over the last two years in the context of these three chapters. My other general sources are *Time*, the national TV network news and the syndicated columns of the *Tallahassee Democrat*.

Strategy and transport

The governance of seaways, air corridors and other international routes is most closely concerned with the twin issues of trade and strategy. Whether power is to be wielded for economic gain or whether economic strength is a means to hegemony seems a constant source of controversy over national policy in most states. Whether they are overtly joint issues in political deliberations or not, it is apparent that potential exchange of goods and potential conflict are the chief motivating forces in relations between nations. Trade policy is not only a response to the perceived needs of national economic health but also a means of buying allies and neutrals and handing out punishment or denying resources to potential enemies. Rather than a profitable enterprise, trade is often employed as a pawn in the game of power. The flag of the British Empire was extended far beyond the limits required for lucrative trade, both in terms of the territory covered and in the amount of controlling organization established. Before it, the Spanish Empire obviously did not pay off as a commercial venture for the homeland. The contest between the USA, USSR and China to save the world is a matter of religion and economics becomes another piece to play in the heady game of dominoes, crescents, shatterbelts, pivots and curtains. In this sport there are no fixed points and no certain outcomes. To have a discernible strategy is to invite manipulation by the opposition, and the tactics of the game, at least, are fuel for the internal political process and subject to seemingly arbitrary change with partisan fortunes. If agendas of strategic goals exist they are not made public in any more concrete form than that of the ideological slogans of politicians or the *ex post* geographical simplifications of academics, including past participants such as Henry Kissinger. There is no way of deducing the best trade policy as the optimand of a clearly defined strategic objective. Yet many decisions on trade and, thus, on transport are shaped by the politics of power. The US acquisition of Hawaii, East Samoa, Guam, the Philippines, Puerto Rico, the Virgin Islands and the Panama Canal Zone in the last two decades of the nineteenth century was excused as satisfying the dictates of the USA's 'manifest destiny'. From a less spiritual viewpoint it looked more like the embodiment of Captain Mahan's 'curtain of naval bases' as a basis for world power. Overtly a major function of the Panama Canal was to enable the US fleet to move rapidly between the Atlantic and the Pacific. In all of this the US was emulating the British Empire's control of its main artery with bases and bunkers at Gibraltar, Malta and Cyprus linked by Disraeli's purchase of the Suez Canal in 1875 to Aden, Colombo, Bombay, Calcutta, Singapore and Hong Kong.

The objectives of *Geopolitik*, be they *Lebensraum*, containment, control of oil fields, political domination or integration, have their trade policy and transport policy riders. In its chosen role as world peacemaker, the US has sought to increase the trade dependence of the USSR on the US economy and, thus, reduce the latent strife. To do this it trades with the Soviets on unfavourable terms, and is now negotiating similar arrangements with China. Meanwhile, to obtain a missionary outlet in Africa, China subsidized and built the Tazara Railway. For centuries the British government fostered and protected coastal trade, expecially the Newcastle colliers, as a breeding ground of naval manpower. To sustain the US merchant marine and shipbuilding industry for times of war, the Jones Act insists on interstate shipping using American bottoms, and the Maritime Administration provides construction and operating differential subsidies to US flag carriers. Jean Monnet's goal of European political unity, overcoming its past fragmentation to emerge as an independent centre of influence in global affairs, is being pursued with a trade treaty and the demarcation of a restricted free trade area. This, naturally, does not extend to agriculture, where deep-seated interests are protected by the economic nonsense of the common agricultural policy.

Trade and transport

Trade may be restricted or fostered as an exercise in strategy or in the more clearly delineated interest of material well being. The circumscription of national interest in this does depend on economic doctrine and its supporting body of theory. Mercantilism restrained trade and colonial development to protect home industries and persists in quotas and tariff barriers. A deeper understanding of the mutual benefits from the exploitation of comparative cost advantage through free exchange accompanied the rise of manufacturing on a mass scale requiring expanded markets for their success. These interests, and the theories they nurtured, preached and achieved freer trade. This is still pursued as a General Agreement on Tariffs and Trade (GATT). The interests of developing economies are negotiated in the United Nations Conference on Trade and Development (UNCTAD). Both of these instruments have reduced barriers and increased the volume of international trade and, thus, the demand for transport. The permission or restriction of trade and travel set the limits for international transport. The transport repercussions of changes in trade conditions are not only felt in sea lanes, airways, ports and border crossings but also within national frontiers. The oil embargo of 1973 increased the demand for coal for power generation, putting a strain on the railways linking coal fields to coal-fired plants. The Russian grain sales in 1973, which spun off from Nixon's negotiations for SALT I in 1972, sorely tried the rolling stock capacity of the US rail system, with gondolas and mineral traffic Big Johns being pressed into service to carry wheat. The ramifications of increasing or decreasing overseas trade, then, reach through the points of entry or exit into the networks of their hinter-lands, either directly or through changes in the volumes of import substitutes or in the transported volumes of raw materials and an immediate input for export production. Internal developments can, on the other hand, swing the balance of regional advantages and radically shift the pattern of international trade and demand for transport. In chapter 3 we saw how the Erie Canal cut across the grain of North America, bringing first western New York State and then the southern rim of the lakes closer to seaboard and European markets for wheat. Especially after the repeal of the Corn Laws in 1845, this rapidly eroded the marginal productivity of British and Irish agricultural labourers, already under pressure from Baltic sources, and accelerated their expulsion from the land. The orientation of the American heartland brought about by the Erie Canal did much to swing its attention and trade from heavy dependence on the market of the Cotton Kingdom downriver, thus shifting the centre of gravity of national power northwards. The eventual victory of northern, urban, industrial interests over southern, agrarian, colonial ones, had profound implications for the international relations and policies of the USA. The 'ripple effects' of policy choices do not cease at national boundaries, whether spreading from without or within. Rather they diffuse at varying rates through the channels of the sparsely but extensively linked world economy and community.

International law

The most direct constitutional intervention into the paths and costs of movement between nations is in the actions of government with respect to international law. Relations on the sea have a court in the International Court of Justice at the Hague with a defined jurisdiction and body of precedent. Its potency, however, is limited by its recognition in the observance. Litigants must submit themselves to its arbitration and impose its penalties on themselves. It has no sanctions, playing an emasculated and secular version of one role of the Pope before the fragmentation of Christendom. Between Catholic nations at least, the Holy See can still mediate quite successfully, as in the case of the Argentinian and Chilean dispute over Tierra del Fuego and the Strait of Magellan. Any international rule can be eclipsed by the agreement of sovereign states in a treaty or in the unilateral action of any state if it has the force to support its claim.

International law has been promoted and imposed by those whose interests it served and who had the power to enforce it. The doctrine of freedom of the high seas was a reflection of Dutch and English desire for untrammelled trade routes. This tenet permits a great deal, reducing control costs to a minimum. Although nations may be expected to police their own flag-carrying ships, this is not guaranteed in the case of flags of convenience, and there is no formal means of traffic regulation for safety or cleanliness on the high seas. Governments provide information in the form of charts and weather services to promote safety but there is no means of directing better seamanship with the threat of penalty for non-compliance. The only regular stimulus for right behaviour is the penalty for fault which can be imposed by quasi-juridical process of the examiners of Lloyds of London. The threat of governmental confiscation of property of culpable owners for damage caused by oil spills, for example, may be used to salutary effect. The growth of trade and the increased size and decreased dirigibility of oil tankers in particular have made many high seaways dangerous and collectively costly. This is particularly true of the English Channel and the North Sea. Along with collisions with other vessels or drilling platforms, purposeful or accidental discharge of oil is becoming a significant economic burden and a danger to fragile sea animal and plant life. These are some communities' livelihood. We are coming to the juncture when the advantage of the common treatment of the seas in eradicating mercantile bullying is being outweighed by the disadvantages generated by the lack of responsibility exercised. Efforts at international government in these matters via the International Law Commission have proven unsuccessful.

The most obvious solution in a world of sovereign states is to nationalize seaways by the extension of territorial waters. The confusion of the present on the claims and definitions is symptomatic of this process of redrawing the limits of sovereignty. The limits within which power is customarily exerted to police commercial behaviour are being extended. The objectives are of course many more than merely controlling shipping. A continuing and related concern is with the interception of illegal trade in the form of smuggling. The right of search and seizure has been extended beyond territorial limits to extend the scope of customs operations. The Royal Navy effectively put down the slave trade in this fashion in denial of the freedom of the high seas. Currently the US Customs Service and Coast Guards have been driven to similar measures faced with the burgeoning dope smuggling along Florida's coast of the late 1970s. With increasing domestic demand for marijuana an enormous volume is being brought in from Colombian and Caribbean sources. The *modus operandi* for the seaborne portion of the trade is for a mother ship to stand outside territorial waters and break bulk by the dispatch of small powerboats to the many inlets of the Florida coast. These can usually outrun Coast Guard vessels. The seizure of contraband from the mother ships, an easier task, has been sanctioned by US legal authority. The protection of fisheries for local use, as with Icelandic cod shoals, is another ground for extension, disputed in this case by the UK in the Icelandic 'Cod War'. The recovery of oil, gas and metals from the sea floor has hastened claims of possession. The North Sea Basin has been carved among the adjacent nations. A potential dispute between Scotland and England was avoided by the failure of the bid for devolution to pass muster at the polls. The interests of Scotland with a degree of fiscal independence would be served by parting the waves along a parallel of latitude, which would put the lion's share of the oil field revenues in their exchequer. The English view was that the division should be a projection of the trend of the land frontier, which is nearly north—south, giving a major share of the potential revenues to England. Whatever the cause, the seas are being enclosed *de facto* and *de jure* and in many ways this may have as salutary an effect as the eighteenth—century enclosure of the commons had on English agricultural productivity. This seems the one effective recourse to overcome the diminished responsibility exercised with collectively owned resources. Most immediately, police power is needed to restrain the pumping of bilges offshore and to manage the movement of supertankers especially. Rather than a disputable *ex post* penalty for allowing a vessel to collide or founder on reefs and spill its cargo along the coast of Brittany or Cornwall, agencies should be empowered to insist on obedience to standards of good conduct and seamanship. This would obviously cost a great deal, but the costs of failure to control ships adequately are mounting rapidly in the emergency and clean-up operations involved. The shipowners and charterers ought to be liable for all of the cost of this. A charge incident at terminals would be an apposite way of collecting this due, although it would not reach vessels in passage.

The question of passage has excited some dispute in this context. The Third Law of the Sea Conference meeting at Caracas in 1974, Geneva in 1975 and New York in 1976, achieved some consensus expressed in a Single Negotiating Text which accepted the 12-mile limit as a part of a comprehensive Law of the Sea treaty. This would imply the overlapping national control of more than 100 straits used for international navigation, including the Channel, the Straits of Dover and Bab el Mandeb commanding the Red Sea and the Straits of Hormuz, governing the passage of Persian Gulf oil. The interests of maritime states and, indeed, the majority of nations are incorporated in the

Negotiating Text as a provision for right of unimpeded passage through and over straits used for international navigation by all ships. The objectors are strait states who would restrict use to 'innocent passage' under which submarines would be required to travel on the surface and aircraft to receive permission for overflight. They hold that free transit would interfere with their interest in preventing accidents and defending their security. The fear of maritime nations is that the definition of 'innocence' could be interpreted to prohibit the passage of certain types of ships and cargoes and increase the cost of oil transport in particular.

Right of passage through international waterways such as the Suez and Panama Canals has been guaranteed and also denied. One of the benefits to Israel of its treaty with Egypt will be a reduction of shipping costs occasioned by being allowed to use the Suez route rather than the Cape route to the east again. The Rhine was collectivized as an international waterway by the Convention of Mannheim in 1868 which swept away all previous tolls and restrictions. The state of that river is evidence of the irresponsible actions which common ownership encourages, and calls for the exertion of some authority to prevent its further spoiling.

Roman law recognized no upward limit of sovereignty, and this has been invoked for questions of air passage. It is clearly not observed in space nor at the radius where satellites pass over and sense the doings of sovereign nations with a resolution that can pick out an individual. The clutter of machinery in orbit is in itself creating a traffic problem which may need international resolution in the near future. One hazard of this mass of communications satellites is that bits of the larger among them will survive inevitable re-entry as hefty chunks. The apprehension over pieces of Skylab falling from the sky was not allayed by NASA's odds of 1 in 150 of a person being hit, and its chance impact off the coast of Australia offered no great comfort for the future. Within the limits of conventional manned aircraft there is no absolute right of free passage in practice. In the interest of safety and security national airspace is closely monitored and guarded and overflight must be with permission specific as to lanes, heights, time and equipment. The net of control is not complete, so that several hundred flights a day by small craft and even DC-7s bring cocaine and marijuana in over the US Gulf Coast or the US–Mexican border undetected by civil or military radar. If the most technically advanced nation in the world has difficulty monitoring its airspace, then the pretension of sovereignty over airspace is perhaps an illusion for most nations.

Obviously for legitimate commercial traffic, monitoring and control in the interests of safety is desired by the carriers. The application of navigational rules as operational controls to reduce traffic hazards depends upon monitoring, signalling and enforcement. The obvious benefits make self-interest and training adequate to meet the last requirement for air traffic. For maritime navigation conventional rules of the road, training standards and information by way of tide tables, charts and weather forecasts along with informational signs such as buoys and lighthouses have been adequate until recently. In some places it is necessary to increase the capacity for operational control.

The growing volume of international road transport, especially in Europe, has led to some efforts at standardizing equipment. In 1970 the EEC required the installation of tachographs registering speed and time of operation in all commercial vehicles in the community. On joining in 1973, the UK accepted this regulation, but has subsequently refused to apply it because the Transport and General Workers Union objects to a 'spy in the cab' which will oblige them to observe the law limiting driving hours, thus reducing their overtime pay. Vehicle owners are in favour because it will encourage steadier driving, reducing wear and tear and fuel costs. On the continent the transport unions are its chief supporters, seeing it as a curb on pushing employers and an improvement to safety. The British government finally accepted the ruling of the EEC court of justice that they must be installed in March 1979 and with it the obligation to persuade the unions to comply. Another controversy over equipment concerns the dimensions of trucks, and whether the UK should increase the permitted maximum gross weight from 32 tons to 38 tons to align itself more closely with European standards. Given the objections to 32-ton 'juggernauts' on the grounds of their disruption of peace, quiet and ancient structures, along with the unfair competitive edge they are purported to have over railways by dint of the cross-subsidy of their track costs by other road users, the prospect of 38-tonners should arouse more noise. On the matter of damage to roads caused by vehicle weight, the evidence would suggest that the usual wheel configuration of larger vehicles in fact reduces road damage. The relevant damage factor must take account of the number and arrangement of the axles which transmit the force of the load to the road surface. For a vehicle of gross weight w and an individual axle load x_i, the damage factor is $\sum_i x_i^4 / 10w$. Thus, it is possible to build vehicles to weigh 50 tons fully laden which are less punishing on roads than the British 32-tonner, which is subject only to a 10-ton maximum axle load limit. The characteristic 38-ton articulated truck with five axles has a lower damage factor than the 32-ton four-axle vehicle, while the six-axle 44-tonners now in operation in Denmark, Holland and Italy are even less destructive.

Trade treaties and organizations

The magnitude, direction and composition of trade between nations is not only a response to price differences reflecting factor endowments. It is constrained by tariffs, embargoes, quotas, prohibitions, seasonal restrictions, barter agreements, export subsidies and price supports. At least part of the quadrupling of trade in manufactures and the 50% rise in primary commodity exchange of this century must, therefore, be credited to the relaxation of governmental restrictions on trade. The European common market (EEC) created by the Treaty of Rome in 1957 accounts for nearly a third of world trade. Trade between member nations accounts for 40% of the EEC total. This internal trade has increased three times as fast as the whole in the last decades. It is not clear how much this is a function of the global tendency for greater exchange between increasingly specialized manufacturing nations and how much results from the removal of barriers. It is evident, however, that this latter effect has been potent. The EEC is in its origins an economic alliance between German industry and French agriculture, giving the strength of Germany the elan it lacked but which France gloried in on the diplomatic scene. The UK, in memory of former glory, stood aloof for too long to play a leading role in imparting momentum to the community. The degree of agricultural self-sufficiency the EEC has achieved was France's price for cooperation. This was purchased by the exclusion of the products of efficient meat and wheat producers elsewhere in the world through a system of support prices under a common agricultural policy (CAP). This has created mountains of surplus sugar and butter and lakes of wine, olive oil and milk which have been dumped on the world market with massive export subsidies, ruining the markets of more efficient farmers in developed and under-developed countries alike. Whether British membership, representing a few efficient farmers and a largely urban industrial population concerned with cheap food, can influence and temper the inanities of the CAP and lead to a rationalization of EEC trade remains to be seen.

In the wider forum the EEC has achieved a sufficient constitutional identity, if not unanimity of intent, to present itself as one unit in the GATT negotiation. The GATT organization was established in 1947 to promote freer trade and head off a repetition of the rush to anarchy which followed World War I. It has succeeded in reducing tariffs by one-third. The current round of talks at Geneva is attempting to reduce the non-tariff barriers which now constitute the main blockage against trade. This will in effect mean obtaining a commitment from governments to restrict their discretion and rights. Efforts are being made to require that government purchases be open to international competition and to prevent governments using design standards as covert obstacles to competitive exchange. Given the significance of the EEC in these deliberations, it is not surprising that the GATT objective of free trade has slipped to the Realpolitik one of 'fair' trade, especially over the matter of subsidies, where 'fairness' is a matter of negotiation and would allow governments to protect their producers against 'distruptive' imports and to ensure 'orderly marketing agreements'. The effects of negotiated 'fairness' as opposed to freedom of trade can be seen within the European Common Market, especially in the treatment of agricultural commodities. Trade within the EEC was supposed to be free. To ameliorate the 'disruptive' effects this would have on farm incomes in some countries and consumer expectations as to prices in others, the mad structure of green currencies and monetary compensatory amounts of the CAP was erected to subsidize continued inefficiency and muzzle competition. 'Fair' usually implies the protection of the status quo. It would be a pity if the GATT becomes an instrument to penalize the efficiency of newly emergent manufacturers or of farmers of the underdeveloped world in serving their local markets. UNCTAD is more strongly representative of the interests of developing nations rather than of the existing order, and these nations are seeking to oust GATT from the premier position it plays on trade matters so that rich countries' protective ploys can be more effectively reduced. As well as seeking to improve their access to capital and the stability of their commodity export earnings. the poorer nations are pressing for a larger share of the carriage of their products, by being let in for a bigger cut of both liner and bulk traffic.

Whether for better or worse, trade treaties and agreements govern the global circulation of goods and services and thus the demand for the means of transport by commission as well as permission.

Personal travel for pleasure, business or migration is closely governed by emigration and immigration policy and the operation of the rules governing the issue of visas by both originating and attracting states. The Berlin Wall and the efforts of some Jews to leave the Soviet Union, Pakistanis to enter the UK, Mexicans to get into the USA and the Vietnamese boat people to find a home, bear witness to the stringency of such restrictions. When it is merely a matter of automatic permission, obtaining a passport and a visa presents little hindrance to travel. The relaxation of these requirements in the EEC has probably had little independent effect on holiday or business travel. Whatever its cause, one of the ramifications of the surge of tourist traffic of the second half of the twentieth century is the need to provide the mean for their internal movement often in remote and previously neglected parts of the country.

Restrictions on permanent residence and working in another nation are usually binding restraints which bite in terms of excluding some petitioners. The EEC provision for complete freedom of movement for workers, accomplished finally in 1968, has probably eased the path of Italians to Germany. The possible extension of membership to Spain and Greece and associateship to Turkey would make life easier for Germany's Gastarbeiter population. It would also secure their rights and privileges, reducing their flexibility as a buffer against cyclic fluctuations. They would not be so easy to dislodge in periods of recession.

International regulation of transport competition

If the volumes of cargo and passengers going between countries are not wholly a response to untrammelled competition, neither are the arrangements for their carriage. National governments subsidize their merchant marines for avowedly military reasons. This is the stated intention of the construction and operating differential subsidies and the Federal Ship Mortgage Insurance Program of the US Maritime Administration. The predatory competition for Atlantic and Pacific shipping by the Soviet commercial fleet is presumably for strategy's sake. Governments subsidize national airlines for the sake of pride, to show the flag, picking up their losses and giving them mail contracts with revenues far in excess of costs. Among national airlines probably only El Al and Aer Lingus, with their consistent base loads of diasporic pilgrims, are commercially viable propositions in the long term. Apart from subsidized distortions of price, competition is restrained by cartel arrangements to which governments are party. For traffic not warranting charter on a regular schedule of services, 'liner' operations are mostly organized in 'conferences' according to the routes they ply. The operators fix rates, frequencies of service and even share out revenue from particular trades, Governments collaborate in this endeavour. Conferences are exempt from US antitrust law, for example, although this immunity is being contested in the courts now. One of the objectives of the Manila meeting of UNCTAD in 1979 was to obtain a greater cut of liner cargo for the fleets of poorer nations. Presently generating 60% of the world's cargo, they have less than 8% of the world's ships. A Code of Conduct for Liner Conferences was ratified reserving 40% of liner traffic for the ships of the exporting country and 40% for those of the importing country, leaving 20% for cross-traders, such as the UK, Greece, Japan and Norway. The latter will suffer if this is implemented. Many nations are demanding 'equitable participation' in oil and dry bulk cargoes, in the shape of 50–50 bilateral shares with trading partners. This would reduce the bulk cargo business of the cross-trading nations. Arab oil producers in particular are strongly opposed to the fleets under the flags of convenience of Liberia and Panama, and there is a proposal to phase these out altogether. The UNCTAD secretariat is proposing that richer nations finance this development by providing the money to build bulk fleets for the poorer nations who would gain traffic from these arrangements. The next few years should see a great deal of politicking on this issue.

Regular schedule international air service prices were fixed by the International Air Transport Association cartel (IATA) until November 1978 when that body voted to desist from price fixing. The success of charter operations and Sir Freddie Laker's Skytrain and of the deregulation of domestic air fares in the USA combined with pressure from the US government to separate the trade association functions of IATA, facilitating interline arrangements and governing technical and safety matters, from the control of competition. International fares now become a matter for bilateral agreement. However, IATA continues to provide the forum within which the price-fixing deals are made. The US is leaning on its various partners heavily to reduce fares and restrictions on cheap fares, with some success on transatlantic routes. Arab, African and South American state-owned airlines wish to continue price fixing and may use the UN as a medium for this through the International Civil Aviation Organization. A British–Australian deal, allowing advanced-purchase Apex fares on Quantas and BA, heading off a Laker project for no-booking flights between London and Australia, excludes other nation's carriers and puts a hefty surcharge on stopovers. This hurts the airlines of the five Asian countries and does damage to their stopover tourist traffic. Singapore suffered a 30% drop in hotel business in the first month of the surcharge. The Asian governments have suspended action on a series of bilateral lower airfare deals with Australia and are demanding a multi-lateral agreement. Within Western Europe, with a similar geographical extent and population to the USA, there is only a fifth of the air traffic, largely because fares are double those in the US for the same distance. Higher fuel costs and landing fees account for some part of this , but a major component of higher costs is the inefficiency of the national airline structure and operations. Flights must start or finish in the airline's homeland, denying the more efficient use that is available with round-robin schedules. The cosy pooling arrangements between national carriers have kept a stranglehold on competition and prices high. In March 1979 the EEC commission made the first moves to apply a judgement by the European court in 1973 which in principle empowered the commission to apply the Treaty of Rome's injunction in favour of competition to air transport. Some cautious proposals allowing cut-price 'skybus' operations and relaxing entry restrictions which keep small airlines from offering service on 'dormant' routes are being submitted to EEC ministers. National airlines are stridently against anything which will put downward pressure on fares within Europe, claiming that the liberal agreements the US has foisted upon them on Atlantic routes will not generate enough revenue to cover costs and will require cross-subsidy from increased European route fares. The battle, however, has been joined.

Equipment

A major argument extended to justify cartelization of the air travel business is that the start-up costs in terms of aircraft purchase are enormous and that aircraft designs are rapidly surpassed by newer, better models. Competition in such circumstances would be very unstable with newcomers profiting from a new plane swamping existing carriers in a market where speed and convenience outweigh price. This might have characterized the field in the 1950s, 1960s and early 1970s. The base load was business travel, where time cost was the binding consideration. The market is now evenly divided between business and private travel and the trend is currently projected to result in a four-to-one predominance for non-business travel by 1985. For these travellers, not on expense accounts, fare is generally more important than time in transit. On top of this aircraft technology has reached a plateau in performance so that improvements are now considered in trade-off terms between greater fuel efficiency, seat capacity, freight capacity and engine reliability. In the formative years of the industry much of the carriers' management was drawn from ex-flyers who saw things in operational rather than financial and economic terms. Advice on the future market and fleet strategy was taken from the airplane manufacturers who had the staff and presented well-packaged analysis. The very restrictions on price competition justified by rapid technical advance meant that quality competition decided market shares, and this was chiefly a matter of speed. The plane makers naturally liked to design and build new, faster craft. The era of speed as the dominant factor reached its debacle with Concorde. Although supersonic travel has not been completely set aside, despite the objections of people under flight paths, fleet planning decisions are now a shrewder response to aircraft price, finance and operating economics. Among other considerations it has come to light that the life of aircraft, originally given as 15 years can be extended safely well into the 20s.

However, in all of this politics and nationalism intervene to form choice. The aircraft-making industry is a large employer of skilled labour. The decision to build and use Concorde for Britain was conditioned as much by its large employment of people in Bristol as by the market for its services. In recognition of the burden of having to buy and operate the white elephant for the nation, British Airways have been relieved of Concorde's depreciating costs by the government. United Airlines' order of 30 Boeing 767s (amounting to $1.2 billion in 1973 prices) represents a lot of interest and dividend payments throughout the USA and wages and salaries in Seattle. The pressure to buy the home product is very great and the exact nature of the deals involved does not appear on the surface. Sales of the European Airbus will depend on an intricate game played between politicians and airline and airplane management. Boeing's sale to United cut the ground from under Airbus Industrie, whose main markets are its associated national carriers Air France and Lufhansa. Air Canada is being sucked in with a package of job-creating component orders for Canadian industry to offset Boeing's traditional use of Candian suppliers. On the production side British Aerospace stood drawn between going in with Boeing to build wings for the medium-range 170-seater 575 or going into partnership with McDonnell Douglas on a medium-sized aircraft or buying back into the European Airbus programme to shoulder part of the cost burden. The fact that 757s will have Rolls-Royce engines came into play in that decision but they finally went for the European option. British Airways' choice of planes may well be influenced by the fortunes of British Aerospace and Rolls-Royce. Purchases affecting the numbers produced will influence the delivered cost of the planes. There are economies of big runs, spreading the design, development and plant costs over more units and affording some economy in component purchases. The game is for high stakes and national pride enters into the balance along with concern for industrial dynamics and profitability.

In this tangle of uncertainty and choice one item shoud be a relatively straightforward matter and that is safety. The whole air travel industry is built on instilling confidence that large and ponderous pieces of machinery can rise, fly and land safely. The manufacturers and airlines go to great lengths to prove and maintain safe equipment. Government regulatory bodies specify safety standards for planes and procedures for their regular inspection and maintenance. Yet structural defects do arise unseen and can have devastating effects such as the May 1979 DC-10 crash at O'Hare, Chicago. The subsequent flurry of feverish hesitancy, and the final grounding despite the disruption to travel, revealed the ignorance and confusion which surrounds this function of government. With all the attention which focuses on the spectacular nature of any failure, the price of a mistake for the manufacturer, the airline and the regulatory body is potentially enormous. The care that this fosters is, however, not enough to detect and correct structural shortcomings in time, with fatal consequences. With such a machine, there is bound to be an element of learning by doing, but it is no consolation to the bereaved that the same mistake will not be made again. But the behaviour of the flying public suggests that either they believe this or have very short memories. It does seem that the convenience of air travel and the general level of safety is sufficient to overwhelm any deterrent effect of the risks for the great majority.

On the oceans the monitoring of safety standards has been with us since Britain bullied other sea-goers into observing Plimsoll's mark indicating safe load depths for various waters. The regulation of sea-worthiness is really a market matter governed by the operation of insurance exchanges.

As in the aircraft business, the support of national shipbuilding industries plays a role determining the purchase of equipment. This can go berserk, as when British shipbuilding subsidies provided cheap vessels to the Polish merchant marine with which to undercut the earnings of the British service during the late 1970s. We have already mentioned the US subsidies which bolster their shipyards.

Up to now the purchase of shipping tonnage has presented a more tricky problem than that of an air fleet. Air passenger travel has been increasing, albeit at a variable rate. The demand for ocean-going cargo space fluctuates in harmony with the fortunes of the world economy in a pattern we have not yet deciphered. Along with doubts about cost and obsolescence go questions as to whether trade will be up or down and for how long, and how much spare capacity other owners will have. The oil tanker spot charter market is one of the chanciest going, and this is what must be read far into the future to buy new tankers. With the increase in vessel size the minimum bet has become greater. Tanker size has increased over 30-fold in the last 30 years to the 540,000 dead-weight tonnage of the supertanker. Other cost-reducing innovations have an increasing amount of other bulk cargoes in larger specialized carriers, such as the liquefied natural gas carriers with their special safety problems. The lower value end of the general cargo spectrum will increasingly be carried in barge carriers such as Lash (lighter aboard ship) or SeaBees (sea barge ship), while more valuable general cargo is already carried in container ships. For short crossings, roll-on-roll-off vessels are handling more and more. For some of these changes the economies accrue on the landward side. More specialized shipping is employed to reduce the costs of handling over the dock and dis-tributing inland by road, rail or water. The application of these changes then depends on the ease with which dock labour can be diverted to other employment. The economics of an ocean-going vessel depend on the fluidity and flexibility of national labour markets at its many potential ports of call.

Routes

We dealt with access to the air and the sea under the heading of inter-national law and saw that it was a matter of the power and interests of sovereign states. The opening of an air corridor where hostility existed before, as between Jerusalem and Cairo, has come to signify the onset of peace. The great Suez and Panama canals of the colonial era were cut as civil engineering ventures, but were possessed as much for strategy as for commerce. In the last throes of the colonial era in 1945 Ernie Bevin, as Foreign Secretary, imposed a treaty on Thailand requiring British consent for the cutting of a canal across the isthmus. Such a route would divert trade between South Asia, Africa, Europe and East Asia from the Malacca Strait and the British colony of Singapore. A scheme for this Kra canal is currently being promoted by a Thai Chinese entrepreneur. The British interest lapsed in 1960 and Singapore, wishing to become a centre of manufacturing and finance rather than a pull-up for ocean carriers, has no objection. Apart from Indonesian apprehension that the canal would give Gulf oil the edge over theirs in the Japanese market and Thai unease about the canal's too-clear demarcation of the Muslim minority on the borders of Malaysia, there are no strategic, political questions involved. Since it is technically feasible it seems that this scheme's viability could be judged quite readily in the economic terms discussed in chapters 6 and 7. The chief question involved is whether the savings in shipping costs attract a large enough volume of ships to pay fees and generate a stream of revenue which will exceed operating costs sufficiently for their net present value to outweigh construction costs of $11 billion. This is what the World Bank and Asian Development Bank must ask in response to Mr Chow's request for construction loans. The auxiliary port, warehouse and industrial developments are already spoken for as obviously profitable by Japanese, French and American private interests.

In addition to passages of air and water, nations are linked by land routes. In most cases providing these is merely a matter of cooperation over the alignment and operation of national road or rail networks. Even East and West Germany have come to an agreement over a new Berlin—Hamburg autobahn. Where physical barriers intervene a more strenuous form of cooperation is called for, such as the tunnelling through the Alps of Switzerland and Italy or the recent completion of the Karakoram Highway rising 18,000 feet as it surmounts the Himalayas, which has cost 600 Chinese and 2,100 Pakistani lives. We mentioned Britain's rejection of the Chunnel in chapter 4. This project has been resurrected by Mr Richard Burke, the EEC's transport commissioner, in his search for a concrete something for the EEC to do. His argument is that for some transport infrastructure schemes the benefits are spread beyond the boundaries of any pair of nations involved, and that benefit to the whole community may justify communal sponsorship. He has laid out a plan to spend £1 billion a year over 20 years, with the EEC paying up to 20% of the cost of schemes. His list includes a road and rail Chunnel; a road and rail crossing of the Fehman Belt between Denmark and Germany; a road and rail tunnel under the Straits of Messina; improved rail links from France to Brussels, Amsterdam, Liège and Cologne, from Brussels to Luxembourg and Strasbourg and from Frankfurt to Cologne and Utrecht, and improved roads from Dublin to Cork, Wexford and Galway (Mr Burke is Irish). The first proposal to be subjected to close scrutiny will be the Chunnel, which can be set alongside the alternative of a single-track rail tunnel which BR and SNCF are considering as a joint venture.

The major international rail route completed over the last decade is the Tazara line (formely known as the Tanzam) laid down primarily to handle the export of Zambian copper. Proposals for a link from the Zambian copper belt to Dar es Salaam were economically scrutinized by East African Railways and Harbours in 1952, by the World Bank in 1963 and by Maxwell Stamp Ltd for a consortium of British and Canadian interests in 1966. The first two studies presumed that over 90% of copper traffic would continue to traverse the Rhodesian railway to Mozambique and that traffic to and from Dar es Salaam would mostly be in general merchandise. The World Bank suggested that money would be better spent on improving the road networks of both nations. The Anglo-Canadian study disputed the capacity of the Rhodesian route, claiming that it was operating near full capacity, and projected that the Tazara would carry a million tons of copper in 1971, increasing to 1.2 million tons by 1981. Examining the competing routes, not only the Rhodesian Railway but also the Benguela Railway running to the Angolan port of Lobito and road routes to Dar es Salaam and eastwards to Mozambique, in terms of their investment requirements per million tons of increased capacity to carry copper, under an assumed total requirement to move 4.3 million tons a year, gave the edge to investment in the Tazara. In the event, the closing of the Rhodesian border in 1973 as a UN response to UDI and the disruption of the Benguela Railway by Unita guerillas in Angola would seem to offer unforeseen support for this positive finding. The Chinese seem to have carried out no economic analysis before deciding to undertake this largest foreign aid project in Africa, being moved more purely by politics. They began work on it in 1973 and completed ahead of schedule in 1975 at a cost of $420 million. President Kaunda's motive in accepting this assistance for Zambia was relief from dependence on white-controlled southern Africa for access to world markets. Nyerere in Tanzania stood to gain from an increase of employment to handle the copper in Dar es Salaam, improved access to Ruhulu—Longea iron-ore and coal, especially after Rhodesian sources in Wankie were cut off, a strengthening of the more radical membership of the East African Community to offset Kenya's conservative influence and the involvement of China, whose official view of the development process was more in tune with African conditions in his eyes. For China, isolated after its split with the Soviets, new allies were needed, and here was a spectacular way of demonstrating leadership of the Third World. In operation the railway has not come up to expectations. Inefficient operations have reduced its daily volume from 1,150 tons in 1977 to 700 tons in 1979. More than half of its locomotives are under repair and a quarter of its rolling stock is off the line at any time, much of it being used elsewhere in Tanzania. Chinese managerial and technical staff who had been withdrawing have been brought back to try and restore it to working order, but they doubt that Zambian and Tanzanian management can do the job without elaborate training and equipment purchases. The port of Dar es Salaam has not proven capable of handling the increased traffic, especially now that Zaire and Burundi traffic has started using it as an outlet, which further overloads its facilities. The result is that in October 1978 2 months' shipments of copper were piled up at the mines while shipments of fertilizer destined for Zambian farmers could not get in. These pressures forced President Kaunda to reopen the Rhodesian border in that month, ignoring UN sanctions, to gain access to the ports of Maputo and East London via Rhodesian Railways. This route is vulnerable to attack by Zimbabwean guerrillas—there was a derailment in April 1979 for example—but it operates. The Benguela Railway was festively reopened, but guerrilla action in Angola reduced operations to naught. In 1983 Zambia and Tanzania will have to start repaying China the $400 million debt. From the looks of things now this will not come from railway revenues. Given the political volatility of the region, the fortunes of the Tazara venture could never be forecast, nor can they now. The risks, doubts and possibilities involved might have been recognized and formally incorporated in an evaluation, however. When the World Bank came to appraise investment in a Tanzam Highway, they did include the uncertainties engendered by the potential of the railway in their calculations (Pouligren 1970), before deciding that it was a worthy project.

Terminals

International air and sea routes end where goods and people must be transferred to domestic means of travel. Providing the place and equipment for this transfer is expensive and establishes a powerful presence in the geography of a nation. Docks and airports complement the institutions of commerce and finance; they focus overland traffic; they provide the opportunity for processing and manufacture at the point of break of bulk; they attract ancillary services and manufacturers who serve the needs of planes and ships; in all of this, along with their own functions, they are major places of employment; they are a source of noise and nuisance and large occupiers of land. There are scale economies involved in the provision of these very costly facilities and their approaches are essentially collective goods, so that the most efficient size of operation is beyond the scope of any one carrier. Thus, sea and airports are usually owned and financed by national or local government and operated by a managerial unit responsible to government. The choice of where to locate dock capacity and airports is, thus, a very public matter. The choice is not merely for the operational convenience of the overseas carrier but also in terms of the domestic transport involved and the externalities imposed on those in its environs. We referred to the machinations which accompanied the search for a third London airport and the decision to suspend judgement in chapter 4. This question will soon raise its head again with the growth of transatlantic air travel consequent on fare decreases, even despite the reduction in aircraft numbers necessary to carry a given amount of traffic due to the introduction of wide-bodied planes. Already the ground is being prepared to review the potential for expanding terminal capacity. The current forecast is of 80 million passengers by 1990. Heathrow may be able to handle 38 million and Gatwick 25 million if facilities are improved. The Department of Trade has set up a study group to consider the accommodation of the remaining 17 million in southeastern airports. Largely ignoring the Roskill Commission's £2 million worth of analysis, this group has come up with six sites, named after the villages they would sacrifice to the bulldozer: Hoggeston, near Leighton Buzzard; Langley, near Royston; Stansted, an existing airport; Willingdale, at the Essex end of the Central Line, and Yardley Chase, lying between Northampton, Bedford and Milton Keynes. The sixth site was selected because it was the Roskill report's favourite, Maplin Sands. At the time of writing it appears that the British Airports Authority will at last be given its way and be allowed to expand the use of Stansted as it wanted to in the late 1950s.

One of the chief considerations in such matters is the flight paths a location implies and the noise projected from these onto people at work and rest. John Adams (1970) has shown that if the relative values implied by the Roskill Commission's selection procedure were applied to all potential sites, then Hyde Park would be the optimal location. He was horrified when a retired air commodore, oblivious to the irony, proclaimed in a letter to *The Times* that this vindicated his long-held belief that that was indeed the right use for the Park. There is evidently difference of opinion on the value of quiet and open space and a range of prices that people would be willing to pay for them. Since they are not marketed as such, we cannot ascertain a market clearing price, and thus, we must employ ourselves in the compromising exercise of politics to establish their social worth. We can avail ourselves of standards and prohibitions, insisting that noise be suppressed by operating procedures; limiting take-off times; requiring noise abating equipment and banning particularly noisy aircraft. This was the fate of Concorde, excluded from New York airports by the myth of its supersonic roaring.

Apart from site requirements of flat land and unimpeded and minimally disturbing approaches, the accessibility of an airport in terms of surface transport from its market is the chief locational consideration. With the growth and spread of the market for international travel, the need to concentrate passengers at a limited number of national gateways has decreased as sufficient volume to justify service from regional centres builds up. In the USA, Customs and Immigration services are being put in to go along with international flights from smaller but growing hubs such as Atlanta and even Disneyworld. Since the British Airports Authority has a monopoly in the UK, there is at least the framework for an efficient allocation of capacity. There is, on the other hand, no competitive spur.

Over the last quarter-century seaports have faced the dual problem of catering for new types of vessels and phasing out outmoded accommodations and redundant dock labour. Container ports, with deep water berths and elaborate handling machinery, turn vessels around very fast and enjoy considerable scale economies. Apart from this potential limitation on the efficient number of container harbours in a nation, extensive, flat storage areas and good road and rail access are important locational factors. The potential for surplus capacity due to competition among ports led to the setting up of the National Ports Council in the UK to advise the Minister of Transport, who has power of veto over projects costing more than £½ million under the 1964 Harbours Act. The Council has generally not inhibited competition, which some hold against it. The veto was employed by Barbara Castle in the case of the Portbury proposal by the Port of Bristol, basing her finding on gravity model forecasts of traffic (Ministry of Transport 1966). Roll-on-roll-off vessels, carrying trailers of high value cargo to be hooked up to tractors for distribution by road, seek to shorten the water leg of the trip and get trucks on the road as soon as possible. No expensive machinery is required, merely a place where vessels can berth at any state of the tide and drive trailers on and off, just like a car ferry. Barge-shedding vessels stand offshore and can then distribute their cargo far inland by river and canal. Supertankers, which require 8 miles to come to a stop from cruising speed, enormous turning circles and deep channels, cannot penetrate many conventional ports of the world with ease. For distribution to the European market a consortium of oil companies persuaded the Irish government to allow them to set up a supertanker terminal in the Bantry Bay ria with a storage farm on Whiddy Island from which smaller tankers could make local deliveries to European ports. Charmed by the prospect of some employment in West Cork and the importance of it, the goverment obliged. Some of the unforeseen costs came to light in January 1979 when 50 people died when an offloading French tanker exploded. The cost of the spills and bilge pumping in the waters off Cork and Kerry are yet to be counted.

These developments leave existing docks closer in to the centre of the urban coagulation with an underemployed labour force and under-used berths and gear. The short-run problem of redundant dock labour has inhibited development of new docks as national unions exert their political muscle to resist change. Insistence on stuffing and unstuffing containers with dock labour at the port makes a nonsense of the economy they offer. Both cargo handlers and dockers are antipathetic to the closing of the older inner docks of Rotterdam in favour of the Maasvlakte development on reclaimed land below Europort. The city alderman in charge of the port has plans to switch all container traffic from Waalhaven and Eeemhaven in the middle reaches of the New Maas to Maasvlakte. The city of Rotterdam is filling older docks and building houses on them, boosting its revenue base for central government funds which are doled out on the basis of population. The dockers do not wish to travel 20 miles to work from Rotterdam, especially since there is virtually no public transport. The container-handling firms would prefer to expand *in situ*. The effort to shift activity to the mouth of the Maas, however, has a wider economic context. It is the strategic hope of the city council to offset the loss of employment in oil refining and petrochemicals the city has suffered by providing more efficient port facilities tied in with stockpiles, power generating and manufacturing activities without sprawling over pleasant countryside.

The Port of London Authority lost £8 million in 1977 at a time when the National Ports Council reported a surplus of £41 million. One of its shortcomings is poor labour productivity and relations. A strike in 1974 led to the diversion of much of its traffic to smaller ports where it has stayed. London's upper docks are geared to conventional cargo which dropped by 3 million tons between 1970 and 1971 while containerized cargo rose by 15 million tons. Container traffic is handled at Tilbury and larger container ships will be brought into Fleetwood Hope. Although it has managed to shed 16,000 of its labour force by attrition and juicy severance payments, the Port is still overmanned and inefficient. The Port Authority are battling to close the upper docks, which handle less than 40% of the total port traffic, turning them over to public and private real estate enterprise. The Callaghan government, however, to preserve employment in the East End, gave the Authority £35 million to transfer cargo upstream from the Royal Docks to the India and Millwall Docks to keep them open. They have now asked the Thatcher government for £45 million, £35 million to bribe dockers in the the upper docks to quit and £20 million to enhance Tilbury as a deepwater port. In the meanwhile the growing container traffic goes to Dover, Felixstowe, Southampton and Harwich, where traffic has increased fourfold over the last ten years. The chief growth in trade is with Europe, and this will favour roll-on-roll-off operations, which are expanding where the sea crossing is shortest, especially at Dover. Whenever it occurs, the freeing of an acreage equal to the extent of the City and West End on their eastern side presents developers and planners with a challenging opportunity. It is rumoured that the Royal Docks site is being viewed as a prospect for the 1988 Olympics.

Ports may suffer from more that technological obsolescence; changes in the pattern of trade can drastically curtail traffic. Marseilles, Europe's second port, has had a decline of fortunes which started with the closing of Suez and the diversion of Oriental traffic around the Cape. The withdrawel from its African empire and fervent participation in the creation of a European economy by France has considerably reduced the significance of its Mediterranean outlet.

With this brief discussion of the problems of terminals for international intercourse we bring the international economy's ebb and flow into the streams of the national economy and can move on to discuss the provisions for these motions, first at the broader, regional scope and then within the daily range of local community bounds.

CHAPTER 11

Interregional Transport

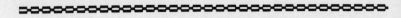

Institutional reform

Lapses of faith in the market economy's ability to foster efficiency in the best public interest through competition have resulted in restrictions on entry and price in the transport sector wielded by regulatory bodies such as the Interstate Commerce Commission (ICC) and the Civil Aeronautics Board (CAB) in the US and the now defunct Transport Tribunal in the UK. Those departures from the competitive norm have been justified in terms of the geographical natural monopoly of railways in their early days. This monopoly was never complete and has rapidly eroded with competition from road vehicles, waterways, planes and pipelines. What strengthened the grip of regulation was the general economic depression of the 1930s. On both sides of the Atlantic this encouraged dirigiste intervention to protect the interests best represented to the body public, i.e. the railways, bigger operators and unions. The competitive position was congealed where it stood and small truck owner-operators willing to provide service at competitive rates were frozen out. In return for entry restrictions sheltering their market shares, the railways and existing operators accepted some public control of prices. This never amounted to much in the UK and was complicated by the nationalization of British railways which eventually were given complete commercial freedom in a frantic effort to enable them to meet their break-even financial remit. In the USA pricing controls remain and the ICC continues to struggle valiantly to discern and impose prices based on marginal costs.

The most serious contortion resulting from the British scheme of regulation was that imposed on the expanding road haulage sector. Given restrictive licensing of hauliers plying for hire, which required proof positive from customers that no alternative existed and encouraged automatic objection by existing carriers, the only way for many shippers to enjoy the convenience and speed of trucks was to purchase their own fleets. Since there were no limits on the licensing of vehicles purely for carriage of the shipper's own goods, much of the expansion in the number of commercial vehicles in the 1933-68 period was in the form of such fleets. The restrictions on the use of these resulted in low efficiency. Things could seldom be arranged so as to ensure backloads or fill-in time not related to the production cycle of their owner. The cost of their management and operation was lost in the general overhead of the production division of the firm and there was little incentive to managerial efficiency. The transport function did not appear as a separate profit centre in the accounts. The locus of vehicles plying for hire or reward was, in addition, circumscribed geographically so that they had to return to their home base periodically. This meant that as the geography of the economy evolved the provision of road haulage services retained the shape of 1930s demand. In regions of decline there came to be a surplus of hauliers while shippers in waxing areas suffered a shortfall of service. This seriously distorted prices as operators in an area of surplus, such as South Wales for example, would take a load out of the region at less than cost rates to get into the lucrative Midlands and southeastern markets where they could get in a circuit of profitable trade before returning to the slim pickings of their home base.

A premier consideration in the politics of competitive control was the inroads a more efficient and uncontrolled road haulage sector would make into the railways' share of freight. Labour doctrine and union interests required protection for the railways. There was little debate over whether decontrol would increase efficiency. The vested interests of the opposition to decontrol were largely voiced in the tones of the 1930s, citing chaos and instability as the fruits of competition. The events leading to the relaxation of the vehicle licensing control of competition are an object lesson in the importance of the pragmatic exploitation of circumstance in the affairs of men. Barbara Castle, the Labour Minister for Transport, in her 1967 Transport Bill proposed a more stringent direction of shares of traffic between road and rail with quantity licensing providing the control. To accomplish this it was necessary to dismantle the vehicle licensing system of the Road and Rail Act of 1933. The two separate functions of licensing, to ensure minimum standards of vehicle safety and operational competence and to control competition, were to be disentangled. This first, quality licensing, was to give permission to operate on the basis of meeting safety and stability objectives. The market share control was to be exercised through quantity licensing. With the change in government in 1970, the Tories took the opportunity to amend the law in execution and bring about free competition. They executed the dismantling of the old licensing system, instituted quality control on entry but simply scrapped the quantity licensing provisions. Thus, the government retains entry control in terms of the roadworthiness of the vehicles and an applicant's capacity to maintain vehicles and run a business. These are essentially police matters. Entry control on economic grounds was effectively removed. Since that time competition and stability of supply in the road haulage industry has not been a significant policy issue. The outcome of this improved competition seems to have been accepted as positively beneficial by everyone, except British Rail apologists, railway unions and those who would nationalize the whole transport sector for doctrinal purity and Clause Four. Freight rates have declined relative to other prices. Service is better than under regulated entry. There was no flood of failures and disruption of supply. The inefficiencies of empty backhauls and low load factors imposed by regulation were reduced. And, most importantly, the grossly under-used private fleets have been phased out where inappropriate. In many cases industry was able to turn to the less costly hire of specialized hauliers. There has been no remarkable diminution of the level of service provided to small isolated communities, as opponents prophesied, but the reverse (Moore 1976).

In the USA the battle for deregulation was joined more explicitly with President Carter's appointment of Alfred Kahn to the chairmanship of the CAB in 1976. Kahn had championed deregulation in his *Economics of Regulation*, published in 1970. Senator Edward Kennedy had laid much of the legislative groundwork for this effort in his role as chairman of the anti-trust subcommittee of the Senate. He was the sponsor of the Federal Aviation Act of 1978 which gave Kahn the opportunity to dismantle the price and entry control functions of the CAB. The price decreases fostered by the new competitive ambience produced a large increase in demand for intercity air travel. Kahn proved to the airlines what the majority of them had refused to believe in their defence of the regulatory control, that demand for their services was elastic to a decrease in price. The largest of them, United, had realized this and supported the legislation. United and the doubters have profited greatly from Kahn's lesson. The surge of demand has caused some problems in overloading terminal facilities, but in part this is a reflection of the irrational pricing of airport berth space, whereby a single landing fee is charged no matter the time of day, week or season. A suitable variation of prices to reflect temporal scarcity of terminal facilities, which would be translated to fare schedules, might go far in smoothing out the bunching of demand. It is evident that for personal travel the friction of distance has been reduced in a very real fashion everywhere. The dreaded withdrawal of service to small communities has not come about, although in places it has changed in nature and now more closely reflects needs and costs.

The Carter administration has the extension of deregulation to trucking as a component of their anti-inflationary policy package. Kennedy had pursued the issue with hearings on the trucking industry in his anti-trust subcommittee. Carter and Kennedy, although political rivals, came to an accommodation on this and Kennedy introduced an administration bill to the Senate in June 1979. Carter appointed Daniel O'Neal, who was sympathetic to deregulation, to the chairmanship of the ICC in April 1977 and the board was packed with economists, such as Marcus Alexis, who would cooperate in an abdication of power. A bill giving railroads more freedom in setting rates is supported by the railroads, for it would essentially mean rate increases. A trucking deregulation bill is faced with greater opposition. The American Trucking Association, representing the big operators, is opposed and powerful, as is the Teamsters Union under Frank Fitzsimmons. Since the services of road haulage are seldom directly employed by the public, there is little popular interest in the matter. Ralph Nader, the consumer activist, is a proponent, however, in cahoots with the National Association of Manufacturers and some economically conservative pressure groups such as the American Conservative Union and the American Enterprise Institute. In the Carter cabinet, the first Secretary of Transportation, Brock Adams, aspired to assume the mantle of Hubert Humphrey in his special relationship with organized labour, and has not been an enthusiast of deregulation. Although it was outside his bailiwick, his voice carried some weight in these matters. His successor, Neil Goldschmidt, former mayor of Portland, Oregon, has a more urban constituency and is concerned with federal support for urban public transport rather than with intercity freight matters. However, a counterweight to deregulation arose from the programme to contain wage inflation which involved the administration in negotiation with the Teamsters. Deregulation may obviously become a pawn in this game. What has been made clear is that the price of continued regulation is high. Estimates of the increment in rates caused by the cartel-like operation of regulated competition among motor carriers average out to 62%. The administration has released figures giving the annual savings which could be achieved by deregulation as $5 billion. The American Trucking Association is willing to pay $2 million in a public relations battle against deregulation, a sure sign that privilege is at stake.

Within state lines, there is a wide variation in the nature and level of control of transport competition. Florida, for example, is one of the states with a more stringent set of entry controls but it also has a state constitutional provision which makes it necessary for the legislature to review them and reinstate, amend or repeal the governing laws in 1979. The Sunset law requires periodic review of all legislative programmes and it is the Public Service Commission and motor vehicle regulation's turn. The battle in Florida may then provide a test case for more general deregulatory efforts, and the vested interests and acute local politicians seeking to enhance their reputations on the national scene are mounting campaigns on the two sides.

Whether at the federal or local level the arguments are similar. Although there is some controversy over trucking costs and whether they are constant or decreasing, natural monopoly is not the chief argument used by those in favour of retaining control. The premier objection is that freer entry will cause chaotic instability in the trucking industry and costly uncertainty as to supply for shippers. Putting this in measurable terms what is implied is higher rates of entry, a lower chance of survival and higher rates of bankrupt exit than is usual in business. The argument is redolent of the economic climate of the 1930s when the restrictions were introduced. As a counter to this it is pointed out that the UK and Australia have lifted entry control recently without chaos ensuing. Within the USA, agricultural product trucking is exempt from regulation and enjoys freedom of entry. Examination of bankruptcy rates in this sector may provide evidence. Objectors hold that freer entry allows in 'cowboys' who will charge customers less than compensatory rates, giving rise to an excessive rate of bankruptcies as truckers fail to turn a profit or even cover costs. Cut-throat competition and bankruptcy results in a transfer of wealth away from truckers' creditors, and the final incidence of this transfer usually falls on the other customers for these creditors' goods, as higher profits. Thus, a high rate of bankruptcy is undesirable from the consumer's viewpoint. Data from exempt trucking suggests entry rates in 1973 slightly ahead of those for auto repair or dry-cleaning but on a par with those for restaurants. 1973 was an exceptional year, however, as you would expect a surge of entrants following US wheat sales to the USSR. In 1973, the bankruptcy rate for exempt trucking was 17 per 10,000 firms, as opposed to 28 per 10,000 in trucking as a whole. The average for manufacturing establishments was 55 per 10,000 while for retailing it was 40 per 10,000 establishments. These values are consistent with bankruptcy rates in trucking in Great Britain prior to the imposition of entry restrictions in the 1930s (MacLeod and Walters 1956). British data prove that, contrary to myth, bankruptcy rates in unregulated trucking were lower than those in most other activities with similar start-up requirements. The steady state of the industry in Britain since deregulation has borne this out.

What is charged in favour of retaining regulation is that exempt agricultural carriers consistently fail to meet harvest demands. Failure to provide service in the unregulated sector is then made into a case against easing entry restrictions in trucking as a whole. The fact is, of course, that agricultural demands are the most notoriously peaked transport demands in the world, and no amount of government control will ensure the capacity to meet it. Railways are everywhere closely controlled and they regularly fail to muster sufficient capacity for the wheat harvest. Peaked demands of all kinds generate problems for even the most tightly controlled suppliers. Power companies have been known to fail in the peak. Taxi service is everywhere strictly controlled in terms of entry and daily fails to satisfy rushes of demand.

Another objection raised against free entry is that it will destroy the value of the licences or certificates in currency and strip existing holders of a valuable asset and their credit-worthiness. This, it is held, will impair their ability to provide service and be a dis-service to the public. It is claimed that deregulation will deprive holders of certificates of 'need and necessity' of 'property'. It seems questionable that a public licence can be accounted private property. There was an active market for these certificates at the interstate and intra-state levels and the price paid for them was a clear indicator of excess profits in the industry. For such rights to change hands for large sums of money would appear to be *prima facie* evidence of excessive profits. If the level of competition is adequate to ensure efficiency, then people should be earning just enough to keep them in business. If regulation had been geared to achieving efficiency then certificate values should be negligible. When people spend a lot of money to get into a business by buying entry rights, then it is obviously an exceptionally profitable business. Willingness to pay to get in implies special opportunities which probably result from restrictions on entry. It has been argued that certificate owners have borrowed money using the certificates as collateral and if their value goes to zero, then loans will go into default and trucking services will be impaired. This does not follow.

The value of real assets, trucks and plant, will not be changed if current certificate holders suffer a financial reverse as the government takes away monopoly profits which its actions enable in the first place. Efficient firms will be able to earn an adequate return on their physical assets and to prosper even though their certificates' value will evaporate. Existing firms will still have a competitive edge over potential entrants, being established with goodwill. Since deregulation has been in the air, trucking shares have declined in value and the market for certificates is drying up. The existence of positive certificate values is evidence of inequity. It is difficult to claim harm from the correction of an inequity, although there are proposals for compensation to incumbents.

On the geographical extent of service, a fear is voiced in objection to freer entry that small communities, which it is alleged are currently provided with cross-subsidized service by existing certificate holders, will lose their lifeline to the mainstream of the economy if competition drives prices everywhere to equal incremental costs. There is, of course, no statutory obligation to provide such cross-subsidies at present, and no convincing evidence that it is being done to any great extent or that less than compensatory rates are being charged to people in isolated communities now. From the perspective of national efficiency, if such cross-subsidies are in effect, they are encouraging people to produce and live in inefficient locations and ought to be curtailed so that they realize the real cost of their locational choice and can behave accordingly. Now, politically that may be a difficult thing to say, but the economics of the case ought to be clearly understood.

We have already remarked on the resort to nationalization to ameliorate the effects of declining market shares and financial disarray for railways in the face of worn-out tracks and equipment, antiquated labour contracts and growing competition. This has evidently not succeeded in achieving commercial viability in Britain after a third of a century. Even though railway management was given complete freedom in pricing and has managed to prune the network geographically, the losses mount and the extent of the government subsidy runs at over £500 million, some 0.4% of gross domestic product. It is evident that the art of graceful management of decline has not yet been mastered, and the institutional arrangement to provide the appropriate incentives for good conduct has not been devised. Persistent annual losses with the Exchequer picking up the deficit, however this is disguised, produce a demoralizing atmosphere.

Despite the example of BR, faced with the financial failure of the six northeastern railroads in similar circumstances, the US political response was effectively the same, with the creation of the Consolidated Rail Corporation (Conrail). Thus in 1976 Central of New Jersey, Erie Lackawanna, Lehigh and Hudson River, Lehigh Valley, Penn Central and the Reading were put together, given a $2 billion once-off grant with management answerable to the Congress through the US Railway Association in return for federal underwriting of their operation. This is nationalization in all but name. By 1979 the whole was losing some $400 million, more than the sum of the parts has been losing. Plagued by high featherbedded labour costs and uneconomic routes which politicians are loath to let be closed, and worn-out power units, rolling stock and track, it would be difficult to do otherwise with the best will in the world. Deregulation which relaxes the heavy hand of the ICC on rates and services may well make financial integrity less difficult to achieve.

Prior to the formation of Conrail, the railroads had eagerly cooperated in the nationwide nationalization of intercity passenger services with the creation of the National Railroad Passenger Corporation (Amtrak), in order to rid themselves of the burden of the remnants of this traffic. The operation was intended to make money, but, geographically constrained by congressional politics in its ability to withdraw service where it does not pay, the losses have mounted to $578 million in 1978, about $2 from the fisc for every $1 taken in fares. For both of these systems, a major determinant of their performance and viability lies in the ability of management to control the extent of service. This is mostly a matter of withdrawing from unviable markets. This is a question of structural amendment to which we will return at the end of this chapter.

Regulation of competition

In the USA the ICC now stands as a bastion of bureaucratic control over the provision of transport, attacked from within and without. The brief of this agency was to regulate entry, merger, exit and rates for road, rail and waterway transport. Agricultural commodities carried by truck or barge are exempt from this. In the case of trucks, the ICC can designate the commodity and route a carrier can use. The date from which trucking was controlled is significant. It was the 1935 Motor Carrier Act which brought road haulage under the ICC. The agency vets rate proposals made by firms or resulting from collusion in rate bureaux, to ensure that they are 'just and reasonable, compensatory and neither unduly discriminating nor preferential'. The setting of trucking rates by cartels was granted immunity from anti-trust laws by the Reed-Bulwinkle Act of 1948. Rates are commodity specific and ad valorem. The operation of rate regulation has most seriously distressed the railroads. Judging 'compensatory' in terms of every traffic bearing some portion of unassignable overhead costs in line with a notion of 'fully distributed' costs, has hindered railroad competition with road and water carriers. The rigidity and grinding slowness of the vetting process has limited railroads in responding to market changes and offering innovative services. In times of inflation, the lag involved in the price adjustment has forced prolonged periods of providing service at less than cost. By the time any adjustment is through the bureaucratic mill, it has been surpassed by inflation and losses persist. This was the occasion of the independent truckers' withdrawal of service in June 1979. This event brought the question of regulation to the public notice dramatically enough to make it an auspicious time for Carter and Kennedy to introduce their deregulatory legislation.

The transport market is additionally distorted by the uneven treatment of the different means in the form of subsidies and taxes. Railroads must pay property taxes on all their facilities and corporate income tax, while road carriers' routes and water carriers' routes and terminals are not subject to these, since they are government property. This clearly distorts the cost basis for pricing. In freight transport, barges enjoy subsidies from the government amounting to 40-50% of total expenditure while rail and road operators get less than 1% and air freight gets a 2% subsidy (Morlok 1978, p. 481). Railroad management is particularly bitter about the lack of user charges imposed on waterways. The Corps of Engineers provides facilities in accordance with the Northwest Ordinance of 1787 which specified that they should be 'forever free'. Charges which fully recover the cost of construction, operation and maintenance of locks, dams, channels and harbours would certainly swing the balance of advantage for some traffic towards the railroads. This continues to be a matter for debate. It may well be, however, that the desire to reduce inflation and to conserve energy may promote the correction of the gross distortions which bleed the economy currently.

Regulation for safety

One argument employed to justify governmental regulation of transport operations is that it is necessary to control entry to ensure that operators will behave responsibly. It is implied that owner operators clamouring to be let into the business will irresponsibly cut corners in maintaining and running their vehicles to the detriment of public safety. From this viewpoint it is evident that big, long-established carriers behave properly and do not put people's lives at risk. This is, of course, nonsense. That the police function can be satisfactorily separated from the control of competition is demonstrated by the conventional practice with most goods and services and by their successful divorce in GB road freight. It is evident that the close regulation of large firms has not reduced the propensity of trains to derail or of DC-10 engines to fall off. If anything it would seem more likely that small firms, who risk their very existence in an accident, will be less prone to take the risks of using untried equipment or operational shortcuts. The effects of economic regulation are not invariably favourable to safety. It could be argued that the regulation of railroad rates and services in the US exacerbated the financial difficulties of an industry which needed to trim back its overextended network in the face of changed demands and competitors. Slim earnings were used to meet operating expenses, and track and stock maintenance was deferred. This has led to their appalling safety record. There was a series of accidents involving hazardous materials at the end of the 1960s when the maximum limit for tank cars was raised to 60,000 gallons. This prompted a reduction in the allowable limit to 34,500 gallons. In 1970 the Rail Safety Act gave the Department of Transportation jurisdiction over all matters of railroad safety. These measures, without incentives to improve the condition of the track, have not notably improved the record and in the late 1970s there were a series of disastrous derailments. with poisonous cargoes contaminating their surrounds and killing people on roads alongside the railroad.

Road vehicle construction is subject to safety regulation and this is not inevitably successful in seeing errors in new designs and reacts after the event of accidents revealing flaws by demanding recall and adjustment. One area of design regulation concerning intercity traffic safety which generates heated discussion is the limits on freight vehicle size. We have touched on this matter in connection with wear and tear on road surfaces. With regard to safety, many people appear to be intimidated by sheer mass. Those who write to papers and start campaigns perceive bigger vehicles to be more dangerous. This perception is not borne out by the facts in the case of US statistics at least. Damage and the probability of death resulting from an accident are slightly greater the larger the vehicle involved but the propensity to crash is less with larger vehicles. This is possibly because drivers of big rigs are usually better qualified and because these vehicles are restricted to travel on higher-quality roads. Braking is if anything improved by greater mass and bow wave effects are not significantly related to vehicle size. Longer vehicles do expose any cars passing them to danger for a longer time on undivided roads. Data from states in the US where higher size and weight limits are in effect indicate that larger rigs operate at least as safely as conventionally sized ones. The quality of the driver and the care employed in maintenance rather than the weight or configuration of the vehicle are the most important contributions to safety.

Another safety item on the political agenda is the US 55 mph speed limit. This was introduced as an energy-conserving measure in 1974 and made law in 1975. It was well observed in its first year of operation and road deaths fell by 16%. By the end of 1977 surveys suggested that 75% of drivers were exceeding the limit as a matter of course when the opportunity presented itself. Especially in western states it was not enforced with any zeal and penalties had been reduced to a nominal level. The Federal government exerted pressure on states to ensure that the limit is binding by requiring annual affirmation by governors as a condition for receiving federal road grants. There is no constitutional provision which can impose such a standard. In January 1979 the Wyoming legislature voted to raise its limit to 65 mph and damn the consequences. These were a potential loss of $50 million in road funds and increase in Wyoming's national lead in road death statistics. Senator Hayakawa of California has introduced a bill to Congress to repeal the limit entirely. The independent truckers press for a higher limit on the grounds that 55 is not their most efficient speed. The large hauliers, represented by the American Trucking Association, continue to support the present limit in their propaganda at least. These moves are afoot despite evidence that the limit is beneficial in saving lives. It is evident that life is not priceless. The struggle between securing greater safety and avoiding the restrictions on personal freedom of rules and regulations finds expression in the seat belt issue. There is strong evidence that they save lives. The Transport and Road Research Laboratory suggests that if all drivers and front seat passengers wore them, as many as 12,000 fewer people would be killed or injured every year. Most west European countries exert compulsion in this manner. Mr Rodgers, the transport minister in the Callaghan government, had introduced a bill to make them compulsory and brought it through its second reading in the Commons. The new Tory

minister, Mr Fowler, withdrew the bill on the grounds of its encroachment on rights of personal decision. Neil Carmichael introduced a
private members' Seat Belts Bill which passed its second reading in the
Commons by 134 to 50 over the objection of Mr Fowler in July 1979
and stands a good chance of becoming law.

On grounds of both safety and peace and quiet, there were plans
at one time to designate a very restricted set of lorry routes in the UK,
to segregate heavy vehicles from local and pedestrian circulation and
from residences. The cost of greater circuity and constricted accessibility seemed too great to pursue this as a whole. Obviously prohibiting
access for lorries to particular streets or areas can be effective and
less costly.

Operational control

In discussing speed and route designation for safety purposes we phase
from regulatory to operational control, since such limits are a matter
of signalling and can in principle be varied according to operational
circumstances. Reverse lanes to carry the tidal flow of the daily rush
are an instance in point. Restricting hours for deliveries to downtown
ships is a similar control.

The use of signals to control the circulation of traffic is an internal
matter for railways as they came to be constituted after the opening
of the Manchester-Liverpool in 1830. This set the mould of carriers
monopolizing their own track. Where a desire to extend coverage of
the network at a low cost resulted in insufficient segregation from
road traffic, there is potential conflict and need for control at grade
crossings. This is frequently inadequate and dangerous. It augured
something that the first of Amtrak's shiny new French-built trains on
its maiden run concertinaed when it hit a farmers' pick-up stopped on
a grade crossing north of Springfield, Illinois. The need for a complex and costly signalling system for the functioning of a railway
does involve the general fisc when it is used as an argument to justify
subsidy. The argument runs that signalling costs are a fixed requirement of operations which do not vary with the volume of traffic.
For such a decreasing cost activity, efficient prices and levels of output
can only be achieved by the collective shouldering of the fixed element
of costs. This then becomes a justification for government covering
railway losses. It depends on the assumption that signalling costs are
fixed. It has, however, been shown in practice that the costs of monitoring and control can be reduced in line with reduced volume. Coras

Iompair Eireann (CIE), for example, employed a method whereby a single key physically controls access to a length of track and is then passed on to the next user. For lightly trafficked lines this seems foolproof and cheap if slightly inconvenient.

As far as road traffic is concerned signalled control of circulation is only necessary in the dense streams of urban traffic. On intercity routes signs and signals indicate speed and safety rules, advise on location, direction and services or warn of hazards.

The safe, orderly and expeditious movement of aircraft in the air and on the ground requires a considerable public outlay in air traffic control centres and towers, routes and airport surveillance radars, radar beacons and flight service stations along with navigational assistance by way of information transmitting and measuring devices, radio beacons and instrument landing systems. At present much of the cost of this is recovered by indirect means such as user taxes. Since the military employ some parts of the system, some of its costs should be collectively borne. In the USA, at least, moves are afoot to bring about closer equation of the burden of cost and actual costs imposed by users on the system in the form of user charges. Given that the tight surveillance of individual vehicles is already in place, this should involve little extra administrative cost, merely the addition of a billing mechanism. As traffic builds up towards dangerously congested levels, the controls of a variable user charge may be an invaluable supplement to technical ingenuity in keeping the skyways safe. One potentially very dangerous component of air traffic in the USA is general aviation, private and corporate planes, and this bears a disproportionately small share of the cost burden currently. Cost-based user charges might well induce a reduction in this traffic, which is difficult to monitor and govern and can jeopardize the lives of many in bigger aircraft.

One instance where price in the form of a user charge could be used with profit to overcome a congestion problem operationally is on US waterways. It is not the channels but the locks which generate queues on the Mississippi. The locks which provide passage past flood control dams are old and of limited capacity. The Corps of Engineers' solution would be to rebuild these locks and dams with greater throughput capacity. A more obvious and immediate solution is to ration the limited capacity with a variable user charge which might also operate to even out peaks and troughs of demand through time. This is met with counter claims that the structures are ancient and unsound and need replacement anyway. The retort suggests that they can be made sound by repair at far less cost. The test case over which this argument rages is Alton Lock and Dam 26, where the Illinois River joins the Mississippi. This instance of conflict between operational, pricing solutions and structural solutions to a transport problem aptly leads into an examination of decisions involving making new facilities.

Structural decisions

Shortcomings in the ease with which people and goods move between parts of a nation can be ameliorated not only by legal controls and operational manipulation but also by making new ways and means of travel or improving old ones. Such structural solutions to the problem of inadequate mobility may involve the moving components of the system. Decisions on vehicle improvement and replacement are usually taken at the household or firm level with the public sector setting the limits in terms of performance and dimensional standards, or encouraging certain desirable trends by exhortion and subsidy. Obviously for a nationalized operation the public sector is directly involved in such decisions. This is especially true if the corporation in question is a financial loser, which is the case for most national railways and airlines. In this case purchases will be government financed. Decisions on a vehicle fleet are not always independent of the state and nature of the track they pass over and the place at which they end their journey. Often the two issues are joint, as with railway electrification. Where vehicle operation and the provision of track are independent, notably on roads, the extent, location and quality of routeway is a political matter and this constitutes the most important role of the state in transport. Even if it is not directly responsible for links and terminals, it is usually deemed strategically and politically essential that government have the final word on the extent of networks. This has presented railways with a major difficulty in trying to divest themselves of excessive geographical coverage, since political control presents the opportunity for partisan politicking. Among potential links in a transport network the most geographically significant are perhaps those which round out a nation's action space by crossing estuaries or mountain barriers. These are most costly and their impacts potentially more dramatic, and thus uncertain per mile. For internal air travel, as with international flying, the critical public decision is on the location and capacity of terminals. The main concerns of this section then will be with vehicle improvement, route and terminal planning and bridges.

Vehicle improvement

Although the government may exhort and encourage improved truck,
plane and car design from the point of view of technical efficiency and
safety and set the limiting constraints within which designs must fit,
the chief research and development effort is undertaken by the vehicle
manufacturers. Indeed from the DC-10 case following the O'Hare crash
in May 1979, it appears that government could not muster the expertise
and depended on the plane makers' engineers for tests and judgements
on safety. This must always leave the suspicion that commercial objectives can lead to design short-cuts. On the demand side, choice weighs
the prospect of financial success or personal convenience against cost.
The most significant development in aircraft of the last decade was the
introduction of the wide-bodied jet with the Boeing 747 in 1970,
followed by the DC-10 in 1971, the L 1011 in 1972 and the Airbus in
1974. These can operate on the same runways as older craft with
capacity per vehicle increased by nearly 200%, seating up to 550
passengers. These jumbo jets carrying an increasing load of passengers,
with little or no increase in numbers of flights, expanded airport
runway capacity and took the pressure off the search for new locations
in the mid 1970s. Heathrow's passenger numbers increased by 41%
between 1971 and 1977, but aircraft movements fell by 0.7%. The
congestion in passenger and baggage facilities is obviously not relieved
by these new aircraft. Indeed, it is exacerbated by a concentration of
throughput into larger quantities of people disgorged at one time.
The General Electric, Pratt and Whitney and Rolls-Royce turbofan
engines of these large aircraft are cleaner and quieter than previous
models and have improved the lot of residents about airports. Eventually the improvement might be deemed enough to warrant relaxing
the curfew on night operations in many airports. This would spread
the volume out and stretch existing airport capacity further (Gates
1979).

Mechanically, road vehicle engines have reached a plateau of development and will only be marginally improved in performance by micro-
chip automatic control devices. There is some prospect of improved
efficiency through a reduction of aerodynamic drag. The modifications to the horse-drawn landau or a phaeton which have constituted
automobile design up till recently are being replaced by some serious
aerodynamic work which may improve fuel efficiency by some 15%.
The streamlining of a box presents greater difficulties but this is what is
called for as far as the truck is concerned. However, already the modifi-

cation of vehicles operating now with bolt-on cab-roof wind deflectors is reducing fuel consumption significantly, and vehicles purposely designed to that end may be even more successful. This interest in fuel efficiency has, of course, been fostered by the relative increase in gasoline prices since 1973 and it is reflected in the shift towards smaller cars. This is most striking in the increased market share of foreign compacts in the US traffic mix and the bids of the big five to find competitive models. The design and dimensions of the car present a particular difficulty in that it is used for many quite different purposes. Cars are driven into the teeming centres of cities and parked in narrow confines while waiting to do the second half-hour lap of their daily round. They are used to ferry children and haul weekly shopping. They are used to make weekend sallies of 100 miles or more and annual expeditions across continents. The large size of the US gas-guzzler had customer comfort and the long haul as its binding design limits which, of course, coincided with the interest of Fords or GM in selling more cars and was not inhibited by the price of fuel. As the price at the pump rises and expectations dim, so the proportion of smaller vehicles in the national fleet has increased. With more households owning two or more cars and more second cars being bought new, the three main purposes — commuting, local haulage and long-distance travel — are being done in vehicles more appropriate to their nature. Increasingly commuting is done in a small car while driving the kids around, shopping and long-distance travel is done in a station wagon. This obviously is a matter for discussion in the next chapter when we treat local travel. Sufficient to say for now that there is the appearance that the size of vehicle purchased is sensitive to the cost of fuel and, outside the Environmental Protection Agency regulation of average gasoline consumption over a manufacturer's output, the response of customers is having its effect on car design. The world car or X car is not only a response to scale economies achievable with a global market but also the response of domestic users to rising fuel prices.

The major technical advance in railway operation since the peaking out of steam technology in the 1860s has been electrification. The operating costs of electric trains are 30% below those for diesels at current oil prices. However, what goes along with new power units and special rolling stock is the network cost of hooking up the power supply and stringing overhead lines on supports over the track. This is expensive. Switzerland, Norway, Sweden and Italy, with cheap hydro-electric power, have much of their route mileage electrified.

British railways electrified commuter lines in the 1920s and 1930s, but these carry current on third rails, which is no use for high-speed operations. In the 1960s the London-Birmingham-Manchester-Liverpool-Glasgow route was electrified, and BR are now pressing for £400 million to extend electrification to the London-Bristol-South Wales, and London-Leeds-Newcastle-Edinburgh trunk, bringing the total to 41,000 miles, 37% of the total network. This is promoted as a hedge against the soaring cost of diesel fuel in the next decades. The investment proposal faces the serious political difficulty of coming from a public enterprise which has consistently lost money since its foundation and being addressed to a government pledged to retrench the public domain in the economy. On the other side of the national politics of the issue, the ability of an electrified system to convert the output of power stations fuelled from a variety of sources into mobility may be seen as a strategic advantage when it becomes necessary to conserve oil for use in road vehicles, planes and plastic and chemical factories. Aside from questions of political viability, the rate of return on the investment will obviously depend on the future path of fuel prices. If the worst expectations about oil supplies and prices come true, then the operating cost savings may be greater than 30% in the near future and the discounted traction cost benefits may overwhelm the immediate electrification costs to produce a positively attractive return on outlay. Even if oil prices continue to bear a similar relation to other power prices for some time to come, the savings on electric over diesel traction may still warrant the investment, but the magnitude of the savings will depend crucially on the amount of traffic which railways are predicted to carry. Different trajectories of total demand and railway shares will result in different yields. Since electric locomotives are cheaper (in Europe), longer lived and more reliable than diesels, there is a good prospect that this will be undertaken and prove successful. Taken a route at a time the investment analysis is not too convincing, and BR resort to a 'systems' economy argument, claiming that the benefits accruing to the entire system are greater than those which can be calculated for the sum of the parts because of route overlaps and the common use of track, signals and power supplies. In the USA, there is little electrified track. Amtrak proposed to electrify the 155 miles between Boston and New Haven, but since the railroads have unloaded their passenger traffic they do not have the dense routes requiring high speeds which justify electification. Nor do they have the financial track records to attract capital. What is more, they can buy ready-made diesel units from General Motors for a third of the price of electric trains, which strongly affects the balance of advantages.

Routes and terminals

In these days new railway routes are built ostensibly for mineral traffic but the underlying motive is often national prestige and global strategy. We have examined the case of the Tazara Railway. In the USSR the Baikal-Amur Mainline (BAM) is being laid across 2,000 miles of wilderness at a cost of $15 billion to parallel the Tsarist-built Trans-Siberian route 200 miles to the South. This has a distinctly colonial flavour to it, opening the mineral and forest resources of eastern Siberia to fuel Russian ambitions for economic power. It will enhance the Soviet presence in the Pacific and increase the trade-based dependence of Japan and Korea on the Soviet resource base. There is no evidence of any cost-accounting perspective on this enterprise. It is cut from a more heroic mould in the best Soviet tradition of archaic romance. This was perhaps best exemplified by Stalin's completion of Peter the Great's dream of a Volga-Don Canal in 1952, in a country where everything freezes for half the year. In transport technology as well as politics the Soviet leaders are men of the nineteenth century.

The accent on high-order transport facilities in poorer countries is strangely out of tune with anti-colonial rhetoric. The highly hierarchical network structures of railways are usually geared to collect and remove some mineral or agricultural product efficiently for export to the industrial world. This was the function of the railways of the Raj, along with the administration and policing of a large territory. It could be said that this had the dual detrimental effects of overblowing the national consciousness of India and its international posturing, while encouraging its continued dependence on overseas markets rather than the evolution of an integrated domestic economy for development. The emphasis on rail transport and the neglect of roads produced an economy arranged in branched harmony with an overcentralized bureaucracy, with little means for the development of local markets and more intimate geographical specialization and efficiencies. During Robert MacNamara's term as chairman of the World Bank, the emphasis in aid distribution has shifted towards rural development and more locally focused projects. The World Bank's refusal to fund the Tazara Railway pointed out that Zambia and Tanzania could get eleven times the length of good road for the same price.

In urban, industrial nations the railway structural problem is one of over-extension, and the obvious solution the deletion of unprofitable links from the network. Lines built in the rush to monopolize a market in the last half of the nineteenth century are now made redundant by the greater suitability of road vehicles for their light traffic in goods and people. Regulation, drawn on the railways initially by the very monopoly they sought, has severely limited their freedom to withdraw services, including the closing of branch lines. These restrictions have been carried over into an era when railways by no means enjoy monopoly power, and have been a major source of financial difficulty. In Ireland CIE's experience in cutting back railways foreshadowed the problem elsewhere because the problem was extreme and simplified in this island lightly touched by the nineteenth-century industrialization of Europe. The lessons learned there, however, had to be relearned elsewhere. Faced with a revenue loss problem and the need to replace capital run down in the 1930s and 1940s, the rail system incurred a revenue loss of £10.2 million, had capital written off by government to the extent of £10.6 million and was given grants of £26.7 million between 1945 and 1963. By 1957 it had become plain that this could not be sustained in a country of 3 million people. This was clearly a serious misallocation of resources. In that year the Beddy Committee (Department of Industry and Commerce 1957), recognizing that Ireland had the lowest rail passenger and freight densities in Europe, the lowest use of track and stock, the highest labour-to-traffic ratio and many redundant services and stations, suggested that the rail system should be pruned drastically. CIE's policy of favouring rail over its road undertakings was deprecated and it was suggested that the corporation should operate as a commercial undertaking, freed of common carrier obligations. These recommendations were embodied in the 1958 Transport Act, which empowered CIE to close down uneconomic services without reference to any tribunal. The board of CIE, however, continued to shoulder an obligation to cater for a 'need' sector in transport defined on social grounds. The Beddy Report envisaged reducing the rail network to 850 miles, and CIE did close nearly 700 route miles and 218 stations during the 1960s, reducing the system to less then 1,400 miles. Before closing a branch line, CIE analyzed the cost of operation and the revenue of rail services and of substitute road services. Where there was no prospect of commercial success and where CIE's net receipts would increase from the substitution of road for rail services, the branch was closed. The West Clare line, famed in song, was costing the general exchequer £23,000 a year before it was closed. Substituting road services reduced the loss to

£4,000. The West Cork line loss was £56,000 a year, and in their first year of operation bus and truck services on the route made a profit of £8,000 — a betterment of £64,000. The 30% of the network closed had carried less than 5% of the traffic for 6% of the revenue. The result of these closings was to reduce the deficit from £1.2 million in 1958 to £0.5 million in 1960. These advances were rapidly eroded by higher labour costs. Despite this trimming, improved use of equipment, dieselization and an increase in volume of traffic, the railway was unable to recoup increased costs in competition with road transport.

In 1962 CIE reviewed the profitability of its components and examined some different configuration for the transport system (Coras Iompair Eireann 1963). It was shown that the six largest stations accounted for over half the rail revenue and that 750 miles of line were unprofitable. It was held, however, that closing these lines would reduce the system below the threshold of viability. A 400-mile railway was felt to be below the critical mass. The conclusion of the analysis was that there was little chance of breaking even in rail operations while social and political ends have to be served. In the 1964 Transport Act, the political desire to maintain a national railway was combined with the realization that this could not be done commercially in a country with a maximum radius of operation of 160 miles about the Dublin focus and virtually no mineral traffic, to provide for an annual subsidy of £2 million, with which the corporation was expected to break even. The fact that railway employees comprise 1% of the national labour force and that CIE was the largest employer in the country obviously had some bearing on this decision. However, in the 1963 report the five optional configurations that CIE considered for cost comparison purposes looked suspiciously like an agenda for gradual dismantlement of the rail network. If this was the intent, it was lightly disguised by the order in which the options were presented. Putting them in sequence of diminishing rail structure with road service replacing the deletions, they look like a reasonable plan for graceful withdrawal: a mainline passenger/freight railhead system with only Dublin suburban passenger services; a Dublin passenger service only and, finally, an all-road system. As yet the system is operating in the first stage.

In the UK, Dr (now Lord) Beeching, formerly of Imperial Chemical Industries, was appointed chairman of the British Railways Board. His report and plan for the future in 1963 included the eradication of many branch lines and the withdrawal of passenger services, reducing maintenance costs to freight standards. This it was hoped would cut a loss of some £30 million a year. BR's ability to achieve this was wholly dependent on government approval. Stewart Joy (1973) has chronicled the internal, inter-governmental and national politics of subsequent developments from the perspective of a former chief economist to the British Railways Board. The voices of preservationists and railway buffs were probably not so powerful in slowing the progress of closure as the position of the railway unions in the councils of the Labour movement. The opposing tensions of economic efficiency and social and political obligations were temporarily reconciled by the government contracting with BR for the provision of 'socially necessary' services at a cost of £400 million a year. Even with this BR have failed to break even and in 1979 they were again pressing the government on loss-making local services. With the succession of a Tory administration, this subsidy has been cut and BR efforts to shut down lines are likely to be met with greater sympathy. Negotiations with the National Bus Corporation to provide replacement services are under way. On slightly heavier-trafficked lines, low cost diesel rail-buses being built by Leylands will replace expensive rail cars.

In the USA, the Railroad Revitalization and Regulatory Reform Act of 1976, which established Conrail to ensure continued service after the bankruptcy of six northeastern and midwestern railroads, acknowledged that private railroads should no longer be forced to provide unprofitable services on high-density lines. Federal subsidies were provided to underwrite losses on such lines which the public wished to continue, and these could be used to provide substitutes for rail service where this is more cost-efficient. The Act, however, clearly indicated that this was to be a transitional palliative. When it came down to cases, Congressmen blocked efforts at abandonment, including those by Conrail to surmount the problem which brought its predecessors to their knees. Constitutionally the iron grip of the ICC on freight lines in effect since 1887 is still binding and is subject to political manipulation. The Carter administration is moving towards the total relaxation of this control by 1984. Among other things this would make abandonment on the grounds of operating losses merely a matter of giving 30 days' notice. Politicians who have interfered to please their constituents and keep lines within their own bailiwicks open, may more readily accept the general proposition and an institutional change which removes the decision from their purview. One organizational ploy which has brought some short lines back above the threshold viability is their sale to small operators who can run them at lower costs by avoiding union rates and rules. This has been going on in southern Illinois for some time. It started when a group of ex-railroad employee enthusiasts bought locomotives and cars from a scrap merchant. Conrail has succeeded in making some such deals.

The Amtrak network of passenger services was designed in 1971 and has proven poor in detail and of too great an extent. In 1978 the government was making up losses of $578 million. This amounted to $2 subsidy for every $1 taken in fares. In March 1979 the Secretary of Transport, Brock Adams, with the support of Amtrak's president Alan Boyd, proposed to cut the system from 27,500 miles to 15,500 miles eliminating thinly used services mostly in the South and West. These included such romantic reminders of past glories as the Crescent running from the capital through Atlanta to New Orleans; the Montrealer, connecting DC with New England and Canada; the National Limited from New York to Kansas City; the Silver Meteor and the Champion from New York to Florida and the North Coast Hiawatha from Chicago to Seattle. The much reduced network would still reach 91% of present passengers and would connect with the 25 largest cities, barring Atlanta, Cincinnati and Dallas-Fort Worth, while saving $1.4 billion in subsidies over the next four years according to Adams. Since neither house voted the proposal down by the end of May 1979, it automatically went into effect in October 1979. It might not have got through so readily if the queues at the gas pumps had not been confined to California in May 1979. A month later, with riots over gas in Levittown Pennsylvania and with the disruption of intercity travel due to grounded DC-10s and a surge of Amtrak bookings, it might have seemed inpolitic.

The influence of the World Bank, the premier lending agency for road building to the poorer nations of the world, has been exerted for the more widespread extension of a rudimentary road network to encourage agricultural commerce. Yet some of the grandiose schemes of the underdeveloped world are conceived in terms of national macho and militaristic vision rather than commercial speculation. The building of the Belem-Brasilia highway in 1964 as the first leg of an Amazon Basin network was primarily a matter of establishing territorial domination and precluding incursions by Venezuela, Ecuador, Colombia and Peru in a region where territorial issues are settled by the principle of *uti possidetis de facto*. Settlement to establish squatters' rights requires roads.

In the richer nations where the frontier is closed, new roads are built to enhance an existing dense network and provide facilities more in keeping with the needs of motor vehicles. In 1924 Piero Puricelli,

a Milanese engineer and entrepreneur, with the backing of the Italian
Touring Club and Benito Mussolini, showed the way with an auto-
strada connecting Milano and Varese. In 1934 Hitler established a
unified road construction agency and by 1939 2,300 miles of Auto-
bahnen had been built. It was not till after the War that the opportunity
presented itself to promoters elsewhere. In the USA, the Eisenhower
administration sold the Interstate system to congress as a civil defence
measure. Few would gainsay such a project in 1956. Economic appriasal
came after the event. Friedlaender's (1965) ex post evaluation of the
network suggests that *in toto* the system produces a positive net present
value; however, it is far from being the best possible investment of
funds in transport. In many rural areas, the likely level of traffic is too
small to justify Interstate standard roads. Because no minimum standards were imposed and because the states bore only 10% of the total
cost, state highway departments which built the roads had little incentive to ensure economy and efficiency. Concrete was poured far in
excess of any conceivable need. Two-lane roads would have achieved
essentially the same operating costs as four-lane roads in many cases.
The cost of the whole system could have been considerably lowered
without any appreciable reduction in benefits. This does not hold for
the lengths of Interstate which penetrate metropolitan settlements,
where they satisfied a strong pent-up demand. It is possible to argue,
however, that marginal cost pricing of urban road space might well
reduce congestion and increase benefits. The geographical impact of
the Interstate system was appraised by Promboin (1971). He found
that he could not reject the possibility that the stock of Interstate
Highways had no effect on local economies on the basis of state level
statistics. Much of the country, including the Midwest heartland,
appeared to be totally unaffected by the construction of the system
or the additional capacity it provided. In the Mountain states, with
sparse populations, where enormous lengths of road were laid down to
span the open spaces, the system did have a noticeable effect on employment. It was only in the Southeast that the capacity of the system
had a marginally significant positive effect, overcoming a bottleneck
due to limited roadspace. The evidence of changes in employment and
income at the state level, then, does suggest that *if* any regional economy
benefited it was the South. This could be claimed as additionally
meritorious in terms of equity, raising the level of personal well being
in the poorest area up towards that of the rest of the country. What is
clear is that neither at the regional nor the local level is the incidence
of benefits uniform. Not only were regions of the nation differentially

influenced, but also it is plain that in order to trace the distribution of wealth involved we need to go to a very fine geographical level of resolution. Work on the detailed effects of road building in particular areas such as Appalachian Georgia (e.g. Wheeler, Pannel and Farkas 1977) reveals that little urban and industrial activity has accompanied the building of Interstate in such areas, where they operate as routes of passage. Kenyon (1978) examined population changes in Southern Interstate 'corridors' in comparison with the interstices of the lattice, and his results suggest that in the 1960s the corridors did not enjoy a growth rate too different from that of the South as a whole. Parts of corridors adjacent to metropolitan areas grew rapidly, along with these cities.

Figure 35 juxtaposes the rate of county population changes between 1960 and 1970 in the South with the extent of the network in 1979. The growth of the Floridian and coastal population had begun in the 1950s prior to the building of Interstates paralleling the Atlantic and penetrating the peninsula and Gulf coast. It is thus difficult to credit the amenity and oil and gas field based developments causally to increased accessibility. Much of the growth in southwest Florida was far from Interstate exits, as were the bayou developments of Louisiana and the population growth in the Ozarks. Nor is population decline confined to the interstices of the network. I55 cuts through the dwindling population of the Delta country and bottom lands of Arkansas. I77 did not deter the decline of Appalachian population nor did I65 hinder the drop in southern Alabama. The suburban growth of the interior South did spread around the principal foci of the network in Atlanta, Jackson, Little Rock, Nashville, Lexington, Richmond and the Triangle of North Carolina. The system was of course designed to join these places, which had already shown up as the poles of attraction in the flux of population and activities. In strategic terms these centres would probably have grown in size anyway without the Interstate links between them. However, the shape of that growth might have been more compact were it not for the lengths of highway designed to serve the urban diurnal flow. The vast spread of residential and occupational land uses can partly be considered as a local, tactical effect of the junctions of the Interstate system.

In summary we may postulate that although the system emphasized the advantages of pre-ordained foci of growth, it did little to ameliorate the geography of structural decline wrought by agricultural evolution and the passing of hillbound cultural isolation. Indeed, the driving of new roads may well have accelerated these processes by bringing

Figure 35 Percent Change in Population by Counties of the South : 1960-1970, and Interstate Highways as of 1970

0   100   200   300   MILES

Scale   1: 5,000,000

PERCENT   CHANGE

GAIN   LOSS

■ 13.3 OR OVER   □ 10 OR OVER

▨ UNDER 13.3   □ UNDER 10

—— INTERSTATE

urban society closer.

In bringing the resources and markets of the South nearer to those in the rest of the continent, the Interstate may have merely reduced the movement costs of developments which would have taken place anyway. To employ the simple, static theory of land value of chapter 2, pushing a road into an agricultural interior from a point on the coast will merely change the location of a given amount of production if demand for the product is perfectly inelastic. In this case the benefits of the road will be merely in the reduction of movement costs for existing production. At the other extreme, with perfectly elastic demand, the maximum expansion of production will occur, extending the margins of commercial intercourse nearly everywhere. In the case of the South, the expanding use of the amenities of the region and its resources do not constitute a mobile use of land, and much the same areas would have been inhabited by a growing population without the new roads. Changing comparative advantage in the post-war decades resulted in the replacement of much cotton acreage with poultry, soybean, dairy, beef and horticultural production. Cotton is traded on the world market and from the local viewpoint demand is very elastic. The newer products are for domestic and even local consumption and the demand for them tends to be more inelastic. Winsberg (1979) could find little statistical evidence that the Interstates have influenced the location of agricultural production significantly. There was greater growth along north-south corridors as compared with east-west alignments, but this suggests the influence of the South's terms of trade with the rest of the economy rather than an independent consequence of road building.

In gauging the utility of a public work to set against its cost, the appropriate measure is the consumer surplus generated over and above that which would arise from inaction. If a road does not generate trade and travel which would not have flowed in its absence, then its benefits consist merely of the reduction in movement cost it occasioned for the given flow. It is difficult to avoid the conclusion that a considerable part of the present volume of traffic would have flowed in, out and within the South in the absence of the Interstate network. As to its savings in transport costs, given that the system in some cases increases the circuity of journeys and, since 1973, can only legally be used at less than its design speed, there must be some reservation even about these. To count against whatever savings it generated must go the surplus of social capital it created. This is not only visible in wasted road space but also in the ancillary facilities of road travel, gas stations, eating places, motels and the settlements they support. The pathetic prodigality of this can be seen along US 41 through Georgia and ALT 27 in Florida, redounded by I75. This superficial glance at the facts would encourage the conclusion that 'this most massive public works project in the history of mankind' has had a negligible economic effect on the well being and geography of people in the South and that its rate of return on investment is woefully inadequate, representing a misplacement of resources. What benefits were generated could have been achieved with a much more modest outlay. Perhaps the strongest and most historically significant results of these roads are the intangible, 'embodied' effects as Fogel (1964) called them. These are the lasting marks a particular technology can leave on polity and society. Although it signalled no great technical departure, the uniformity and standardization encouraged by the Interstate system may have played its role in eroding the separate regional identity of the South as much in terms of diffusing Southern style throughout the land as imposing Yankee ways on the South.

The lobby for a UK motorway network dates back to the turn of the century when the Prime Minister, Balfour, favoured 'great highways constructed for rapid motor traffic and confined to motor traffic'. Motorists, hauliers, engineers and car makers formed the Road Improvement Association in 1905, harnessing the energies of Lord Montagu of Beaulieu. A paper on 'The Economics of Motorways' read by R. Gresham Cooke before the Institute of Highway Engineers in November 1947, suggesting that the economic case should be impressed upon the government, triggered the formation of a Joint Committee of the British Road Federation, Institution of Highway Engineers and Society for Motor Manufacturers and Traders to press the suit. This bore fruit finally in the Macmillan era where the power of the Special Roads Act of 1949 was used to authorize the Preston by-pass section of what was to become the M6, which was completed in 1958. The first economic appraisal by Coburn, Beesley and Reynolds (1960) was after the fact of the building of its subject, the M1. By the time a bureaucratic, formal procedure for economic appraisal had been elaborated the main members of the network were in place and it was brought to bear on the marginal components and the urban stretches which were put off till last because of the political difficulties they presented. In the 1960s economists' doubts about the focus of a complete standardized national network as opposed to the more local relief of bottlenecks fed a growing opposition from the 'environmental' lobby, decrying a threat to the landscape. Extension of the M6 intruded on the fringes of the Lake District and it was proposed to cut the M40 across the Chiltern escarpment and the M3 through the meadows of the Itchen valley in sight of Winchester Cathedral. The linking of the ends of roads terminating in London and the ringing of London with a circumferential motorway proved a sticking point. In 1978 the Leitch Committee proposed changes both in the manner of forecasting the appraisal and in procedural matters, so that interested parties could take part in the design and planning process, not merely in the final adjudication of a given plan. This, if accepted, will help reduce the impression that the road builders are foisting pet schemes upon the public for their professional aggrandizement. There is still pressure from areas of high unemployment, such as the north-east, for road building to provide a developmental stimulus. The evidence is now coming in that these hopes are false or exaggerated. Dodgson's study of the effects of the trans-Pennine M62 (1974) came up with manufacturing cost savings due to motorway building of the order of 0.3%, which translated into a minuscule potential increase in employment in the vicinity of the road. This advantage evaporates if there is substantial road building elsewhere in the country. In long-established industrial economies it does seem that the effectiveness of road building in stimulating regional growth is limited and uncertain. Indeed, reducing transport costs to the peripheral or remote areas of an economy, such as England's northeast or Appalachia, may have a reverse effect from the one desired. For products and services which enjoy decreasing costs presently produced in both the affluent centre of the economy and the economically declining fringe, protected there from competition by high transport costs, lower transport costs may result in greater concentration of production at the centre and further deceleration at the fringe as its formerly monopolized market is penetrated by central producers. In such light it is not surprising that in times when government expenditure must be cut back there is no hesitation in cutting the road programme by either party. The post-election Tory budget of June 1979 cut it by £10 million. In many instances Interstate and motorway-type construction is providing surplus capacity. That should not mask the fact that in poorer nations where transport facilities are vestigial, lack of roads may present a bottleneck to regional or national growth or, indeed, national existence.

Bridges and tunnels

Because of their enormous cost and because they traverse impediments which have inhibited interaction previously, bridges and tunnels constitute a special class of network investment. Because they are frequently linking places between which traffic has been light in the past, their outcomes and, thus, their expected benefits are more speculative than most transport investments. These risky propositions have given the public sector some cause for pause and contemplation. It could be said that welfare economics was invented to deal with bridge investment. Dupuit certainly laid the groundwork as a member of the Départment des Ponts et Chaussées. Many issues have been clarified in the light of these exceptional forms of transport link. Quarmby's study of the Morecambe Bay Barrage (1970) did much to clarify the importance of the geographical framework employed in an analysis. Costs and benefits change radically according to the geographical limits within which they are accounted. The benefit of increased employment, counted within a narrow definition of the relevant territory, may be cancelled out if the scope of accounting is expanded to the regional or national level, since the investment may merely have redistributed an exogenously determined total of activity, having no independent effect. One locality's gain is merely others' losses, signifying nothing in terms of overall national well being.

To the engineer works of this nature present the biggest challenge and greatest satisfaction in their design and completion, so their professional enthusiasm is not unnatural. The difficulties of design and construction also make these the most prone to potentially catastrophic error. A case in point in terms of fortune of design foresight was the Tacoma Narrows suspension Bridge in Washington which collapsed after achieving a harmonic resonance in its vibrations. The Severn Bridge, opened in 1966 to shorten the connection to South Wales, has proven faulty, but only to the point that its strength and carrying capacity are reduced pending repair. The need for more difficult repairs and, thus, closing of lanes is likely to continue into the future. The dramatic example of failure in construction was the nearly simultaneous collapse of the Yarra Bridge in Australia and the Milford Haven Bridge in Wales. These box-girder structures are perfectly sound when complete, but before they are finally tied in, carelessness over a few bolts can cause disaster. On the positive side successful innovation in engineering can radically reduce the cost of overcoming physical barriers. In recent decades, methods of tunnelling in both hard and soft ground have been enormously improved and thus may generate more subterranean proposals in the future.

For the politician the symbolic value of these structures is enormous. It seems that every river crossing in Louisiana was accomplished by the efforts of Governor Huey Long. Such public works, continuously employed by travellers, are the most widely remarkable and visible of advertisements that your constituents are getting their votes' worth. The Humber Estuary Bridge, for example, evidently had its origin in a promise by Barbara Castle in the Hull by-election campaign of 1968. Now it is clear that the decision to go ahead with this project was informed by gross underestimates of cost, which have risen from £11 million to £67 million, and overestimates of potential traffic. Recent extensions of the M62 and M18 make the route redundant apart from traffic to and from Grimsby, which has no reason to amount to much. The statutory authority set up to repay the government the 75% of the construction cost that they loaned will face a stern, if not impossible task. Current estimates by the parliamentary public accounts committee of potential traffic suggest that even tolls of 80p for a car and over £6 for the heaviest truck will not recoup sufficient to pay even the interest on the loan for twenty years to come, and will, indeed, deter potential traffic.

Tunnels and bridges, with their limited access points, make it possible to exclude non-payers from their use at very little cost. Market allocation by a price is readily achieved. The cost of pricing consists of toll booth operation and police back-up plus the waiting time of users at toll stations. This may be greatly reduced by automatic basket collection, which France and the US discovered long ago but Britain for some reason ignores. If a user charge system is politically acceptable, the *ex ante* investment analysis can be reduced to a comparison of discounted revenue and costs. *Ex post facto,* however, when the resources used in construction are a bygone and have no opportunity cost, recouping investment cost and pricing considerations become divorced. The appropriate pricing question is what price at least covers operating costs and makes the maximal contribution to debt repayment. It is inappropriate to charge a price reflecting some average expected contribution to funding the debt.

Canals

Waterborne traffic has increased in significance lately as radar has made night-time operations feasible on big rivers and as pushing power units have increased efficiency of traction. The introduction of ocean carriers that carry and distribute their cargo in barges, by-passing ports, and containerization have added to the potential. Since it suits the style of France's engineering administrative elite it is not surprising that the Rhone-Rhine Canal will be completed in 1985. Increasing Rhine and Danube traffic in ore, phosphates and building materials, etc., have encouraged Germany to join these two with a canal in the best traditions of the Mittelland Canal connecting the Oder to the Rhine. In the USA, the delight with which the Corps of Engineers scar the land with trenches is being called into question. This, of course, was the agency which invented cost-benefit analysis to clothe their activity with the economic respectability the twentieth century has come to require. The most controversial of their current projects is the Tennessee-Tombigbee waterway which they claim will turn northeastern Mississippi into a new Ruhr. Many farmers, state officials, and environmentalists do not see this as an unmixed blessing. The Louisville and Nashville Railroad which currently carries Kentucky and West Virginia coal to the Gulf coast, naturally objects and has combined with the Environmental Defence Fund to halt the scheme with a lawsuit charging that the Corps decision to increase channel width from 170 feet to 300 feet in order to be 'modern and efficient' was not legally authorized. The railroad also point out that they could carry the coal traffic for 200 years for the cost of this project. A major source of disquiet over Corps of Engineers' economic calculations is their use of the government borrowing rate at the time of initial authorization as a discount rate. In the case of the Tennessee-Tombigbee the date was 1946 and the rate 3%. This obviously does not represent the opportunity cost of resources being used now. The rate of return of $1.20 for every dollar of the $2 billion which will be spent, the Corps calculates, would not survive an increase in the discount rate. There are precedents which must make the Corps nervous of this situation. The Cross-Florida Barge Canal, authorized in 1936, on which construction was suspended in 1972, was finally killed in 1979. The major objectors were again the environmentalists' lobby and the railroads. In this case the Corps were hard pressed to defend the project in terms of potential traffic and would never reveal the source of their projections, claiming that disclosure would violate the interests of the enterprises involved.

Pipelines

Pipelines too have been subject to opposition on grounds of environmental degradation both at their terminals and along their length. The public reason for Sohio's decision in March 1979 to cancel a scheme to convert an old gas pipeline to carry its Alaskan crude from the southern California coast to points east, was the tangle of environmental regulations which presented a cost in aggravation sufficient to tilt a break-even proposition into a loser. Oil companies can stand aggravation when it pays, and in reality the evaporation of a West coast glut and the Iranian shortfall probably swung the balance of advantage in favour of shipping by small tanker through the Panama Canal when necessary. This has dashed the hopes of the Los Angeles area air-quality management agency that it could use leverage over the pipeline to get oil company cooperation in reducing air pollution. The Alaskan pipeline to Valdez overcame environmentalist objections about its effect on permafrost and animal migration. The negotiations involved diplomatic and political jostling between federal and state government, oil multi-nationals and, because the options involved pipes or rails through Canada, Ottawa. The strategies involved go much deeper than appears on the surface. Although it was earmarked for the US domestic market, a major extractor of North Slope oil is BP, who would find it convenient to serve their Japanese market from Alaska, thereby releasing more of their Middle Eastern output for the European and US east coast market. From a global viewpoint this would be the most efficient disposition. Whether good sense or US patriotic fervour prevails will depend on many things. After the calculations of cost and the avowed intentions of treaties between states and corporations, we are left with the manoeuvring in the leeway and loopholes left open for the future moves in this game of chance to decide the actual course of events. The prospects of piping coal in slurry from the Wyoming Basin to the Midwest and East have been costed, computed and compared. The eventual outcome will depend on judgements on the water supply and its alternative uses; the price of crude oil; the political power of the railroads individually — for some, such as Union Pacific, are coal owners; the strength of the agricultural and environmentalist lobby and the balance of power among various energy-related interests.

Airports

We viewed the principal interests involved in locating air travel terminals in the discussion of international transport of the last chapter. What makes this a question worth raising both at the international and domestic levels is the 17% per annum increase in air travel of the past couple of years. Competitive pressure on the North Atlantic routes and domestic deregulation and traffic growth in the US are having an effect by example and leverage throughout the globe. The downward pressure on air fares is certainly being felt on intra-European routes and the EEC Transport Commissioner is encouraging these adjustments. The potential in Europe is possibly greater than in the US since the state airline cartel has held prices at three times their US level. It has been projected that air travel will grow tenfold between 1970 and 2000 and the trend is well under way. The introduction of wide-bodied aircraft held off the press on runway capacity but terminal building and services capacity is sorely pressed. More rational pricing and better layout planning may sustain much of the growth and reduce the capacity choke but undoubtedly new airports will be necessary, and already plans for offshore facilities and more fanciful solutions are coming off the drawing board. Having learned once that it is a logistic rather than an exponential world we live in, maybe greater flexibility will be incorporated in the search for a solution to this problem in the future than was displayed in the Roskill exercise on London's third airport in the early 1970s. Already it is dawning on the economists that the current surge of demand was carried on a general upswing of affluence and may as easily attenuate with a recession of activity.

CHAPTER 12

Local Transport

Institutional arrangements

Our daily encounter with the ways and means of circulation within our own community, be it in town or country, is our closest involvement with the transport system. This intimacy and the fact that such facilities are provided collectively, or closely governed by legal controls, means that here we can exert influence as voters. Not only do most of us use roads, buses or railways daily, but also many are employed in furnishing such services. Employment in providing transport creates a potential source of political patronage and a pressure group in favour of certain forms of transport. The problems of personal, daily travel then become highly sensitive political issues. The cost and convenience of people's journey to work in particular is a major item in the household budget and consciousness. It is related to the cost of housing in terms of the price paid for accessibility in the bundle of qualities that give real estate its value. The joint consideration of the ease of travel and the value of property makes governmental handling of travel-related matters a potentially crucial test of political success. What drove Carter's support away in the summer of 1979 was the administration's failure to manage the shortage of gasoline. According to the opinion polls, Salt II, the Egyptian-Israeli pact and all else dwindled to insignificance for a public faced with queues at the gas pump. Anything that makes getting to work or to the store more irksome must visit itself on the heads of those who attained power on the promise of curing the ills of life.

The governmental provision of roads is justified in terms of their being essentially collective in nature and difficult to exclude non-payers from using. Whatever efforts are made at generating pseudo-revenues as streams of social benefit in cost-benefit calculations, in the last resort decisions on road building are political. The functionary vested with decisive authority may delegate it to an administrative formula, but this in itself represents a political judgement. Although such bureaucratic procedures may screen out the more obviously unviable pet schemes, promoters do learn to jump through the hoops. Besides which, the margins of uncertainty involved are so great and the intangible considerations so potent in the more important cases that precise numerical thresholds are inappropriate. Shrewd political resolution of conflicting interests is the apposite art.

A longstanding institutional problem for growing towns has been the failure of the geographical definition of the local government jurisdiction to keep pace with the growth of the community. The underbounding of what operates as an articulate local economy leads to problems of spillover. Facilities built or subsidized for collective enjoyment by the central city's exchequer are available to those beyond its taxing jurisdiction. Roads and railways within the city are used to suburbanites who are not in the city's tax base. This usually represents a serious maldistribution of wealth. The city frequently houses the poorer sections of society, more prone to unemployment, while suburbanites are characteristically better off in secure jobs. The collective provision or subsidy of transport facilities by the government of the city redistributes wealth to the peripheral commuter from inner city residents. This is compounded by the fact that it is the suburban commuter who makes the strongly focused trip to the white-collar jobs of the centre, while working-class jobs are more diffusely scattered and take less advantage of the intensely used radial routes on which collective attention is usually lavished. Associated with this problem of fragmented authority is that of coordinating network planning among a multiplicity of local governments.

In many cities bus and rail operations have been purchased by government, usually to assure the continuation of cheap service. If this is not so, such public transport prices and services are stringently controlled by regulatory bodies. The case for public ownership or strict regulation arose from the clamour of larger operators to put down competition. In London claims of cut-throat and 'wasteful' competition and 'piracy' by small bus companies, threatening public safety by their frantic efforts to serve customers, causing congestion and 'creaming-off' traffic at temporal and geographical peaks, were raised by the monopolistic Underground Group, which had acquired a controlling interest in tubes, trams and buses by 1918. Having the ear of Parliament, the monopoly was rewarded with the London Traffic Act in 1924, which gave the Minister of Transport power to regulate or prohibit bus traffic on certain streets while the licensing authority, the Metropolitan

Police Commissioner, could designate approved routes for bus operations. This effectively put down the competition, leaving the way open for the monopoly to take over many of the independents. The act did not abolish the traffic congestion which had been used to justify it, but its continuation was used as evidence to justify the strangling of competition. The official view was that 'no lasting solution of the London passenger transport problem can be secured as long as the present competitive methods are pursued. The unified management of the underground and local railways, tramways and omnibuses will provide the only permanent solution of the whole problem.' The Tory bid to effect a private sector monopoly to 'coordinate' transport was defeated in 1928 but the succeeding Labour government provided for a public monopoly with the 1933 London Passenger Transport Act. The leader of the private Underground Group was made chairman of the public London Passenger Transport Board, with a monopoly of passenger transport, apart from cars, taxis and mainline railways, over an area of 2,000 square miles, charged with providing 'adequate travelling facilities in the Metropolitan Area upon a remunerative basis and at reasonable economic fares'. The fare structure was standardized and this resulted in a great deal of cross-subsidy, with paying services carrying losers. The creation of this largest transport undertaking in the world has been repeated in spirit with the New York Metropolitan Transit Authority and Chicago Transit Authority, and on around the world. In the USA, of late the mainline railroads have fallen over themselves to unload their commuter services on to the public sector. In Chicago this accompanied an extension of the geographical limits of the monopoly to cover the mainline rail commuting hinterland as the Regional Transportation Authority. The justification for these monopolies with their varying degrees of political control and financial support thus lies in the conditions of the 1920s and 1930s and a myth of the delights of 'coordination', which never seem to have quite come off. Characteristically public transport is in the red and unsatisfactory.

Another institutional response to urban transport problems took shape in the 1950s, as central government required the planning of extensions to the road network to be on a geographical base which encompassed the daily travel hinterland of major cities. In 1954 the Detroit Area Transportation Study was established to be followed in 1958 by the Chicago Area Transportation Study, which extended its domain across state lines, curling around the southern end of Lake Michigan into Lake and Porter counties of Indiana. These agencies coordinated the efforts of cities, suburbs and states to plan road building and attract Federal funds for this purpose. In 1961 the fashion extended itself across the Atlantic and the London Traffic Survey employed the methods and some personnel from the USA to forecast traffic for road network planning purposes. Sir Colin Buchanan's report *Traffic in Towns* in 1963 stressed the need for a concerted effort to plan land uses and transport facilities jointly. This was taken up by the Ministers of Transport and of Local Government, who put out a joint circular in 1964 stressing the need for land use/transportation studies. The Ministry of Transport offered expert advice and to cover 50% of the cost of these exercises. The West Midlands, Teesside, Manchester, Merseyside and the West Riding had taken up the opportunity by 1967. That the strategic, long-term planning of roads could not be conducted in isolation from land use plans and projections was obvious. That the structural amendment of the road system could not be carried out independently of rail planning was clear. What became clearer as experience taught its lessons was that these structural questions were intimately connected with short-term operational matters, such as parking charges, traffic controls and public transportation prices. For rail or bus system planning where funding depends to some extent on potential revenue, short-run questions of price and the fare box are of fundamental importance in investment appraisal. The questions of the geographical extent of an operable rail network and the necessary tax base to subsidize building a system which would most likely not cover its costs out of fare revenue jointly occasioned the foundation of the Bay Area Rapid Transit system, after residents of the communities around San Francisco Bay voted in its favour as an electoral proposition.

In a centralized state such as the UK, where local authority is delegated from the national level, it is feasible to catch up with the expansion of the growth of agglomerations of activities by reforming local government so that its boundaries and functional organizations conform to changed circumstances. This can seldom be done without opposition from associations and interests which will be damaged in the change. Its shape is bound to be distorted from the pure needs of administrative efficiency by the partisan interests of the reforming government; however, many spillover and planning coordination problems can be resolved in part by constitutional change. London again acted as front runner, and the Greater London Council (GLC) was established by the London Government Act of 1963 as the strategic planning authority responsible for major arterial roads, outside the trunk road system. The Transport (London) Act of 1969 added responsibility for London Transport, formerly vested in the Minister for

Transport. The GLC was empowered to determine levels of service and financial objectives and to make current and capital grants to London Transport and to British Rail for metropolitan services, and to plan the transport system entire. Local government reform in the rest of the country under the 1966 Local Government Act was accompanied by the establishment of Passenger Transport Authorities (PTA) for the four major conurbations centering on Liverpool, Manchester, Birmingham and Newcastle, by the 1968 Transport Act. The operations of individual municipal services were combined for day-to-day management under a professional executive reporting to the representatives of constituent local authorities who composed the PTA. Cooperation with the nationalized railways and newly formed National Bus Company was also required in the form of agreements on fare levels and service patterns and railway services to be sustained by subsidies from local sources. Whether all of this coordination and integration has had a salutary effect is not visible in terms of either service or financial performance or in terms of the quality of planning. If anything coordination has meant a good deal of confusion as to responsibility and objectives. In the GLC the integration of transport planning and land use planning was secured by the creation of an agency for liaison whose chief function seems to have been to keep the planners out of the engineers' hair. At the level of central government, the integration was embodied in the creation of the Department of the Environment, combining the Ministries of Transport, Housing and Local Government and the Board of Works. The drive of the Ministry of Transport to build roads was to be tamed by the influence of sharing a common roof and super-minister with the bureaucracies dealing with the other components of the good life. The old ministerial divisions remained divided by more than their location in the separate blocks of the 'toast-rack' on Marsham Street. The rivalry and antipathy to the others' viewpoint was in many ways heightened by proximity, and the opposition between engineers, economists and planners broke into acrimonious vituperation on occasions. The super-ministry has now been disassembled and with it perhaps the tensions of sibling rivalry among bureaucratic specialists.

The federal system of the USA does not permit sweeping change of local government, for its authority is not delegated but constitutionally defined by exception. The Constitution of the US in effect lists the exceptions arrogated by the federal triumvirate of legislature, executive and judiciary. The partisan and personal interests tied up in the structure of local government make it unlikely that it will in general be radically altered to reflect the appropriate scale of community for efficient transport planning and administration. The rapidly expanding cities of the south and west, such as Houston, Miami and Atlanta, are not encircled by long-established urban communities in the way that Chicago, for example, is. Annexation of rural land presents no great difficulty and the city boundaries can follow the subdivider and developer. The built-up area and the jurisdiction coincide fairly well. Hemmed in by Evanston, Skokie, Oak Park, Cicero, Berwyn, Oak Lawn, Calumet City and the Indiana line, the city of Chicago cannot extend its jurisdiction over its commuting hinterland. To acquire federal road-building dollars CATS was set up as a quasi-government. Now in the realm of mass transit the Chicago Transit Authority, which ran services beyond the city which governed it, has been combined with municipal bus services into the Regional Transportation Authority (RTA), responsible for elevated rail, bus and mainline rail services. A flaw in the organization which weakens it politically lies in its broad geographical limits. The RTA takes in Cook and the surrounding tier of five counties. This pushes the boundary far beyond the area of Chicago's dominance as a place of work. Communities in west McHenry county, for example, are chagrined at having to bear a burden of which they are innocent. No amount of subsidized bus services which they do not need will make up for having to carry part of the burden of Chicago's rail services.

Regulation and subsidy

The regulation of price, entry, service standards, vehicle design and the exercise of the taxation and expenditure functions of government have all been used with varying degrees of success to achieve politically desired ends in providing for local circulation. We have seen how price and entry controls and, indeed, police powers were employed in the creation of monopolies such as London Transport with the stated objective of providing 'adequate' service at 'reasonable' fares. Given their quasi-political status, such monopolies frequently find that 'reasonable' has a political definition and is not necessarily compatible with the objective of 'remunerative' operation which is also in their founding remit. It is very difficult to persuade political masters to allow fare increases in line with rising costs, especially when they are fighting inflation or an electoral campaign. The 'first past the post' constituency arrangements of the US and UK accentuate the significance of marginal constituencies which change political complexion easily. These are characteristically white-collar suburbs. From this it follows that the needs of commuters are very close to politicians' and ministers' hearts.

More directly than this, the financial failures of public transport are partly owed to their employment of large numbers of people at high wages in secure, undemanding jobs. In the case of Chicago, there is more than a suspicion that the statutory obligations to provide a high service level with 24-hour service on the elevated rail network and bus service on a mile-square grid throughout the city, which burdens the CTA, is not unrelated to the rich source of job patronage this provides for the Democratic party machine. The employees of the CTA were one of Richard Daley's chief sources of strength, a strength that kept him mayor and the Democratic party in power for over a quarter of a century.

The licensing of taxis is in places such as London a matter of the police exercising their authority in the interest of public safety. In London's case the excessively high standards set and the limitation of entry by this means contort the market seriously — especially beyond the limits of the strict control of pricing. When a large demand exists for travel beyond the radius where fares are strictly prescribed, as in the case of travel from Heathrow to the West End, the limited supply of taxis increases the potential for price gouging. The extension of the Piccadilly Line to the airport obviously diminishes this temptation. To circumvent stringent police requirements for vehicles and drivers, first mini-cab and then a host of radio-controlled, moonlighting private car operations were spawned. This is competition for some part of the market but it does leave a margin of inconvenience in having to phone rather than hail a cab, which protects the short-haul, downtown trade for the licensed hackney. The extent of undersupply which licensing systems can lead to is evident when licences can be bought and sold, as is the case in US cities. The price of a cabby's shield in New York or Chicago is proof positive that entry restrictions are keeping numbers below the level which the balance of public revealed preference and the cost of providing service would dictate. The limitation on entry and the prices set are generating profits in excess of normal returns, sufficient to warrant paying a hefty chunk of cash for the privilege of plying for hire. Where monopoly profits are made available with the acquisition of a licence from a government agency, then the potential for corruption exists and it has not always been shunned. In the case of taxicabs, safety and economic regulation have been badly confused in many places. Many innovatory enterprises which would convenience the travelling public have been severely restricted or driven to a clandestine and insecure mode of operation. It was only the oil crisis of 1973 which finally lifted the restriction on making payments for a shared car or minibus ride in the UK, thereby solving many rural or low-density industrial area commuting problems. Making a payment to a mate who drives a van load to the pit is the most suitable arrangement for many South Wales coal-mining commuters. This was illegal before the panic brought about by OPEC'S machinations. Lifted as an emergency measure, the regulations have not been reinstated.

As opposed to the underprovision fostered by regulations in dense urban markets, local transport for rural communities is frequently kept in excess of needs by bureaucratic control. As part of the price for monopoly over a lucrative route, railways or bus companies were expected to cross-subsidize lightly patronized routes which would not pay at regular scheduled prices. Those who used a lucrative route were charged in excess of cost by a monopolist who then applied some part of the surplus to cover the failure of the fare charged to people on the unremunerative route to meet the cost of service there. Whether the implied transfer of income was desirable in terms of equity, whether it was progressive or not, was not taken into account. When applied in a metropolitan market, it would normally mean that inner city residents on dense bus or rail lines were paying the subsidy for those who dwelt in suburban sparsity. This would involve a reduction of working-class incomes and effectively raise middle-class incomes. Thus a major objection to regulated cross-subsidies is that they carry no guarantee of equity and indeed, given the social structure of our urban world, for personal travel they have an inbuilt regressive bias. In terms of the political structure, the over-representation of rural interests in electoral systems makes such subsidies politically prudent. A more efficacious solution to the problem of providing mobility to those who do not have a car in the suburbs or the country, particularly the old or infirm, is to identify them individually and provide them with the wherewithal to hire a taxi when they need it. If this was accompanied by a relaxation of restrictions on the number and variety of services which could be made available, then much of the rural mobility problem would evaporate. To provide full-blown bus or train scheduled services for the smattering of those without access to a car is wasteful.

There are bases for regulatory intervention which, although they have economic ramifications, do not operate directly to distort markets. The regulation of vehicle designs and standards for the sake of safety, cleanliness and the conservation of energy is an increasingly significant role of government. The various objectives of the role are somewhat confused if not in diametric opposition to each other, particularly in the USA. General Motors, Ford and Chrysler are faced with a deadline of 1985 to meet a raft of regulations requiring improved fuel economy, reduced noxious emissions and improved safety. The Secretary of Transportation has set a goal for the national fleet of cars of an average of 50 miles per gallon by 2000. The National Highway Traffic Safety Administration is empowered to set corporate average fuel economy levels which the output of each car maker must comply with. These decree that companies' fleet averages must improve by 2 mpg till 1983, by 1 mpg in 1984 and ½ mpg in 1985 to achieve an average of 27.5 mpg in that year. The industry is arguing for an even spread of gains stretched out to 1988. Even without regulatory pressure, the increasing cost of fuel, even if visited upon the public as queues at the pump with controlled prices, is having an effect on the demand for new cars. There is every sign that demand is elastic to a rise in fuel costs in terms of the size and fuel efficiency of vehicles. The composition of the US fleet has changed radically since 1973, and this has been marked by the success of Japanese and European manufacturers in the US market. Detroit is responding with the search for a 'world car' to compete not only at home but also throughout the world. Ford's Fiesta, GM's Chevettes and X cars are the first steps in this battle. As well as reductions in size and weight and a switch to front-wheel drive, aerodynamic improvements are being sought to enable cars to slip through the air with a 10-20% reduction in energy required. For power, the diesel alternative is being pursued by GM, but the particular emissions involved may come up against a limit which the Environmental Protection Agency is proposing to set in 1979. The soot output can only be reduced at the cost of a loss of efficiency. Ford are seeking to by-pass the more costly manufacturing noise, vibration and power performance of the diesel by betting on the stratified-charge, programmed combustion engine, which increases mileage by 20% with lower pollutant output. The pumps and fuel injectors for this require machining to microscopic tolerances, and whether these can be mass produced remains to be seen. GM is leading in the search for a battery-operated electric car. Currently the Electrovette can get up to 55 mph but needs recharging every 50 miles.

The efforts to improve the energy efficiency of conventional engines as well as diesels clash with pollution regulations. The mandatory catalytic converter, requiring the use of unleaded fuel, results in a 5-10% increase in consumption. Emissions have been reduced by 80% since controls were introduced in 1967. The rules require a 96% reduction by 1981. The car industry argue that the marginal cost of reduction increases steeply and that it will cost $59 million for every gain of a percentage point. Combining these costs with those of meeting mileage and safety regulations, it has been estimated that the big three will spend $18 billion between 1979 and 1985. Currently the cost of federal regulations amounts to over 10% of the price of a car at $666. According to the President of GM the price of a GM car by 1985 will be $945 more than it would have been without regulations. Obviously the price of these collective desiderata will be very visible and the weight of the benefit achieved by control will be contested, by the manufacturers at least.

One quite different form of intervention which held promise of reducing the cost and irritation of the daily tidal flow of urban travel is the institution of flexitime whereby employers lay down the minimum and maximum hours to be worked each day and employees carry 'debit' or 'credit' hours for up to a month. In World War II staggering of work hours was directly imposed explicitly to even out the load on public transport. 'Gleitzeit' was introduced on a voluntary basis in Germany in the 1960s with more general objectives of improving staff relationships and reducing absenteeism. However, these are achieved largely by presenting the opportunity to avoid the peak of the rush hour. The institution was exported to the UK in 1972 and government fostered it by example and exhortation rather than by impost. Over a quarter of Britain's office workers are now employed on this basis. The cost is some loss of productivity due to key people not being at their posts when needed. Coordinating a bureaucratic process when the work day is open-ended does present a serious problem. There are signs that the practice has diminished the intensity of the surges just before 9.00 a.m. and just after 5.00 p.m., which tax the means of travel and the temper of travellers so harshly. Although it is not imposed, we could look upon flexitime as a permissive instrument allowing a wider margin of autonomy and thus for more beneficial system performance through self-regulation of the individual participants. In effect it is an autonomous form of the operational methods of control which we turn to later.

In a more radical intervention in the customary timing of life, the Greek government have determined to cut down the break for lunch and a siesta in the middle of the day. The midday break is accompanied by a congested surge of traffic as people head to and from home. To reduce this will not only alleviate the traffic congestion of Athens but also cut fuel consumption by 15%, it is estimated.

Road pricing

The regulation of use of limited road capacity by some form of pricing has venerable, if not wholly successful, antecedents. It is still widely used in the form of a toll for bridges and tunnels. In the US prior to the inception of the Interstate programme, several localities built stretches of limited access urban road, financed by bond issues to be serviced by toll revenues. The Chicago Skyway coming in over Gary, Hammond and East Chicago to the south side is such a facility. The Tri-State Tollway was completed as part of the Interstate network to provide an outer belt by-pass of the congestion of the metropolitan core. With road budgets being cut back as austerity measures, with pressure from the continued increases in demand and with governments prone to market solutions gaining power, perhaps tolling will be resorted to as a means of financing new building elsewhere. It is not outside the realm of possibility to contemplate private road companies.

Aside from the question of finance of new construction, road pricing in the form of supplementary licensing has been contemplated, and indeed used, to dole out the use of limited existing capacity. Singapore undertook a bold experiment along these lines in 1974. Costly daily licences were required for cars entering the central area of the city through police-controlled portals. There is evidence that, initially at least, the price was set so high as to drive peak-hour volume far below the socially acceptable level. This represents a social waste, commuter adjustment took the form of travelling before the police inspection for the morning peak started. The surge of travel was shifted an hour forward in the day and the cost visited itself on society as the wasted time of workers spent hanging around downtown in the morning before business hours. Since no control was instituted for the evening peak on the grounds that only what goes in need come out, the evening peak retained its magnitude and time. Supplementary licensing was contemplated and rejected for London in 1975, largely on the grounds that it would diminish retail and service custom. The fact that commuter peak traffic runs quite smoothly and that the snarls of vehicles occur when 'essential' delivery vans and shopping traffic conflict during business hours, make it plain that a Singapore solution would be a waste of effort. In the USA similar proposals have proven equally unacceptable. Predictably the citizens of Madison, Wisconsin and Berkeley, California toyed with the idea of restraining traffic entering their downtown areas as a demonstration project funded by the Urban Mass Transportation Administration, even though neither city suffers severe traffic congestion. Similar plans were laid to restrict entry to Manhattan by high tolls on bridges. The legality of this is disputed between the Environmental Protection Agency with the support of the

US Court of Appeals, and the City of New York and the US Department of Transportation. Such efforts are usually met with opposition from owners of property and businesses downtown, who fear adverse effects on their income if traffic is deterred.

Physical restraint

As an alternative to price as a regulator there have been proposals and, indeed, experiments using queues as a controlled device for rationing or restricting traffic flowing into town centres. Such a scheme was rejected for London, but Nottingham instituted a 'ring and collar' arrangement of physical restraint whereby traffic lights were deliberately set to cause punitive waits on incoming routes in the morning. This was supplemented with a set of peripheral car parks and subsidized bus services into town. Singapore had employed the same device in their project. Nottingham, however, had no enormous traffic problem to start with, and the whole episode seems to have been an over-enthusiastic display of power by an ambitious mayor.

The more usual use of traffic signalling and control is to minimize the friction of traffic and maximize the efficiency with which the system is used. The initial calculation involves determining whether automatic signalled control saves more time for motorists than self-regulation at halt signs. For major intersections the British tradition includes the roundabout option, which terrifies drivers and engineers elsewhere, depending as it does on a level of courtesy and care which is beyond their expectations. The roundabout is really a cheap alternative to grade separation and a clover leaf of connecting ramps. For lower-order junctions, signals come into their own at volumes where the regulated throughput of consolidated slugs of traffic diminishes the waiting times resulting from seeking an acceptable gap to join or cross an opposing stream of traffic. If volumes are low enough, a degree of autonomy may be retained with pad-activated lights. At higher volumes a regular setting tied in with the other junctions in the vicinity or along a route is more suitable to coordinate flows and achieve platooning on main routes. It is evident that the systems effects in a road network become pronounced and widespread in towns, where link lengths are short and traffic volumes high. A hitch in the smooth operation of the system at one junction is rapidly transmitted back upstream to directly and indirectly connected parts of the network. The shortcomings of directing traffic at one junction with a limited scope of vision are obvious whenever a traffic light fails and a policeman attempts to establish order based on the limits of his eyesight. Usually traffic would fare better without his attentions. The effective control of traffic clearly needs to be informed by a broad area field of current knowledge of the state of the system. Chicago's freeway system, for example, is monitored on a regionwide basis with sensors picking up volumes and velocities continuously throughout the metropolitan area. This information is recorded and used for current traffic reports by radio stations, which in itself improves the self-regulation of traffic. Although intended to aid in real-time control it has not yet been hooked up to on and off ramp signals with a set of controlling rules and mechanisms. The data are subject to error for one thing. Trains passing close to roads register as surges of thousands of vehicles. The automatically sensed information needs visual checking and confirmation, which in Chicago can be done from the top of the Sears and the John Hancock towers on clear days, or from police helicopters. The gathering and broadcasting of knowledge of the current speeds and volumes on various routes does greatly help individuals in making their choices and results in a collective benefit by reducing congestion. Such surveillance systems have in addition been put to use in informing control devices such as the West London and Liverpool area traffic control schemes. In the Liverpool case the chief objective is to disentangle north—south traffic parallel to the Mersey from the east—west flow headed for the tunnels, the Pierhead and the ferries across the river to the Wirral in the rush hours. To this end, when electronic sensors embedded in the road surface at junctions pick up congestion as a reduction in speed, the controlling algorithm relieves the pressure by switching signals to red back upstream to prevent excessive bunching which will clog crossings and hinder the flow of the opposing stream of traffic. Thus, delays at the tunnel entrances are prevented from creating a continuous queue downtown along east—west routes, but are held back in short slugs further upstream. This enables north—south traffic to continue to flow. Signals or adjustable physical barriers can, of course, be used to adjust the capacity of the road network according to the needs of the time of day. This is usually done on a regualr daily basis along with the turn of the tidal flow of traffic entering and leaving the town centre. Overhead signals can adjust the direction of travel for which a lane is available. In the case of Chicago's Lake Shore Drive adjustable medians are used to separate the two lanes for counter-tidal flow from the six lanes of the main direction of travel. More discriminatory restrictions have been tried as in the case of Los Angeles' diamond lanes which were for vehicles with at least one passenger in them. This led to a roaring trade for hitch-hikers requiring payment to take a ride and a serious legal debate over whether a corpse in a hearse constituted a passenger. Similar discrimination over tolls on the Oakland Bridge in San Francisco was accompanied by a brisk sale of tailor's dummies. To encourage the use of buses, lanes have been allotted to their use only, with severe penalties to keep private cars off. Experiments in England along these lines had the effect of improving the flow of car traffic, as illegal parking in the kerbside bus lane was strictly policed, and the removal of buses from the other traffic lanes significantly improved speeds. The net effect was a greater encouragement to car use and indeed, an increase in car use along the route was detected. Closer in to the heart of the city, reserving entire streets for bus, taxi and commercial traffic, as in the case of London's Oxford Street, seems not to have grossly inconvenienced private car users, and to have benefited public transport somewhat. The widening of pedestrian pavements was probably of greater significance for this thoroughfare, whose shop-keepers depend so greatly on the casual perusal of their goods to make a living.

The indicative control of traffic with signs and road lines and small physical impediments, with penalties for violation, has done a great deal to accommodate urban structures designed for pedestrians and horses to the car. One-way systems can reduce traffic conflict and increase capacity, although they can also increase circuity and reduce accessibility. The balance can be struck positively with care and attention to detail. Trial-and-error experimentation with readily movable barriers can do a lot to shelter residential areas from rat-running commuter traffic. The restriction of hours when goods can be delivered to shops in busy town centres seems necessary, since parked delivery vans and trucks are the chief culprits in disrupting the flow of vehicles. However, the cost of this in terms of labour and inconvenience in many cases outweighs traffic considerations. More elaborate schemes to close off roads to all vehicle traffic, creating pedestrian malls, often involve something more refined than a bucket of white paint and a few signs and verge on the structural as solutions to problems created by transport. However, before large-scale investment or long-term commitment to subsidize public transport is made, it is of value to seek the best use of the existing system. This means that the entire range of movements of people and goods must be considered, conflicts minimized, congestion reduced and some road space set aside for the exclusive use of those who use it most economically. What is called for is comprehensive traffic management, coordinating the sometimes separate, sometimes interacting circulation traceries of pedestrians, bicycles, cars, commercial vehicles, buses and taxis. The management objective must clearly be broader than the maximization of vehicle usuage. It must seek a balance among the desires and needs of walkers, drivers, riders and goods and those living or working along routes of travel. One aim must obviously be to eliminate extraneous traffic from residential or shopping streets. Since it is unlikely that all desires can be fully met, management will involve rationing on the basis of priority for the use of road space, allocating some parts of the network to particular users, for example pedestrians, buses or delivery vehicles. Expertise in applying this type of solution is largely a matter of experience, intuition and common sense. Learning by doing is possible and not too costly for control measures which are not too costly or disruptive to install. All traffic management is inexpensive compared to new construction. However, large-scale comprehensive management schemes could lead to changes in travel behaviour and even in the locations selected for certain activities, and so as much care should be expended in their design as is lavished on more capital-intensive solutions.

Structural modification

In the latter half of this century, it has become apparent that the mobility requirements of both people and goods call increasingly for the kind of general accessibility best provided by independently controlled vehicles in a network with universal coverage, ie., by a road system. The movement needs predicated by evolving production, consumption, residential and recreational preferences are at variance with the limited coverage, catering for heavily channelled flows, which special-track public transport can provide. The accessibility provided by the road network and the convenience and flexibility of cars and trucks are superior qualities whose value cannot be denied. The temporal and geographical spread of much personal and commercial movement is such that it can only be carried by road. In many directions the amount of travel in total is insufficient to sustain public transport even in the limited form of a bus service, let alone rail. Rail is at its most effective over longer distances and with large blocks of people or goods moving between centres where there is a substantial level of travel demand. There still remains the need to distribute traffic from railheads, and the demand for movement by road reappears.

The principal transport problem facing most societies, therefore, is how to cope with rising travel demand on the road network. Most components of national networks have adequate capacity, but there is a substantial mileage of roads which are increasingly congested at least for part of the day. There are three ways of solving the problem. The first is to exert controls to reduce demand to the level of existing network capacity. This is a long-term proposition and would involve restructuring land use and activity patterns so as to minimize movement. The little we know about the relations of location to movement needs and the adminsitrative and political difficulties of re-planning society geographically might cause us to hesitate in this. The autonomous regulation of prices in the markets for real estate, jobs and travel will bring about an adjustment in greater harmony with personal tastes and preferences than land use planning ever can. We considered the regulatory and operational management solutions in previous sections and now need to turn to large-scale investment in new road buildings. The essentials of this problem are the determination of the correct criteria and their relative importance to apply in seeking a socially desirable equation of requirements and provision of road space. Solutions offered in the past have suffered from a mis-specification of both demand and capacity sides of the equation, and a failure to take account of a broadening spectrum of politically perceived externalities in the calculations.

Taking events from the end of World War II, as the growth of traffic in the 1950s began to cause isolated points of congestion, especially in towns, *ad hoc* construction schemes were devised to relieve them. These were designed to cater for extrapolated and unrestrained all-purpose traffic growth. As civil engineers' confidence and understanding of the relations of the parts of the urban system grew in the late 1950s in the USA, methods for testing whole networks were elaborated. In the 1950s and 1960s the pourer of concrete had his heyday in trying to solve the problem of urban circulation by building road networks to meet the needs of the car, modifying the existing fabric to accommodate the desire for individual mobility. This approach was exported to the UK and advocated in a more subtle fashion by Sir Colin Buchanan in his report on traffic in towns. The modelling and computational efforts involved in the design of such networks provided the data which were to curtail their implementation. Attempts to provide an economic justification for such system designs revealed the flaw of the Buchanan prescription. Given the inertial force of urban land use arrangements in cities which were formed in the last century, with a strong centrifugal tendency and radial structures which for the most part evolved in accord with the use of public transport facilities, the road building proposals which seek to compliment this structure are in competition with high-density uses of land. Therefore, primary network schemes near the centre of town failed to show a good return on investment.

The evidence on returns to schemes is very patchy. The analysis of the benefits accruing to three £10 million schemes and eight £½ million schemes in the Manchester area failed to produce a positive yield. The Berry by-pass, for example, only yielded a cost benefit ratio of 0.19, while the M602 yielded 0.17 and the Manchester inner ring only 0.42. An exercise with data from Coventry on fifty individual schemes produced a range of first-year rates of return from 0% to 200%, with a median value of 20%. The argument which proposers level at these exercises is that they fail to take into account the symbiotic systems effects which mean that the returns to the whole network exceed those from the sum of the parts. However, cost benefit ratios have been estimated for proposed networks in five conurbation studies in the UK and none of these exceeded unity.

	Cost-benefit ratio
Merseyside	0.67
SELNEC	0.52
Tyneside	0.35
West Midlands	0.69
West Yorkshire	0.51

Thus, if the network strategies are considered on an all-or-nothing basis, they would be dismissed if judged in traffic terms alone. There is unfortunately little information on the returns to minor junction improvements, although there is informed opinion that they must be comparatively enormous since journey speed variations in towns are attributable mainly to time spent waiting at junctions. The addition of queueing lanes at signalled intersections would go far to solving the problem.

The tests conducted with data for Lincoln reported in chapter 9, seeking the field of effects of network improvements, were geared to ascertaining the extent of systems effects. Benefits and rates of return were calculated for each of the five schemes identified individually and in total as a whole network strategy. The individual projects accounted for the following percentages of total strategy costs: (1) outer radial dualling, 10%; (2) new orbital road, 56%; (3) inner ring road, 13%; (4) inner relief road, 6%; (5) inner radial road, 15%. Each of these schemes in turn was embedded in the 1986 base network for the city and compared with a do-nothing base which represented doing very little to restrain central area road use by increased parking changes and restrictions. Estimates of the departures from the base which the schemes generated were made assuming that an individual road scheme would not affect choice of mode or destination, and thus consisted of the assignment of a fixed matrix of trips. Scheme and base network costs and flows were used to calculate the difference in benefits arising from the building of a scheme as:

$$\sum T_1 \ (R_1 - R_2 \ ),$$

where T is the number of trips between a given pair of zones, R is the resource cost of making that trip and 1 and 2 refer to the base and test situations. On this basis, the benefits of the individual schemes summed to 98% of the whole strategy benefits. If the errors arising from the random noise in the model are of the order of $\pm$ 10%, then this result suggests that systems effects are hard to come by. The maps of the extent of traffic changes in Lincoln in figure 27 of chapter 9, and the degree of containment of effects suggested by the exercises undertaken with Bloomington-Normal there, are all strongly counter to the systems effect argument.

When the returns to individual schemes were examined, with some confidence now that the investigators did not fail to capture the effects of their interaction on one another, it became clear that in the case of Lincoln a network strategy's overall performance could hide a wide range of worthiness. The first-year rate of return for the entire network and for the sum of its parts, calculated as the change in benefits over the capital cost times 100, was 16%. The rates of return for the individual schemes on the same basis were: (1) 2%, (2) 24%, (3) 18%, (4) 7% and (5) −1%. Clearly, an overall strategy rate of return may mask considerable variations in worth between its constituent elements and much that is worthless can be carried by one or two good schemes in a strategic appraisal. What was chiefly responsible for the low rates of return was the high cost of urban land. Land costs constitute about one-third of construction costs in the UK and weigh very heavily in the balance.

Local public opposition played some part in causing hesitation and re-evaluation of construction solutions. Canvassing the general public, however, reveals a degree of ambiguity between their desire for greater fluidity of movement as drivers and their revulsion at the disturbance of roads and traffic. The continued increase in car ownership will probably not turn this ambiguity into opposition to road building.

On top of such evidence of the limits of its value, road building has been cut back as a result of the reappraisal of many of the basic assumptions underlying what had become conventional calculations of value. As a result of a slowing of population and income growth, car ownership and use forecasts have had to be adjusted downwards. The upward kicks to oil prices in the mid and late 1970s had their effects on income and on the relative cost of distance, thus bringing down the trajectory of demand for movement. Many local forecasts of bustling office employment in town centres which justified road or rail planning proposals in the 1960s have proven over-enthusiastic. Observation of actual traffic on modern roads revealed that they can cope with far greater volumes than allowed for in standards used for design. Transport Research Laboratory measurements found traffic on the M4 far in excess of its designated absolute capacity at an acceptable speed. Findings such as these led to a revision of design standards in 1974. The effect of this was to increase the flow that different road configurations were deemed capable of handling by 50–100%. It was also found that traffic management schemes could achieve more increased throughput on existing roads than had been expected. These changes conspired to reduce the projected severity of traffic problems and to widen the choice of means considered to solve them, leading on both counts to a more widespread appreciation of low-cost, non-building options.

Assumptions on resource availability for road building were also curtailed. The urban transportation studies undertaken on both sides of the Atlantic and the building programmes they generated were often conceived in innocence of any form of budget constraint. Such budgets as were used have proven optimistic in light of the fortunes of national economies and national priorities. The costings of the schemes which were supposed to fit within these budgets have also turned out to be less than realistic. The realization of these uncertainties, among others, has let to the adoption of a strategy of gradual incrementalism, turning away from the vision of a complete and perfect system for twenty years hence. This focuses attention on low-cost solutions, including traffic restraint, first. Only if these prove beneficial is it worth examing the incremental benefits from more elaborate solutions.

Changing attitudes to public transport and externalities has also played a part in tempering the urge to pour concrete or in modifying where and how it is poured. Early transportation studies treated public transport in an extremely rudimentary fashion, and the needs of buses did not enter into the design of the network. With a serious reappraisal of the future role of the bus, heightened by 1979 queues at the pump, the needs of buses for routing and penetration into residential and central areas may come to play a greater part in design. In terms of public attention at least, the distaste for intrusion by structures and vehicle noise and nuisance would seem to have risen sharply in the last decade. In the past road building schemes had to be proven positively harmful to stop them. If the excesses of emotion which are expended by a few against roads in 'environmental' grounds can be cut away, some objective information is being developed which will enable a more rational and consistent incorporation of the interests of non-users in the design and evaluation of roads. If anything this is likely to lead to conservatism in construction.

These changes have been recognized and have found their way into urban transport plans. For instance the Tyne and Wear Transport Policy and Programme (TPP) statement for 1975/6 admitted:

> it is recognized that the previous programme contained schemes which have an unacceptable effect on the urban fabric. . . .The county council intends to reconsider some other aspects of the Transport Plan, bearing in mind a number of factors including (a) the effect of past road building and the use of road transport; (b) a greater awareness that all resources are limited in some way; (c) changes in the anticipated growth and distribution of population; (d) research in traffic management.

More concretely the Greater London Council TPP for that year, faced with tackling the most widespread problems of congestion in the UK, resolved that:

> The building of a network of urban motorways is no longer acceptable. . .The Council has abandoned the concept of an inner ringway system of urban motorways because of the loss of housing and environmental destruction they would cause. Neither does it intend to substitute widespread widening of existing roads. . . .Nevertheless, it has recognized that, in many situations, physical improvements to the existing main road system provide the only means of achieving transport objectives.

There are cases, however, where these matters are resolved in more immediate partisan political terms. The Chicago Crosstown Expressway was the last element of a high-order road network for the region. Its function was to carry traffic on an inner peripheral by-pass of the Loop and improve the circumferential access between segments of the city. In particular it would increase the availability of jobs in the developing industrial areas on the far west side and around the focus of O'Hare airport to people from the black south side. Without the Cross Town, commuting from the south to the west involved going into the Loop and out again and all that entailed. A coalition of opponents including liberal environmentalists, people with homes or businesses along the proposed alignment, especially along Cicero Avenue, and western suburbanites with darker motives, amounted to enough votes to provide Dan Walker with one of the constituencies he used to gain the governorship of Illinois as an independent Democrat in opposition to the Daley machine. Mayor Daley wanted the scheme not only for its transport merit but also because as an urban interstate it would bring in 90% federal funding and employ construction workers and contractors in the Chicago economy. Since the scheme was just outside the city limits for some of its length, it needed the governor's assent, which the victorious Walker withheld. The gubernatorial success of Republican Bill Thompson in 1977 led to a compromise with Daley which will combine a reduced form of the original road design with some public transport improvements. This will provide a further memorial to Hizzoner's 25-year reign. In the last resort what sways these decisions is not so readily calculable.

Hesitation over building has provided time for a serious consideration of the do-nothing, congestion equilibrium solution to the traffic problem. This is worthy of examination both as a viable option and as being the basis for judging other solutions. London, admittedly, with some degree of restraint, seems to have settled to a stable and acceptable level of network performance. It could be that the gap between the congested private optimum and the ideal social optimum is not great enough to warrant an elaborate pricing mechanism to close it. A queueing allocation of limited supply does have the advantage of more progressive distributional implications than a pricing solution. In addition, an allocative mechanism which bites in terms of time would most strongly affect richer people who, for the most part, have greater discretion over how they dispose their day and thus greater ability to escape the queue and spread the peak.

The one means of restraint already in place is the price and availability of parking in the congested heart of town. Evidence in the UK suggests that the control of parking provision is the most efficacious means of influencing the volume of car traffic headed downtown and of encouraging switches to public transport. It seems that the degree of restraint in terms of parking to achieve something approaching socially optimal network use may not be all that severe. The withdrawel of subsidy for parking space provision and insistence on realistic opport-unity cost-based charges would go a long way towards achieving it in most British cities. If the policy objective were to enhance the viability of public transport by increasing usage, since its spare capacity and major loss in ridership has been in the off-peak, this would imply restricting short-term, shopping parkers rather than long-term parkers. These prescriptions go against the attempts of city fathers to attract customers and defend the returns to capital sunk in city centre shops and services by making parking cheap, and discriminating in favour of the short-term parker. In the USA, the evidence is not quite so sanguine. A study of the effects of a 25% parking tax in San Francisco (Kulash 1974) suggested that the demand to travel is quite inelastic with respect to the price of parking, for work trips being of the order of -0.3. Thus, a doubling of existing parking charges with a tax would only cause a minor reduction in demand. The conclusion from this was that a tax on parking is ineffective in reducing traffic volumes significantly, and as a means of alleviating congestion, pollution and energy problems. Indeed, if higher parking charges encouraged a higher turnover and stops of shorter duration, it could exacerbate the social cost of traffic and pollutants. The chief effect of a tax would be to transfer wealth from parkers to the community as a whole, and whether this is pro-gressive in a nation with nearly universal car ownership is questionable. These findings are based of course on responses to changes in price for a given and, seemingly, generous provision of spaces. Where government can control the availability of parking spaces, as was presumed in the British studies, this does become a strong binding constraint on the use of the car.

Mass transport and new technology

The flexibility and convenience of the car and the social need to achieve some economy of large numbers are best compromised by the bus. Bus service combines the potential for a high density of access and egress points, reducing walking time at both ends of the line haul, with a high energy efficiency. In addition buses require little in the way of unsightly furniture or intrusive structures. The bus is not, however, imbued with much glamour. For some strange reasons, fixed-rail trains somehow excite a more glamorous following. Some would find meaning in the symbolism of trains driving into tunnels and the insistent rhythm of wheels clacking over rail joints, which now disappears with continuously welded rails and rubber wheels. Whatever the source of fascination, railways do exert an attraction which defies logic. Even though they may not generate sufficient patrons they are never without proponents. When we get down to cases, however, it does appear that this zeal is often misplaced. There is a misconception of the relative merits of the means of mass transport, both in terms of conventional measures of economic efficiency and also in the special measurements, such as energy efficiency, which come to the force in periods of political panic. Great play has been made of the environmental and energy efficiency of fixed rail systems, and this played its role in the politics which gave rise to the Bay Area Transit (Bart) network of the San Francisco Bay region and its successors in Washington, D.C.(Metro) and Atlanta (Marta). Happy urbanity and the good life can be reconciled with good-earthmanship through the shiny, electronic medium of trains carrying passengers on fixed railways. Lave (1977) did some calculations to disprove the conventional wisdom that directing commuters from cars to trains saves energy, using the Bart example. Working in BTUs per passenger mile he estimated that the energy expended in construction to provide the same capacity of urban freeway as Bart carries is 25 times less. In terms of operating energy, including both propulsion energy and a pro-rata share of the energy involved in making the vehicle, Bart expended 4,740 BTU per passenger mile, while buses involved 2,900 and cars 8,310. On the lavish assumption that Bart got 46% of its riders out of cars, this saving of 680 BTU per passenger mile annually is so small that it will take over 500 years even to repay the energy invested in building the system, much less save any. In fact most of Bart's new riders are former bus users, so according to Lave's calculations there was an energy waste involved. Given the most favourable circumstances, with a doubling of current ridership, three-quarters of the new riders switching from cars and trains half full on average, it would take 168 years to repay Bart's construction energy, by which time the system would be clapped out and incapable of making a positive contribution. The moral of Lave's arithmetic was that rail transit is an energy waster and that we should emphasize improving car efficiency and encouraging bus use. The actual impact of Bart was worse than this reveals because it generated an increase in car usage in the Bay Area. After the inception of Bart, car miles per head increased. Former bus riders, who used to walk to the corner to catch a bus, now drive three or four miles back up the track to a station, and park and ride. The Congressional Accounting Office endorsed Lave's views with some further calculations for the Senate transportation sub-committee in 1977. They examined the energy efficiency of various modes of commuting, including construction, operation and maintenance costs. Their figures do reinforce Lave's:

	Total BTU per passenger mile
Car — 1 person	8,360
New heavy rail	3,080
New light rail	2,590
Existing heavy rail	2,320
Car pool	2,080
Bus	1,420
Van pool	1,400

Even in very dense corridors of use where conventional wisdom puts rail way ahead, the office suggested that since buses can bring service closer to the doors of those using cars, they can save more energy than rail operators. A new bus trip typically means greater energy savings than a new rail trip. New bus services seldom require new right of way and are less expensive to start up. Commuter car pools are a definite energy saver. Light rail, trolley-type services, are marginally effective over the car, but rank below bus, van pool or car pool in terms of conservation potential. The most energy-efficient mode is a van collecting employees to one site, but this is of limited applicability, requiring a clustering of employee residences, deriving its efficiency from high load factors and door-to-door operation. In line with these kinds of findings the Urban Mass Transit Admistration of the Department of Transportation began to discourage proposals for mass transit rail systems. However, the coincidence of the opening of Marta in Atlanta and the mishandling of regional allocations by the Department of Energy in the summer of 1979, leading to queues for gasoline, may have regilded the tarnished tinsel.

This fascination with rail is part and parcel of the enthusiasm for high-technology solutions which will dismiss the mess of the past at a stroke. Electronic control systems and silvery streamlined rolling stock make conventional railways nearly as alluring as monorails. That vogue died in the UK when an artist's impression of a Bond movie set monorail striding across the city of Coventry was circulated as the cover of a technological and economic appraisal by the Department of the Environment. However, the enthusiasts' capacity to underestimate the cost and disruptive influence of his pet project continues unabated. The

civil engineering profession's ethos makes them particularly prone to
this malady and colours the advice they proffer in some cases. Edward
Merrow of the Rand Corporation has codified this tendency as Merrow's
Law which states that 'optimism tends to expand and fill the scope
available for its exercise'. New technological solutions are persistently
presented with exaggerated benefit and over-modest cost estimates. As
an example consider the case of Dunlop's pedestrian mover belt—Speedaway. Dunlop's engineers developed a means of smoothly accelerating a
moving walkway from the 2 mph suitable for people stepping on to
12 mph, which made its use worthwhile, in a very short space by means
of an ingenious arrangement of plates of the belt moving from long to
lateral position at its ends. Technologically it was constrained to operate
on the flat and straight and achieved economic efficiency with very
high volumes of pedestrians travelling just over half a mile. In the
early 1970s a Minister of Transport made a promise to the management
of Dunlop's to do something for the promotion of this device. Dunlop's
discovered that Liverpool were putting a pedestrian bridge over the
main north—south artery of the city which separates its commercial
heart from the Pierhead. Although only a matter of a hundred yards or
so, this was seen as a suitable place for demonstrating the paces of the
machine. Dunlop's economists did some calculations and produced a
positive cost-benefit ratio in terms of walking time savings. This was
brought to bear as justification for a government grant for a demonstration project. As a Department of the Environment economist I
pointed out that Dunlop's calculations included the waiting time
savings which would result from the bridge anyway, along with the
savings to traffic, and credited them to the Speedaway system. Their
positive result also arose from their illegitimate expansion of benefits at
the going rate of inflation. Investment comparisons must, of course, be
done in constant deflated terms. The simplest calculation of the net
present value of a perpetual stream of legitimate time savings benefits
produced a negative return on the investment. Because of the ministerial
commitment involved the Department was obliged to take things
further than this and took the obvious route of getting an outside
transport planning consultant to seek the market niche for this
technology in the British urban landscape and evaluate its potential
savings. Since the brief was couched in neutral terms and the partner in
Jamieson, MacKay and Partners, whose proposal won the contract, was
a civil engineer, an unfortunate degree of enthusiasm entered into the
proceedings. The engineering elegance of the solution encouraged a
positive bias in the investigation. The consultants requested that they

be released from the standard value of time requirement employed in transport investment appraisals so that the more valuable time of businessmen could work to the credit of the contraption. A similar propagandist's zeal entered into the evaluation of dial-a-ride demonstration projects done for the Transport Research Laboratory by a team from Cranfield University. What was supposed to be an objective evaluation became a crusade. The investigators even wished to re-invent welfare economics so that the benefits of installing a dial-a-ride system could be enlarged beyond what convention allowed. It was necessary for civil service economists and scientists to curb this tempation and douse the fervour with a dash of reality and insistence on theoretical consistency. Even with more modest proposals, excessive zeal may tinge a scheme with fanaticism. The suggestion by Peter Hall that some rail rights of way could be converted to busways for urban circulation may make sense in some limited cases. The cost of such conversion is more than might appear as the roadbed needs complete building. Rail road-bed is designed to bear sleepers and rails, not the axle load of a bus. The use of lightly trafficked rail lines as an integral component of rail system operation for freight severely restricts the possible applications. The case for conversions not only has to work against the political clout of BR and the railway unions but also the antagonism which Edward Smith, Hall's collaborator in this matter, generated by false claims and misplaced zealotry.

Energy, living style and transport

Right now much of our future gazing and prognostication on urban transport is strongly tinged with fear of oil shortages. The US Department of Commerce evidence on reactions to the panic of 1973 suggests that all of those who made the switch from cars to public transport as a result were back in their cars by 1975. Adjustments in vehicle size market shares are more lasting and will outlive the passing of the 1979 panic. How the cumulative effects of such episodes will result in more lasting adjustments of the customary means of travel and choice of density and location of homes is yet to be seen.

These questions of energy policy and transport can be addressed by geographers with the authority of their perception at least, if not of an articulated body of tried and tested theory. In particular, energy policy options for reducing consumption in the transport sector require forecasts involving geographic prescience. In order to estimate the energy savings associated with more energy-efficient technologies and

operations it is necessary, as was suggested in chapter 8, to have a
baseline of expected energy consumption in the absence of new government initiatives—a 'do-nothing' yardstick. In reviewing the best baselines available in 1975 (Koppelman, O'Sullivan and Collum 1976) in
terms of whether they were sound extrapolations of the best empirical
evidence available embedded in a consistent theoretical structure, I
concentrated on the sense the underlying assumptions made in geographical terms. The two baselines examined were the Brookhaven
National Laboratory Reference Energy System and Stanford Research
Institute's projections for Gulf Corporation. The Brookhaven projection derived from the Federal Energy Administration Project
Independence forecasts. These involved trajectories of demand based on
imported crude oil prices of $4, $7 and $11 per barrel (1973 constant
prices). The $4 scenario was an extrapolation of existing trends in
transport energy intensiveness. The $7 and $11 projections made
adjustments in total transport demand, modal shares and energy
efficiency due to increased costs. Brookhaven modified the $7
estimates and thus explicitly allowed for the effect of energy price. The
Stanford projection was the arithmetic mean of the Ford Foundation
Energy Policy Project's Historical Growth and Technical Fix predictions. This averaging did not concern itself with accepting, rejecting
or compromising the assumptions underlying these trajectories, and can
be dismissed as an arbitrary splitting of the difference without a tenable
rationale.

To detail the kinds of assumptions employed in these forecasts we
will only consider car energy use, which accounts for half the total
transport consumption, and freight energy use, which accounts for a
further quarter of the transport total. Total transport uses account for
a quarter of US energy use and over 50% of total petroleum used in
1976. The assumptions made to project these quantities often
incorporate a geographic judgement or thesis. The Brookhaven
prediction of car energy use was based on an assumed growth in urban
vehicle miles of 4% pa to 1985 and 2.5% thereafter. The deceleration
after 1985 was an arbitrary representation of approaching saturation of
the demand for travel without reference to future energy prices. The
load factor for vehicles was assumed constant. The energy efficiency
assumption was taken from the Ford Foundation $7 scenario and was
supposedly based on market responses to increased fuel prices in terms
of use of radials, reduced weight, improved aerodynamics and greater
use of compacts. The use of energy was predicted by dividing vehicle
miles of travel in urban and intercity use by the corresponding energy

efficiencies. These predictions incorporated a response to energy price in terms of fuel efficiency due to technical change and car size market shares. But they did not allow a response in the form of travel patterns, forms of transport or increased load factors.

For road, rail and air freight, the Brookhaven projection assumed some improvements in vehicles and operations which would reduce fuel consumption independent of any increase in crude prices. Some slight additional improvements were allowed at higher fuel prices. Possible product price changes and locational shifts of production were considered in passing but it was deemed that no significant changes in the quantity or geography of production and thus the demand for transport would result from a change in energy price. Clearly we have a geographical hypothesis here. The Brookhaven projection has been improved upon in the Transportation Energy Conservation Network (TECNET) produced for the US Department of Energy by the International Research and Technology Corporation (Doggett, Meyer and Heller 1978). This incorporates indirect as well as direct transport uses of energy so that consumption to produce equipment, infrastructure and support services is taken into account. Although both the Brookhaven projection and its more sophisticated descendant make adjustments in terms of technology and car size market shares, no allowance is made for a response in the form of travel patterns *or* means of transport *or* location of activities. The notion of causality in most predictions is that 'lifestyle' causes the pattern of travel needs. This is exemplified in scenarios constructed for the Department of Energy at Argonne Laboratory (Bernard, LaBelle, Millan and Walbridge 1978). Even if the analysts recognize the historical reality that our way of life is conditioned by the cost of mobility, they proclaim that policy studies must reverse the causality and determine the transport configuration to support a given lifestyle. This presumes too much on social sluggishness. Evidence on the demand for cars in the USA (Leape 1977) does suggest strongly that the ownership and use of cars is governed by a comparison of schedules of travel, leisure, housing density, location and other goods and that there is active substitution among them. There can be little doubt of the historical agency of the internal combustion engine and plentiful petroleum in shaping society geographically and structurally from the 1920s on. Why should a rise in the relative costs of overcoming distance not bring about further adjustments in the social order? Even in a period of constant or decreasing real gas prices in the mid 1970s, there was some evidence of a locational response to increased total costs of travel, of a shift of employment to small towns on the metropolitan fringes of New York and Chicago at least, reducing the burden of daily travel for many clerical and manufacturing workers.

If we imagine a tree-like structure of household preferences among a branched hierarchical ordering of the amenities of life, it is reasonable to conjecture that one major link of the household utility tree partitions the close substitution between residential location, space and mobility off from all other goods. In such circumstances one would expect an increase in the cost of distance as a result of higher fuel prices to have a long-run effect on housing density and travel demand. In the long run we are not all dead, for in the housing market the long run is not far ahead. If 17% of the US population changes residence every year, the choice of travel pattern and housing combination is being made frequently enough to generate a fairly short relaxation time for the process of long-run adjustment. In the context of projections running a generation into the future, we should at least allow for the possibility of a significant downward adjustment in mobility needs, in geographical as well as technological terms. The performance of the deregulated airline industry in the US domestic market has provided a demonstration that intercity travel demands are very elastic to a price decrease. Do we have any reason to believe that the demand for movement is radically less elastic at the urban scale *or* that it is asymmetrically inelastic to a price rise? These essentially geographical questions are in urgent need of both theoretical and empirical investigation. A source of insight for such predictions is to be found in the economic historians' attempts to evaluate technical changes. Looking backwards they have to construct a 'counterfactual' trajectory of events, a notional do-nothing base against which to measure the impact of their objective phenomenon. In attempting this for US railroads, Fogel (1964) suggested that much of the geographical arrangement of the economy, but not its industrial structure and magnitude, is an 'embodied' effect of marginal differences in cost between transport technologies. Much of our settlement structure contains an inertial reflection of trains on steel rails as modified by the flexible and cheap mobility of cars and trucks on tarmac or concrete since 1908 when Henry Ford opened his Highland Park plant. The loci of population, manufacturing and agriculture have changed significantly in that period, partly as an embodied result of cheap oil. Another seventy years and costlier traction for individual vehicles might result in a different geographical embodiment that that suggested by the extrapolation of past trends.

Much of the predictive effort directed at informing the making of transport energy policy suffers the malady we uncovered in chapter 8 when considering investment decision-making rules. Forecasting is still geared to producing a precise path describing the effect of a particular strategy in what is viewed as a determinate world. Insufficient recognition of uncertainty is allowed for. Trajectories of energy consumption have to be traced in a fashion so beset with limiting assumptions as to make the placing of a numerical likelihood on any particular outcome inappropriate. We do not know what will happen to crude oil prices. Spot prices in the summer of 1979 hit $20 a barrel but what will happen when Mexico comes on stream is unclear. We can only surmise about the processes of societal response to changing petrol prices. We do not know how the tastes and preferences of society will change or even how society will be composed with any certainty or precision. Trying to come up with precise paths of energy consumption with or without some particular intervention is somewhat ambitious. We are faced with making choices under ignorance. It is only reasonable to identify some possible futures. They cannot be accorded a cardinal or ordinal likelihood. The problem will evolve through time, requiring a sequence of decisions in the light of unfolding reality, In such a setting what should be sought is the current actions which keep the largest number of acceptable futures open as long as possible, so that as the unforeseen emerges the fewest avenues for socially desirable advance have been precluded. This is not a prescription for the 'durchwursteln' of the Austro-Hungarian Empire or British 'muddling through'. It demands a great deal of hard predictive effort and honestly come-by foresight. Ingenuity and exertion should be concentrated on identifying and mapping all the possible futures so that we can do the best for ourselves now in such a way as to limit our truncation of future choices available.

CHAPTER· 13

Community and Mobility

▭◇▭◇▭◇▭◇▭◇▭◇▭◇▭◇▭◇▭◇▭◇▭◇▭◇▭◇▭◇▭◇▭◇▭◇▭◇

The current shape of our social and economic tissue has grown up on the basis of cheap petrol and cars and trucks on roads, In varying degrees the travel and commerce of the richer nations and the poorer nations of the world is predominantly carried in small vehicles over a widely cast network, achieving the maximum in flexibility and customer convenience. This geographical mobility, although satisfying a derived demand, seemed to achieve the status of the ultimate superior good. The first thing increased income is applied to is acquiring wheels. The correlation between household income and car ownership in every nation is the tightest thing in statistics. The difference in performance between road and rail hauliers for the great mass of freight traffic, which occurs within a 200-mile radius, is so big as to lead to the in-exorable growth of road carriage. The relaxation of the geographical constraints imposed by the confinement of long-distance travel and freight to the use of rail and local circulation to rail, walking or horse-drawn vehicles, has radically influenced where we live and work, do business and spend our time and money. Continuous tracts of separate houses at four to six to the acre spreading up to 50 miles from the clustered core of the city reflect the ubiquity of access provided by the car. Chains of industrial linkage between factories, warehouses and retail outlets scattered over broader ranges in the industrial belts of Europe and North America are held together chiefly by the truck. Within the matrix provided by this expansive arrangement different social attitudes and bonds were adopted. After a generation of Americans were conceived in the back seats of Model T Fords, friends as well as mates could be sought over a wider range. As children could be driven to school, schools were enlarged. Contact, generating friend-ship as well as antipathy, was no longer limited by the requirement of geographical propinquity. Parents with cars reinforced these noncontiguous bondings by their willingness to act as chauffeurs and later subsidize the use of cars by youths. In the workplace car commuting reduced the force which had kept people close and living among their workmates. Those you worked with and, thus, knew best came to be scattered widely. Neighbours, workmates and friends were no longer necessarily drawn from the same small circle. Shopping was no longer a daily matter within a neighbourhood but became a more efficient, impersonal affair in a supermarket or at a mall in the midst of its acres of parking lot. The choice of three or so of these within easy reach in metropolitan suburbia or a middle-sized town provided comparison and competition. For the American middle classes who experienced this first, the weight of social responsibility devolved on the nuclear family divorced from a local community defined in terms of neighbourhood. The signs of strain are manifest in the frequency of failure. The opportunities for cheating on the marital commitment that held this unit together were vastly enlarged for both wife and husband by the car. The conventional venue for such infidelity was, naturally, the motel. The focus of life turned in on the hearth, and rather than using commercial or public communal facilities such as bars, cinemas and parks, the wherewithal for private, self-sufficient enjoyment was devised and acquired, further diminishing the significance of neighbourhood.

Self-sufficiency and nucleation lead to a degree of isolation, and this is part of the price of mobility as she has been used. Individual control over a vehicle encasing the occupants in steel and glass separates people from their fellows and their surroundings. People and places flash by. The feel, noise and smell of life and discomfort of weather are banished by air conditioning, heating and a tape deck. The loss of exertion of muscles atrophies the limbs and broadens the beam. To counter these losses, more vigorous, anachronistic forms of locomotion — walking, running, horse-riding, sailing and bicycling — are used to fill the leisure time released from the requirements of travelling by the car. It is even customary to drive the car some distance to a safe or pleasant place to run or ride around in circles. The crazes for jogging and bicycling express the fear of physical degeneration which accompanies dependence on the car for everyday movement. Sailing boats and cantering around on horses are more expensive and higher-class manifestations of this fear. In all of this, the lower orders of society are aping what the landed gentry and industrial rich did before them as they gained greater mobility and leisure.

It is not only the car which releases the bonds of place and smooths the abrasive power of distance. The plane has brought the world closer

together at the intercity and international scale of interaction. More of
the time of more of the people has been brought into Melvin Webber's
'urban non-place realm'. More of us can and do traverse continents and
oceans in hours at a cost we can afford once every few years. Emigration is no longer a one-way ticket and unfulfilled dreams of home.
The ties of family and friends can be sustained in the flesh rather than
in the memory and the mail. Far-away places with strange-sounding
names are no longer merely the stuff of geography lessons or the news
but are attainable sources of curiosity. For a few, the globe becomes
part of the daily round. Henry Kissinger's frantic attempt at omni-
presence in the mid-1970s was the pinnacle of this. At the level of
policy for the elite, of commerce for the salesman and entrepreneur, of
adventurous experience for a holiday maker and passage for the migrant,
cheap air travel has pushed horizons to the limits of the earth. With this
has come some release from ignorance and the chauvinism it engendered. However, we have not yet come to grips with the perspective
this medium offers, and the life and vision adopted to accommodate
the exigencies of travel over vast expanses lose touch with our
pedestrian and social nature. To overcome distance we isolate ourselves
from our surrounds, contort out bodies' time keeping and bring the
comforts of home along in the shape of a Sheraton or Hilton. Our
curiosity and sense of adventure is carefully limited so that no real
element of danger or involvement will hinder 'enjoyment'. The world
becomes places to be seen and collected but not touched or tasted.
Although statesmen, merchants and citizens see more of each other in
the flesh, whether they become more familiar as a result of the greater
capacity to travel is in doubt. The ease with which you come is equalled
by the ease with which you go and haste does not foster acquaintance
with persons or places. Even in the carefully selected venues of world
tourism a membrane keeps the visitor and the native apart to coddle the
traveller in as much of the trappings of his home niche as are trans-
ferable. Even within a nation the desire to reduce uncertainty and
potential contamination by a different culture has bred the standardized
auxiliaries of travel. In the USA, travel by Interstate or air can be a
procession from one Holiday Inn, McDonald's and Howard Johnson's
to the next, unmarked by the produce or style of the surrounding
country except in the accent of the staff — what they say having been
learned as part of the standard package. The cost of certainty as to
price and quality is an eradication of the nuance of geographical
variety. A commonly felt ambiguity, if not antipathy, to the results of
the conquest of distance finds elegant literary expression in John

Fowles' *The French Lieutenant's Woman* (1969):

> Yet this distance, all those abysses unbridged and then unbridgeable by radio, television, cheap travel and the rest, was not wholly bad. People knew less of each other, perhaps, but they felt more free of each other, and so were more individual. The entire world was not for them only a push or a switch away. Strangers were strange, and sometimes with an exciting, beautiful strangeness. It may be better for humanity that we should communicate more and more. But I am a heretic. I think our ancestors' isolation was like the greater space they enjoyed: it can only be envied. The world is only too literally too much with us now.

Membership in a social, economic and political sphere, not constrained by the requirement of geographical contiguity, is becoming available to more people for more of their time. Social forms and arrangements have evolved with this conquest of distance and greater control over the stuff of life. Material culture is merging and the barriers which nurtured its variance are torn down as the reduction of effective distance causes a convergence of places. At the same time that our speech and ways of doing things become less disparate, what we do becomes more specialized, limited, structured and interdependent. As communities, politics and markets expand, the potential for enjoying the benefits of specialization increase with them. Even now the urban masses most of us in the developed world inhabit are intensely complex structures of specialized and interlocked roles. This makes for greater efficiency and productivity in the arrangements of life, politics and production. The price of this is the greater fragility of the intricate functional formation necessary for consistent and smooth operation. The intense specialization of mass production in manufacturing, as opposed to craftsmanship, means that the whole process can be disrupted by the failure to produce one part out of thousands. A strike in a small machine shop can bring the whole industry to a halt. In agriculture, commercial monoculture, as compared with mixed family farming, faces the uncertainties of weather, disease and market with the spectre of a total wipe-out for one or several years. One response to the intensification of such risks due to specialization is to be seen in ownership. A larger unit with a corporate structure can carry the disruptions and losses resulting from the vagaries of nature and markets over a long enough period for the benefits of specialized production to tell. This happened in the early stages of industrialization in manufacturing and is happening in agriculture now. Risks can be spread by the selection of portfolios of assests by an investor so as to limit the likelihood of coincidental failure. The other response is to try to build a degree of adaptability into the production process or infrastructure in question. In the Swedish car industry, the assembly line has been replaced by team assembly so that each person is responsible for many tasks in the course of operations, and this has proven successful. For individual careers there is growing recognition and facility for retraining to meet the rapid evolution of society's needs and technology. Education is being geared to instilling a greater flexibility with respect to required skills. In agriculture, monocultural operations are being diversified by combining them with a variety of other crops and livestock, not necessarily in a contiguous land holding. As far as transport facilities are concerned the beginning of wisdom lies in the understanding that the more rigid the lines and limited the coverage of a system, the greater the prospect of failure to satisfy future needs. For road investment in the conurbations of the developed world, the inadequacy of building high-standard limited access thoroughfares as compared with improving the quality of a higher density network of conventional roads is becoming clear. This, not only in terms of circulation for a given arrangement of activities but also in terms of fostering a geographical spread of land uses less conducive to congestion bottlenecks. This is also the strategy which most helps modes of travel other than the car, such as bikes and buses, thereby enhancing flexibility in another dimension. In underveloped economies, road rather than rail construction and the spinning of a dense net of lower-standard roads to encourage agricultural commercialization, rather than a sparse web of high-quality intercity roads, are similarly robust inclinations in policy.

In the urban conglomerations of the industrialized world we are now in the process of stepping back from a tendency to sole dependence on the car and building up our entire social and economic structure around this extremely efficient but dangerously singular solution. In the third quarter of the twentieth century increasing numbers of Americans and Australians, followed by Europeans at some lag, have embarked on a way of life founded on what is for the individual the ultimate in flexible mobility. At the national level, providing the vehicles and fuel for this has built rigidities into the options available and reduced collective freedom of action. There can be no doubt, however, of the freedom of place and time it bestowed on the individual. This unleashing reached its zenith in Los Angeles where its fastest population growth was accompanied by the nearly universal use of the car. The resulting autometropolis took shape with little reference to the rail lines of the nineteenth century and the strong monocentric focusing they encouraged. Rather a multiplicity of focuses of employment and business emerged, laced together by a net of freeways. The limits of the geographical licence provided were explored in an apocryphal tale of a family who lived on the move in a camper on the freeways, coming to a halt in parking lots to sleep, feed and copulate — although some sexual encounters are evidently managed while travelling at the legal limit. Driving is even used as a sedative, providing a shell of banal sounds and sights and a sequence of nearly automatic actions, cocooning consciousness from the disturbances of living in the midst of others' wants and lack of concern. When driving and feelings towards others, in general or particular, get mixed up, the effects can be lethal. Aggression, whatever its causes, by someone on foot is bad enough. When it is at the controls of a 350-horsepower V8 in a steel projectile, it can be devastating, as a recent outbreak of berserk behaviour in Los Angeles has demonstrated. There are signs, however, that having explored the extremities of car culture, consciousness of its costs has given people, in their individual and political roles, cause for hesitation and reappraisal. The flurry of panic buying queues and price rises for petrol in the early summer of 1979 did have an effect on local traffic and long-distance vacation traffic. Sales of gas-guzzling big cars dropped sharply and small car sales increased. There was a surge of interest in bicycles, and the sales of backyard swimming pools, as a substitute for weekend trips to the coast, soared. The lesson that petrol prices are likely to continue to increase in relative terms in the future has probably been driven home, and some permanent tendencies to reduce the overwhelming involvement with the car are under way. The frailty of reliance on petrol-powered wheels for all of your connections with the rest of society becomes obvious as the dawn of falling oil production appears on a horizon within the range of life expectancy. The effects of disrupted supplies have been demonstrated. Questions about the effects of increasing travel costs on property values begin to enter the deliberations of families, businesses and local governments. Excessive dependence on one means of mobility begins to look like a weak trait in the competition for social survival, and experiments to reduce this and produce a hardier organization are in order.

Recent trends

If we examine the recent trends in residential growth in the USA it is plain that overall the process of suburbanization is decelerating. The following table gives the proportion of housing units in central cities, suburbs and non-metropolitan areas in 1960, 1975 and 1976, for the US:

Percentage distribution of housing units in the USA,

1960, 1975 and 1976

	1960	*1975*	*1976*
Central cities	35.0	30.7	30.4
Suburbs	31.2	36.4	36.3
Non-metropolitan	33.8	32.9	33.3

Source: US Bureau of the Census, Current Housing Reports, series H-150, Annual Housing Survey Part A, General Housing Characteristics for the United States and Regions.

Although the flight from the central city into the suburbs and the trickle off the land continued through the 1960s and early 1970s, after the oil crisis of 1973-4 there was a significant shift of development to non-metropolitan areas, as the pace of suburban spread slowed. This was not a mass return to the land but, as far as can be discerned, largely consisted of a movement into smaller towns beyond the metropolitan bounds. Towns such as Rockford, Illinois or the Long Island Sound settlements of Connecticut are cases in point. In some cases, bureaucratic processing operations sought a convenient place for the employment of their clerical labour force, hiving off those company headquarter functions not requiring the immediate access and centrality of Manhattan or the Loop. Manufacturers employing a comparatively small and skilled labour force have followed a similar track. This could be construed as the start of a search by a certain range of activities for a less widespread communal setting which is less expensive to their labour force in terms of daily travel costs. This has happened to an extent within the suburbs already as manufacturing left the downtown fringe and service industries for the community population grew. Many suburbs are highly self-reliant in employment terms. The archetypal dormitory suburban area of Westchester county only send 20% of its workers into New York. Even the post World War II development of Queens has its local sources of employment in and around Kennedy and La Guardia airports. The phenomenon of reverse commuting from the central city to the suburbs is widespread and large. The 300,00 cars entering the city of Chicago every day are matched by 100,000 leaving for the suburbs. The poly-nuclear city has been with us for a while and not only within the limits of Los Angeles and Orange counties. In a way the planned growth of British new and expanded towns beyond conurbation green belts was a precursor to these market responses and for a certain type of activity this may be an appropriate form of settlement. The small but persistent industrial growth in the shire towns of rural England portends the same. The small town setting may well suit some economic functions and personal inclinations, but not all. The 'new town blues' and commuting to big city jobs by many second-generation residents make this clear. Parents content with a steady job for life in a small uniform community do not necessarily beget children so inclined.

Counter to this centrifugal dispersion a smaller centripetal tendency has been noted. There has been a discernible movement of higher income people back into the central city, remarked in both the USA and the UK. What in England is called the gentrification of former poorer quarters near the core of the city is a way of escaping the tyranny of the car in the suburbs. The desire to be at the seething heart of the thronging mass calls for some denial of car-borne convenience. Parking downtown is scarce and costly and the delivery vehicles and taxis which dominate the circumfluence increase the tension of driving. But walking and public transport are viable propositions to touch bases with a regular round of acquaintance and business. The wealthiest, of course, combine the country life which suburbia simulates with a place in town. The more recently affluent seek to emulate this with a second dwelling on coast or lakeshore, in the hills or in the abandoned homes of those who have fled the land. The availability of cheap and fast transport allows the compromise of the suburban villa to be decomposed into its contradictory components of living in the countryside and working in the town. As working hours are reduced, time spent away from the city expands and the requirements for shelter between workdays may become more modest. The combination of a rural or coastal homestead and a mere *pied-à-terre* in town may become a viable proposition for more people. Obviously it would be awkward for those with children attending local schools or whose composure requires tranquil even routine. From the opposite direction, in places such as the country around Shannon Industrial Zone, Gaston and Carrobus counties North Carolina or the outskirts of Stuttgart, people whose value as farmers has declined commute from their bucolic bases to small outliers of industrialism at some remove from the major urban massifs. Their journeys can be long and costly, but much of such development is in small compact towns such as Shelby and Riedsville, North Carolina. The success of small Southern towns and England's country towns in attracting manufacturing plants is already remarkable. There are an increasing number of products which can be produced efficiently on a small scale and for which the amenity of their small, highly skilled work force, and the perks offered by government, are the dominant local considerations. As the science parks of Palo Alto and the two Cambridges bring new products with little material input to readiness for mass manufacture, so the delights of country life and bribes of land, buildings, cheap loans and tax holidays, in Ireland for example, have proven most attractive. The assembly and distribution costs of such industries are minuscule beside the value of their products. Their markets are worldwide, and specifications and orders can be transmitted anywhere at similar cost. Like the makers of films, airframes, ballistic missiles and rockets before them, these firms are footloose in terms of the transport of materials and products. In addition, as in the watchmaking of the Jura, the scale of production necessary to satisfy the world market is quite limited and not likely to swamp a rural or small town setting. There is, thus, the prospect of some dispersal of people engaged in manufacture and the provision for their needs. This would permit the reduction of the expenditure of time and energy on the daily round of travel, though some would use the opportunity to get as far removed from the presence of their fellows as possible. The great bulk of manufacturing and commerce will continue to require most of us to huddle together but, more than previously, smaller clusters will be sufficient.

An exaggerated view of this prospect of greater dispersion provides the basis for a projection of future requirements for mobility in the US by the Stanford Research Institute (1977) done at the bidding of the Department of Transportation.

In their 'Transformation' scenario they postulated a social cleavage with the largest part of society eschewing convential 'achievement' and suburban success in favour of greater material simplicity and 'personal development'. Leaving 40% of the population to extend themselves along the trajectory of the mid-twentieth century consumer society definition of the good life, by 2025 60% of the population seek salvation in simplicity. This comes about as increasing numbers move away from the metropolitan areas back to the land and small towns, where community self-sufficiency is more attainable. There is a retreat to the local realm of geographically contiguous community. The extent of the great urban masses sprawls a little more and experiences further focal diffusion, while the expansion of population is mainly in towns of 25,000 to 150,000. At the cost of a reduction in the rate of national economic growth, the decentralized believers of the 'transformed' persuasion use intermediate technology, consume frugally and defend the environment fiercely. They prefer part-time or intermittent employment to the efficient, centralized, high-technology-using Mammonites. This permits more time for the personal quest for satisfaction. Within the ranks of the transformed, production pays lower wages and uses labour intensively while going easy on energy and capital. The circulatory needs of the transformed are met with fewer miles in more energy-efficient cars plus a greater reliance on walking, bikes, car pooling and public transport, with widespread use of rented electric and hybrid cars. Those who continue in the old ways seek speed and comfort with a variety of types of car and mass transit. Naturally Stanford Research Institute calculated that the net effect would reduce energy consumption. The mutually dependent coexistence of those who are born again to frugality and locality and of the unrepentant urban majority is seen as reducing the role of federal government and the concentration of production and commerce. This is predicted to reduce long-distance travel and freight and increase the intensity of local movement of goods, with telecommunications substituting for much business traffic. An increase in political involvement of more people at the local level is translated into the emergence of areas where the community has elected to subsidize public transport at a variety of intensities and restrain private travel to reduce car ownership.

A forecast based on the projection of a rate of conversion to a new way of life and the delineation of its geography must be regarded as heroically tenuous. The division of visible tendencies in current behaviour into two 'lifestyles' and their extrapolation over two generations to predict our demand for transport energy in somewhat crass and Manichean. The reality is more likely to be an unfolding of a variety of compromises between the material and spiritual within the individual. The outcome will undoubtedly be more complicated and various. However, the signs of flight from the centre by some at least are visible and the future will in all likelihood be less congregated. In underdeveloped lands with a high rural density, there is the prospect that the emergence of manufacturing and service activities may be achieved with less agglomeration, serving less extensive market areas from more frequently distributed production points achieving the necessary minimum scale of production. The landscapes of industrialized China and India as they emerge may have smaller regional economies and lower transport expenditures than the empty economic spaces of the USA and Soviet Union have called for. Part of the global adjustment will undoubtedly be the progressive self-denial of mobility by those who have built a society on rubber wheels and petrol, in the USA in particular. Given the geography of world oil reserves, the growing demands of the rest of the world and the potency of envy as a political motive, the market and political prudence may well bring about a reduction in the use of the car in the USA. Just as the British aristocracy yielded not merely their relative but also their absolute superiority in wealth in the late nineteenth and early twentieth centuries in order to avoid a radical and violent redress of marked inequality and survive with some privileges intact, so the middle classes of America may reduce their relatively lavish enjoyment of mobility and comfort in a global social setting.

Rather than the excesses of banning the car and building fixed rail networks to serve movement needs *en masse*, there are small readily adopted ways of cutting down on car use which are open to individual option. One serious contender for much local travel is the bike. Even if a surge of enthusiasm does not sustain the crest of a coming wave of pedalling, this most efficient machine may come into its own in many places over the long haul, combining as it does adequate speed, reliability, convenience and healthy exercise. For a range of trips up to five miles, a three-speed bike provides no more than a minimum requirement for daily exercise into the middle years in most urban terrain. In that, it has the advantage of not jolting joints as the pounding on pavement of running does. San Francisco, Pittsburgh, and Sheffield might present some problems. The exposure to weather involved can be ameliorated by protective clothing against cold and wet and little clothing in heat. The provision of changing and washing rooms in places of work would help. The bike allows literally for door-to-door travel in most instances, takes little parking space and can be secured against theft simply. It is a robust machine requiring only muscle power and is easy to repair and maintain. Running repairs for the most frequent failures are not beyond the mental and manual capacities of most people. In the last resort it can always be pushed or carried. The material and energy used in its manufacture are minimal. It can be used on the existing network of local streets without too great conflict with car traffic travelling at less than 30 mpg. There is a danger of death or injury from tangling with motor traffic but few singular accidents with bikes are fatal. As the numbers of bikes on the road increases and while bike riders occupy an ambiguous legal position between pedestrians and motorists, the antipathy of drivers presents an added danger. Where bike riding is taken as an outward sign of liberalism in a community with a lot of truck-driving rednecks, running bikes off the road becomes a sport and political gesture. Frustration with the low speed, unsteady progress, arrogance and indifference to traffic signals and rules of riders reinforces the temptation. Education is needed on both sides for peaceful coexistence. Drivers must understand that bikes cannot stop in their tracks, do require a bit more than the width of a rump and operate best if they can maintain momentum. Once the converted rider has learned to keep his balance, steer, pace and change gears as a matter of course, then attention to traffic should improve. If bike volumes reach a certain threshold it may pay to provide a separate track. This has been accomplished with a pot of paint and a few signs coverting sidewalks in some towns, If there is little walking done this may be satisfactory. As a microcosm of society and a sign of things to come, university towns have increasingly adopted the bike over the last decades. What people learn in the way of style in their student days will undoubtedly diffuse itself more widely through society with some rapidity in the USA, where some 40% of the population go to college.

For long neglected, provision of bikes and for pedestrians is being incorporated in civic design with more attention to detail. Some *ad hoc* efforts like bikeway designation or pedestrian malls are quite effective. The thoroughgoing recognition of the special needs of people out of cars is for the most part confined to the design of buildings or assemblages such as campuses or shopping malls. The simple contrivance of leaving mass movement to stamp out a beaten path between buildings before laying down a formal arrangement to accommodate walkers has been employed in a few places, and geometrical symmetry in plan is still imposed. Some small effort to avoid conflict between riders and walkers is called for to reduce minor injuries and altercations. That special arrangements need to be made in town planning for those on foot may seem redundant to a European, where the viewpoint of the majority and the perspective of design is still pedestrian. In American suburbia, however, the layout was designed for the mounted and sidewalks are seldom provided. It is difficult and, indeed, hazardous to walk beyond the quiet internal streets of a neighbourhood. The only arrangement for people on foot is around schools. Walking along a traffic artery involves scrambling along an overgrown verge or drainage ditch on a talus of broken bottles and empty cans. In many cities to take a reasonably short route between two places involves illegally climbing through the tangle of ramps and embankments of the freeways, leaping over crash barriers and median strips and sprinting across fifty-foot stretches of scorched concrete in the face of instant death. To be struck in a stream of cars doing 55 mph is usually fatal to someone on foot. With sidewalks and the closer scale of society, lost to the embrace of the car, have gone the independence and adventure of walking to school and much else that was humane. Greeting people on the road, chance encounter and the exchange of gossip are inhibited. The rolling drunkard returning from his revels is transformed into the potentially murderous drunk driver. Perhaps the greatest loss is the opportunity for rumination ˉand reflection. Being our natural gait, walking requires little of our consciousness and leaves it free for contemplation. Driving and, indeed, running, swimming or riding a bike, require more mental effort, and any train of thought is constantly interrupted by the need for minor alterations of direction or pace. The sequence of ideas is broken by the need to adjust a wobble, avoid a pothole, get back in lane, allow for a passing vehicle, increase the stroke to maintain buoyancy. Even though there are interruptions to walking and in Manhattan grim determination turns it into an imitation of the Indy 500, these are fewer and can be avoided by stopping, which is relatively easy to do. Commuting by mainline rail is probably the only other regular form of travel which is calm enough for prolonged meditation. Buses and stopping passenger rail services provide too much diversion of the senses. Frequent stops and passing sights and fellow passengers excite observation rather than analysis. Walking also presents a more comfortable personal space for dealing with others in many instances. What is difficult to achieve standing or sitting face to face sometimes comes easier at a stroll. The action of walking quiets the distraction of minor motions and mannerisms and concentrates attention on the matter in hand. For those who do not know each other well enough to sieve out extraneous noises and twitches, this does seem to work well as a natural filter. Aside from exercising the mind, walking does bring our surroundings most closely to our notice. It is the best pace for seeing and marking the land, the seasons and man's handiwork. The hurried passage of a car or plane or train provides a superficial glance of a greater expanse of territory in the same time interval, but it misses the finework and actual density of variegation which surrounds us. The increasing velocity and mobility of recent decades and the instant coverage of the globe by television news, does not seem to have heightened geographical awareness. If distance friction has been abolished, so has variation in the grain of the land. To a generation that flies above the clouds or drives in air-conditioned isolation on an Interstate or Motorway, the subtleties of the landscape are lost. When this happens in the environs of our daily life, then we have lost some of our humanity. It is evident that recognition of this is widespread, and the first frantic efforts to resist the degeneration of our bodies and atrophy of our senses are planting the seeds for a variety of more physically, socially and mentally satisfying ways of dealing with each other and making a living. Hopefully these will draw us back from the over-indulgence in rapidity, petroleum, steel, glass, rubber and concrete with which we have experimented since the end of World War II. The personal, social and economic gains of the motor vehicle have been great and real. Based on a dwindling source of power, the direct costs of this mobility are bound to mount. Experience, discourse and controversy have heightened perception of the indirect costs involved. After a frenzy of geographical freedom we are coming to recognize where it becomes licentious and set it off against other desires over a more prolonged term in our personal and political judgements and actions.

Bibliography

Adams, J. (1970) 'Westminster: the fourth London airport', *Area* 2, 1-9.

Ahmed, Y., O'Sullivan, P., Sujuno and Wilson, D. (1976) *Road Investment Programming for Developing Countries: an Indonesian Example*, Evanston Ill.

Arensberg, C. M. and Kimbal, S. T. (1968) *Family and Community in Ireland*, Cambridge Mass.

Batty, M. and Masser, I. (1975) 'Spatial decomposition and partitions in urban modelling' in Cripps, E. L., ed. *Regional Science: new Concepts and old Problems*, London.

Beckmann, M. (1952) 'A continuous model of transportation', *Econometrica* 20, 643-60.

(1967) 'Principles of optimum location for transportation networks' in Garrison W. L. and Marble, D. F. (eds) *Quantitative Geography, Part I: Economic and Cultural Topics*, Evanston Ill.

Bernard, M. J., LaBelle, S. J., Millan, M. and Walbridge, E. W. (1978) *Transportation Energy Scenario Analysis (ANL/EES-TM-1)*, Argonne Ill.

Berry, B. J. L. (1966) *Essays on Commodity Flows and the Spatial Structure of the Indian Economy*, Chicago.

Brown, R. H. (1948) *Historical Geography of the United States*, New York.

Bruzelius, N. (1979) *The Value of Travel Time*, London.

Buchanan, C. (1963) *Traffic in Towns*, London.

Bunch, J. E. and Rose, D. J. (1976) *Sparse Matrix Computations*, New York.

Burik, D. and Ormancioglu, L. (1977) *NETWORK: an easily manipulated small network interactive traffic assignment program* (Northwestern University Transportation Center research report), Evanston Ill.

Chenery, H. and Watanabe, T. (1958) 'International comparisons of the structure of production' *Econometrica*, 26, 487-521.

Chisholm, M. and O'Sullivan, P. (1973) *Freight Flows and Spatial Aspects of the British Economy*, London.

Christaller, W. (1966) *Central Places in South Germany* (translated by C. W. Baskin), Englewood Cliffs, N. J.

Coburn, T. M., Beesley, M. E. and Reynolds, D. J. (1960) *The London — Birmingham Motorway, Traffic and Economics* (Road Research Technical Paper No.46), London.

Coras Iompair Eireann (1963) *Report on Internal Public Transport*, Dublin.

Dantzig, G. B. and Wolfe, P. (1960) 'Decomposition principle for linear programs'. *Operations Research*, 8, 101-11.

David, P. E. (1969) 'Transportation innovation and economic growth: Professor Fogel on and off the rails', *Economic History Review*, 2nd series, 22, 506-25.

Department of Industry and Commerce (1957) *Report on the Committee of Inquiry into Internal Transport* (Beddy Committee), Dublin.

Dodgson, J. S. (1974) 'Motorway investment, industrial transport costs and sub-regional growth: a case study of the M62', *Regional Studies*, 8, 75-91.

Doggett, R. M., Meyer, R. and Heller, M. (1978) *Ten Scenarios of Transportation Energy Conservation using TECNET* (IRT-17200/2–R), McLean Va.

Dyos, H. J. and Aldcroft, D. H. (1969) *British Transport: an Economic Survey from the Seventeenth Century to the Twentieth*, Leicester.

Eaton, C. B and Lipsey, R. G. (1975) 'The principle of minimum differentiation reconsidered: some new developments in the theory of spatial competition', *The Review of Economic Studies*, 42, 27-49.

Evans, S. P. (1973) 'A relationship between the gravity model for trip distribution and the transportation problem in linear programming', *Transportation Research*, 7. 39-61.

Fogel, R. W. (1964) *Railroads and American Economic Growth*, Baltimore.

Foster, C. D. and H. Neuberger (1974) 'The ambiguity of the customer's surplus measure of welfare change', *Oxford Economic Paper*, 86, 66-77.

Fowles, J. (1969) *The French Lieutenant's Woman*, London.

Fox, C. (1959) *The Personality of Britain*, Cardiff.

Friedlaender, A. F. (1965) *The Interstate Highway System: a Study in Public Investment*, Amsterdam.

Friend, J. K. and Jessop, W. N. (1969) *Local Government and Strategic Choice*, London.

Frye, F. F. (1962) *The Effect of an Expressway on the Distribution of Traffic and Accidents* (Chicago Area Transportation Study Report No. 1-4, Chicago.

Garrison, W. L. and Marble, D. F. (1958) 'Analysis of highway networks: a linear programming formulation' *Proceedings of the Highway Research Board* 38, 1-17.

—— (1962) *The Structure of Transportation Networks* (Northwestern University Transportation Center research report), Evanston Ill.

Gates, N. (1979) 'Down to earth problems with giant jets', *The Geographical Magazine*, May, 525-32.

Goddard, J. B. (1970) 'Functional regions within the city centre: a study of factor analysis of taxi flows in Central London', *Transactions of the Institute of British Geographers*, 49, 161-82.

Gupta, S. K. and Rosenhead, J. (1968) 'Robustness in sequential investment decisions', *Management Science*, 15, 18-29.

Haggett, P. (1966) *On Certain Statistical Regularities in the Structure of Transport Networks* (University of Bristol, Department of Geography mimeo), Bristol.

Harrison, A. J. and Holtermann, S. E. (1973) *Economic Appraisal of Transport Projects and Urban Planning Objectives* (Department of the Environment, mimeo), London.

Hartwig, J. C. and Linton, W. E. (1974) *Disaggregate Mode Choice Models of Intercity Freight Movement* (Northwestern University Transportation Center research report), Evanston Ill.

Hebert, B. (1966) *Use of Factor Analysis in Graph Theory to Identify an Underlying Structure of Transportation Networks* (Ohio State University, Department of Geography, mimeo), Columbus Ohio.

Hensher, D. and Stopher, P. (1979) *Behavioral Travel Modelling*, London.

Hicks, J. R. (1956) *A Revision of Demand Theory*, Oxford.

Hinkle, J. J. and Frye, F. F. (1965) *The Influence of an Expressway on Travel Parameters — the Dan Ryan Study* (Chicago Area Transportation Study Report no. 10), Chicago.

Johnson, E. A. J. (1970) *The Organization of Space in Developing Countries*,

Cambridge Mass.

Joy, S. (1973) *The Train that Ran Away: a Business History of British Rail 1948-1968*, Shepperton.

Kahn, A.E. (1970) *Economics of Regulation: Principles and Institutions*, New York.

Kenyon, J. B. (1978) *Regional Implications of the Interstate Highway Network in the Southeast*, Athens Ga.

Koppelman, F., O'Sullivan, P. and Collum, T. (1976) *Baseline Energy Consumption Forecasts for Transportation: a Review and Evaluation* (Energy and Environmental Systems Divison, Argonne National Laboratory), Argonne Ill.

Kron, G. (1963) *Diakoptics — Piecewise Solution of Large Scale Systems*, London.

Kuhn, H. W. and Kuenne, R.F. (1962) 'An efficient algorithm for the numerical solution of the generalized Weber problem in spatial economics', *Journal of Regional Science*, 4, 21-34.

Kulash, D. (1974) 'Parking taxes as roadway prices: a case study of the San Francisco experience', *Transportation Research Record*, 494, 25-34.

Lancaster, K. J. (1966) 'A new approach to consumer theory', *Journal of Political Economy*, 84, 132-57.

Lassière, A. (1976) *The environmental evaluation of transport plans* (Department of the Environment Research Report no.8), London.

Lave, C. (1977) 'Negative energy impact of modern rail transit systems', *Science* 19, 595-6.

Leape, J. P. (1977) *An Analysis of the Demand for Automobiles: the Case of Multiple Car Households* (prepared for the US Department of Energy, Division of Transportation Energy Conservation at Harvard and MIT), Cambridge Mass.

LeBlanc, L., Morlok, E. and Pierskalla, W. (1975) 'An efficient approach to solving the road network equilibrium traffic assignment problem' *Transportation Research*, 9, 309-18.

Leitch Committee (1978) *Report on Trunk Road Assessment*, London.

Local Government Operational Research Unit (1976) *Development Plan Evaluation and Robustness*, London.

Lösch, A. (1954) *The Economics of Location* (translated by W.F.Stopler), New Haven Conn.

Louvière, J. (1977) *On the use of Direct Utility Assessment to Identify Functional Form in Utility and Destination Choice Models* (University of Wyoming, Center for Behavioral Research, Paper 10), Laramie Wy.

MacKinnon, J. (1978) *The Ape Within Us*, London.

MacKinnon, R.D. (1970) *Transportation Forecasting* (University of Toronto, Center for Urban and Community Studies, Research paper 33), Toronto.

MacLeod, W.M. and Walters, A.A. (1956) 'A note on bankruptcy in road haulage', *Journal of Industrial Economics*, 5, 63-7.

Marglin, S (1963) *Approaches to Dynamic Investment Planning*, Amsterdam.

McCasland, W.R. (1964) *Traffic Characteristics of the Freeway Interchange Traffic on the Inbound Gulf Freeway* (Texas Transportation Institute Research Report no.24-27), College Station Texas.

McFadden, D. (1973) 'Conditional logic analysis of qualitative choice behaviour', in Zarembka, P. ed., *Frontiers in Econometrics*, New York.

Meister, A.D., Chen, C.C. and Heady, E.O. (1978) *Quadratic Programming Models Applied to Agricultural Policies*, Ames Iowa.

Melut, P. and O'Sullivan, P. (1974) 'A comparison of simple lattice transport networks for a uniform plane', *Geographical Analysis*, 6, 163-73.

Meyer, J.R., Peck, M.J. Stenason, J. and Zwick, C. (1959) *The Economics of Competition in the Transportation Industries*, Cambridge Mass.

Milnor, J. (1954) 'Games against nature' in Thrall, R.M. Combs, C.H. and Davies, R.L., eds, *Decision Processes,* New York.

Ministry of Transport (1966) *Portbury: Reasons for the Minister's Decision not to Authorize the Construction of a new dock at Portbury, Bristol,* London.

(1968) *Road track costs,* London

(1969) *Road pricing: the economic and technical possibilities,* London.

Moore, T.G. (1976) *Trucking Regulation: Lessons from Europe,* Washington D.C.

Morlock, E.K. (1978) *Introduction to Transportation Engineering and Planning,* New York.

Moses, L.N. (1958) 'Location and the theory of production', *The Quarterly Journal of Economics,* 72, 259-72.

O'Sullivan, P. (1978) 'Geographically partitioning a transport network', *South-eastern Geographer,* 18, 125-36.

Holtzclaw, G.D. and Barber, G. (1979) *Transport Network Planning,* London.

and Ralston, B (1974) 'Forecasting intercity commodity transport in the USA', *Regional Studies,* 8, 191-5.

(1978) 'Sensitivity to distance and choice of destinations', *Environment and Planning A,* 10, 365-70.

Pearman, A.D. (1976) 'Transport investment appraisal in the presence of un-certainty', *Transportation Research,* 10, 331-8.

Pecknold, W.M. and Neumann, L.A. (1971) 'Adaptive time-staged strategies for transportation investment', *Proceedings of the IEEE Conference on Decision and Control,* New Orleans, 512-16.

Pouligren, L.Y. (1970) *Risk Analysis in Project Appraisal,* Baltimore.

Promboin, R.L. (1971) *Regional Impact of the US Interstate Highway System: a Macroeconomic Approach* (Stanford University Ph.D. dissertation), Palo Alto California.

Quandt, R.E. (1960) 'Models of transportation and optimal network construction, *Journal of Regional Science,* 27-45.

and Baumol, W.J. (1966) 'The demand for abstract transport modes: theory and measurement', *Journal of Regional Science,* 6, 13-26.

Quarmby, D.A (1967) 'Choice of travel mode for the journey to work: some findings', *Journal of Transport Economics and Policy,* 1, 1-42.

(1970) 'Estimating the transport value of a barrage across Morecambe Bay', *Regional Studies,* 4, 205-39.

Roberts, P.O. (1971) 'Selecting and staging additions to a transport network', in Meyer, J.M. and Straszheim, M.R. *Pricing and project evaluation,* Washington D.C.

Rogers, A. (1976) 'Shrinking large-scale population projection models by ag-gregation and decomposition', *Environment and Planning A,* 8, 515-41.

Rosenhead, J.M., Elton M. and Gupta, S.K. (1972) 'Robustness and optimality as criteria for strategic decisions', *Operational Research Quarterly,* 23, 413-31.

Rostow, W.W. (1960) *The Stages of Economic Growth: a Non-communist Manifesto,* London.

Roy, B. (1971) 'Problems and methods with multiple objective functions', *Mathematical Programming,* 1, 239-66.

Royal Commision on the Third London Airport (1971) *Roskill Report,* London.

Samuelson, P.A. (1947) *Foundations of Economic Analysis,* Cambridge Mass.

(1952) 'Spatial price equilibrium and linear programming', *American Economic Review,* 42, 283-303.

Savage, L.J. (1951) 'The theory of statistical decision', *Journal of the American Statistical Association,* 46, 55-67.

Scott, A.J. (1971) *An Introduction to Spatial Allocation analysis* (Commission on College Geography Resource Paper no. 9), Washington D.C.

Shaked, A. (1975) 'Non-existence of equilibrium for the two-dimension three-firms location problem' *The Review of Economic Studies*, 42, 51-6.

Stanford Research Institute (1977) *Transportation in America's Future: Potenetials for the next Half Century* (report for the US Department of Transportation), Palo Alto Calfornia.

Starkie, D.N.M. and Johnson, D. (1974) *Valuation of Disamenity in Transport Planning* (University of Reading report to Department of the Environment), Reading.

Stevens, B. (1961) 'Linear programming and location rent', *Journal of Regional Science*, 3, 15-26.

Stopher, P.R. and Meyburg, A.H. (1975) *Urban Transportation Modelling and Planning*, Lexington Ma.

Takayama, T. and Judge, G.G. (1964) 'Equilibrium among spatially separated markets: a reformulation', *Econometrica*, 32, 510-24.

Thomas, E.N. and Schofer, J.L. (1966) *Introduction to a System Approach to Transportation Problems* (Northwestern University, Transportation Center report), Evanston Ill.

Ullman, E.L. (1949) 'The railroad pattern of the US', *Geographical Review*, 39, 242-56.

US Department of Transportation (1973) *Traffic Assignment*, Washington D.C.

Wallace, W.H. (1958) 'Railroad traffic densities and patterns', *Annals of the Association of American Georgraphers*, 48, 352-74.

Walters, A.A. (1968) *The Economics of Road User Changes*, Baltimore.

Warner, S.L. (1962) *Stochastic Choice of Mode in Urban Travel: a Study in Binary Choice*, Evanston Ill.

Wheeler, J.O., Pannell, C.W. and Farkas, Z.A. (1977) *The Impact of Expanding Transportation Networks on Potential Economic Development Locations in the North Georgia Area* (University of Georgia, Department of Geography report), Athens G.

Williams, H.C.W.L. (1976) 'Travel demand models, duality relations and user benefit analysis', *Journal of Regional Science*, 16, 147-66.

Willig, R. (1976) 'Consumer's surplus without apology', *The American Economic Review*, 66, 589-97.

Wilson, A.G. (1967) 'A statistical theory of spatial distribution models', *Transportation Research*, 1, 263-9.

and Senior, M.L. (1974) 'Some relationships between entropy maximizing models, mathematical programming models and their duals, *Journal of Regional Science*, 14, 207-15.

Winsberg, M. (1979) 'Agriculture and the Interstate: a note on locational impacts in the South' *Growth and Change*, (in press).

Index